PSYCHOLOGICAL PERSPECTIVES ON CHICANX AND LATINX FAMILIES

Second Edition

By Yvette G. Flores, Ph.D. and
Mónica Torreiro-Casal, Ph.D.

University of California – Davis

cognella®

SAN DIEGO

Bassim Hamadeh, CEO and Publisher
Kristina Stolte, Senior Field Acquisitions Editor
Carrie Baarns, Manager, Revisions and Author Care
Kaela Martin, Project Editor
Abbey Hastings, Production Editor
Emely Villavicencio, Senior Graphic Designer
Alexa Lucido, Licensing Manager
Natalie Piccotti, Director of Marketing
Kassie Graves, Vice President of Editorial
Jamie Giganti, Director of Academic Publishing

Cover image copyright © 2016 iStockphoto LP/Kudryashka.

Printed in the United States of America.

cognella® | ACADEMIC PUBLISHING
3970 Sorrento Valley Blvd., Ste. 500, San Diego, CA 92121

Brief Contents

Contents

Acknowledgments

This book could not have been written without the support of my family. With deep gratitude to my original *familia*, my parents, may they rest in peace; my biological children, Xochitl Maria Henninger (nee Ortiz) and Alejandro Esteban Ortiz; my stepchildren Britt Ortiz and Brigitte De Mille Ortiz; my son-in-law Tyron Henninger; my granddaughters Jessica and Melina Virgen Ortiz, Lei-Lahni Xitlali, and Naturelle Idolly Henninger; and my grandsons Jaali and Tyron Rommello Henninger. I also recognize the invaluable assistance of my extended family and the seven generations who came before me. We are connected by blood and spirit.

This book would not have been possible without the support and encouragement of my circle of friends who nurture and support me, Drs. Hector Rivera-Lopez, Beatriz Pesquera, Lesleigh Franklin, Ellen Lanzone, Regina Armas, Rosa Granadillo-Schwentker, Vilma Wilcoxen, and Marisol Reyna. All of these kind colleagues are a source of continued inspiration.

I dedicate this book to the many generations of students I have had the privilege to teach, especially Drs. Monica Siañez and Dr. Lisceth Brazil-Cruz; Briza Ramirez, my research assistant and dedicated alum; and my professional *familia* in Chicana and Chicano Studies at UC Davis, especially Carlos Jackson, Dr. Natalia Deeb Sossa, Dr. Angie Chabram, and Sergio de la Mora, and our Chicana/o Studies staff, Alyssa West, and Alma Martinez whose commitment to students and building *familia* is a source of inspiration.

—Yvette G. Flores, PhD

I would like to express my deepest gratitude *con respecto y admiración a mi querida profesora* Yvette Flores for inviting me to participate in this book and welcoming me to the Chicana/o department at UC Davis where I teach some of the classes that she created with love and *sabiduría*. I also want to thank the students, families, *mi familia*, and my colleagues who inspire me every day.

—Mónica Torreiro-Casal, MFT, PhD

We both extend our thanks to Dr. Roberto C. Delgadillo at the UC Davis Library for his research support.

Introduction

Latinx Families in the 21st Century

Challenges and Opportunities

As we write the second edition of this book, we are in the midst of a global pandemic that threatens to kill hundreds of thousands of men, women, and children around the world. While health care providers fight the virus to save lives, mental health professionals also must respond to the challenge of supporting the well-being of our communities, attending to our therapy clients' increased anxiety, depression, and trauma. In particular we are called to consider and support those who may be more vulnerable due to age, long-standing health disparities that threaten their health and may render them more susceptible to the virus (preexisting health conditions, lack of access to health insurance, poverty, homelessness), and loss of employment and the potential for losing their homes, whether owned or rented. We are concerned in particular about Latinx immigrants, especially those who are undocumented and are more likely to work in the service sector and construction, both of which are being impacted severely by the pandemic. We do not know what the long-term effects of this global crisis will be on families. It is with a heavy heart and hopeful optimism that we contextualize Latinx families in this book. Most immigrants are very resilient people. It takes courage to leave one's homeland and family ties to escape persecution or poverty and pursue a dream of a better life for one's family. We draw from their strength to continue our pursuit of social justice in our work with Latinx families.

Chicanx/Latinx Families in Context

According to the Pew Research Center (Noe-Bustamante, Lopez & Krogstad, 2020), the U.S. Hispanic population reached 60 million in 2019, up from 47.8 in 2008. Latinxs constitute the largest ethnic minority group in the country and account for more than 50% of the population growth since the 2000 Census. Latinxs in the United States comprise a racial tapestry reflecting the population demographics of the 21 countries that comprise the Americas. The largest subgroup of U.S. Latinx are of Mexican origin (78%). Only Mexico had a larger "Hispanic" population than the United States in 2010, with 112 million (U.S. Census International Data, 2014). Salvadoreans constitute 7.4% of the Latinx population, followed by Guatemalan (6.6%). Another 9.4% of U.S. Latinx residents were of Puerto Rican background. Mexican origin individuals constitute the majority of Latinx in most metropolitan areas of the United States, except for New York and Newark, New Jersey, where Puerto Ricans constitute 26.7% of the population, followed by 21.3% Dominicans, and 13.6% Mexican. Likewise, Miami, Fort Lauderdale, and West Palm Beach in Florida are predominantly Cuban (42.9%), Colombian (9.3%), and Puerto Rican (9.3%). According to the Pew Research Center (2015) 4.6% of adults who are Latinx (or have a Latinx parent or grandparent) have a multiracial background. Multiracial adults are those who say the racial background of themselves, their parents, or their grandparents includes two or more census races, regardless of whether they see their Latinx background as a race. However, the same report finds that most Latinx do not see themselves as multiracial, despite the *mestizaje*, the racial mixing, that occurred when Spaniards first arrived on the continent. Likewise, there is little data on the numbers of indigenous Latinx who inhabit the United States. According to an Associated Press report in 2010, the counting of Indigenous Mexican and Central Americans in the U.S. Census is complicated by language barriers, undercounting, and the fact that individuals may identify by national origin and not Indigenous affiliation. Therefore, the numbers of Zapotec, Miztec, Maya, and other groups in the United States remain unknown. The National Center for Farmworker Health (2018) found that there are around 165,000 Indigenous Mexican farm workers in California, and most of them are originally from the states of Oaxaca and Guerrero. According to a Pew Research Center (2016) report, a fourth of Latinx in the United States identify as Afro-Latino, Afro-Caribbean, or of African descent with roots in Latin America.

Latinxs continue to be a young population. According to the Pew Research Center (2018), Latinxs accounted for 25% of the nation's 54 million K–12 students in 2016, up from 16% in 2000. In 14 states, Latinxs accounted for at least 20% of K–12 students in 2016, up from six states in 2000. States showing an increase in Latinx students in 2016 include Connecticut, Florida, Illinois, New Jersey, New York, Oregon, Rhode Island, and Washington. Latinxs account for about half or more of all K–12 students in three states: New Mexico (61%), California (52%), and Texas (49%). The adult population (Latinx over the age of 18) was 33.3 million in 2010; this represents a 45% increase from 2000. While immigration to the United States from Latin America contributed to the population increase, the migration to the United States has slowed down in recent years. The U.S. born account for 81% of Latinos ages 35 or younger in 2016, compared with 42% of Latinos ages 36 or older.

By 2012 there were 11.6 million Latinx households in the United States. Of these, 63.2% were heterosexual married couples and 60.4% had children younger than 18 years of age. Furthermore, 65.7% of Latinx children were living with two parents in 2012; 45.3% of Latinx children lived in households where both parents worked outside the home (U.S. Census Bureau, 2015). The same report noted that 37.6 million Latinx residents older than 5 years of age spoke Spanish at home; more than half of those residents reported also speaking English very well. Thus, Latinx families often comprise a significant number of bilingual households in the United States.[1] From 2012–2014, Hispanics were the only major population group to simultaneously lower their poverty rate and increase their

---

1   This is an important fact given widespread policies in the United States to ban bilingual education and other discriminatory practices that prohibit the use of languages other than English in the workplace. It may well be that the home is perceived as the only safe place where the ancestral language can be spoken.

annual household income. In 2014, the Hispanic household annual median rose 7.3%, to $42,492, contrasting 2012's $39,600 annual median income (Barraza, 2016). However, the current global pandemic has affected Latinx families significantly. A recent article on the *Washington Post* (Jan & Clement, 2020) poll found that 20% of Latinx adults and 16% of Black people report being laid off or furloughed since the outbreak began in the United States, compared with 11% of White people and 12% of workers of other races. The long-term impact of this economic disparity remains to be seen; however, it is likely to adversely impact overall family well-being.

While divorce rates have escalated in the past few decades among European Americans, the majority of Latinx marry or form long-term domestic partnerships, remain married, and have children. However, their family formations are diverse and face myriad challenges and disparities related to the degree of **structural integration** to U.S. society they have attained (Portes, 1993; Rumbaut, 1994). The most salient of the disparities is related to their economic position. According to the U.S Census in 2019 the Latinx poverty rate was 17.6% and the median household income in the United States rose to $63,688 (Creamer, 2020). For Latinxs, the median family income in 2018 was 50,486 (Statista, 2018). There were differences in family income throughout the country, with the western United States experiencing the greatest decline. For example, Mexican origin families in the congressional district 20 (CD 20), which is considered the poorest in the country based on the Human Development Index (De la Torre et. al., 2013) and includes the agricultural rich central valley of California, had a median family income of $25,441.

While the nation's official poverty rate in 2018 was 11.8%, down 0.5 percentage points from 12.3% in 2017, for Latinxs the poverty rate was 15% (Statista, 2018). Given the high unemployment rate for Latinx as a result of the COVID-19 pandemic, it is very likely that the poverty rate for this group will increase in the following year and beyond.

Family income is related to the types of jobs performed and level of education attained. Among Latinx there is significant variability in educational attainment depending on nativity and generational status. In 2017, only 77.8% of Latino students graduated from high school in 4 years (compared with 88 and 90% among White and Asian students, respectively; 29% of Mexican-origin Latinx aged 25–29 held a high school diploma. Only 12% of that same population held a baccalaureate degree, 2% held a master's degree, and only 0.18% held a doctoral degree. Among the various Latinx subgroups, Venezuelans[2] had the highest degree of college completion at 55% and Guatemalans the lowest at 10% (Pew Research Center, 2017).

Of the various Latinx population groups, Chicanxs had among the lowest educational attainment and one of the highest high school discontinuation rates (Manzo, 2014). The majority of Latinx, 67.4%, work in civilian jobs (including blue collar and service categories). Large numbers of Latinxs, particularly immigrants from rural areas of Mexico, work in agriculture. Latinx also have high rates of participation in the military; in 2011 1.8 million Latinxs were either active military personnel or veterans of the U.S. Armed Forces. According to the Latinx veteran organization Casaba, 17% of active-duty enlisted

---

2   The majority of Venezuelans are college-educated immigrants who have fled their country since 2000. The population of Venezuelan immigrants in the United States has risen 54% since 2015, when it stood at 256,000. By 2018, this population had grown to 394,000, making it the fifth largest South American immigrant population in the United States (Gallardo & Batalova, 2020).

service members are Latinx, on par with the 17.5% of the general U.S. population that is Latinx (Bernal, 2018).

Job categories also influence overall health, as many Latinx are under-insured or have no access to health insurance. According to the Office of Minority Health (2019), in 2017, 38.2% of all Hispanics had public health insurance coverage, as compared to 33.7% for non-Hispanic Whites. However, if the data are disaggregated by nativity and job category, Mexican immigrants and agricultural workers face significantly greater **health disparities** based on lack of access to health care (De la Torre et al., 2010; Flores et al., 2014).

Access to good schooling and well-paid jobs, which may provide individual and family health insurance, also is impacted by citizenship status. While the majority of Latinx are citizens or residents, large numbers also reside in the United States without status. The number of Mexican **unauthorized immigrants** declined since 2007, while the total from other nations increased. Mexicans made up less than half of all unauthorized U.S. immigrants (47%) in 2017 for the first time, according to the Pew Research Center's estimate, compared with 57% in 2007. Their numbers (and share of the total) have been declining in recent years: There were 4.9 million Mexican unauthorized immigrants living in the United States in 2017, down from 6.9 million in 2007. At the same time, the total from other nations, 5.5 million in 2017, increased from 2007, when it was 5.3 million. The number of unauthorized immigrants has grown since 2007 from both Central America and Asia. There were 1.5 million Central American unauthorized immigrants in 2007 and 1.9 million in 2017. This growth was mainly the result of immigration from the Northern Triangle nations of El Salvador, Guatemala, and Honduras.

Clearly Mexican origin and other Latinx will continue to constitute a significant proportion of residents of the United States. Therefore, it is crucial to understand their psychosocial characteristics and the ways in which families support and prepare the ever-growing population of Latinx children in U.S. schools.

This book provides an overview of the major issues affecting Latinx families today and offers a review of theoretical models that promote an understanding of these issues. In particular, we utilize theories that explain how migration and the multigenerational legacies of previous migrations, including the conquest of the Americas, may shape family patterns and contribute to family injustice when it exists. In addition, the book highlights how nativity, race, ethnicity, sexuality, religion, spirituality, and cultural values influence gender roles, parenting styles, and the negotiation of power in family relations within and across generations of Chicanx and Latinx. We also foreground the resiliency of families in the face of structural barriers and discriminatory policies and practices and examine the ways in which Latinx utilize their **cultural capital** (Yosso, 2005) to promote family well-being.

The book is grounded in family psychology. According to the American Psychological Association (2020),

> Family Psychology is a specialty in professional psychology that is focused on the emotions, thoughts, and behavior of individuals, couples, and families in relationships and in the broader environment in which they function. (Division 45. Couple and Family Psychology, American Psychological Association, 2020)

Family Psychology as a Theoretical Foundation

Family psychology is founded on principles of systems theory (Gurman, 1991), where the family as a system is considered the most central focus of study and intervention. Family psychology emerges as an important sub-discipline in the 1960s when a group of psychologists and psychiatrists working with socioeconomically and ethnically diverse populations in the United States began to address the limitations of individual psychology and related psychotherapy approaches in the treatment of people with schizophrenia and other mental health problems. Working in Philadelphia with African American and Puerto Rican families in the late 1950s and early 1960s, Salvador Minuchin, an Argentinean psychoanalytically trained psychiatrist, began to study non-White families and argued that families must be studied, understood, and treated with consideration of their social class, race, and ethnicity (Minuchin et al., 1967). Twenty years later, McGoldrick, Giordano, and Pearce (1984) published the classic text *Ethnicity and Family Therapy*, now in its third edition with Nydia Garcia-Preto as coauthor (McGoldrick, Carter & Garcia-Preto, 2005). This book brought the intersection of race, class, and ethnicity to the forefront of family psychology. Furthermore, by addressing the role of culture and ethnicity in the development and functioning of European American families as well as families of color, the authors contest the supposition held by many mental health professionals that culture and ethnicity were only relevant factors for nondominant culture individuals, which often resulted in blaming the culture and/or ethnicity for the dysfunction in families that were poor and socially marginalized. At the same time, feminist psychologists were foregrounding the importance of gender in the functioning of families, particularly in terms of understanding culturally rooted power dynamics (Goodrich, 1988; McGlodrick et. al., 2011)

Over the past quarter century family psychology has become a well-respected discipline with professional organizations,[3] degree-granting institutions, and thousands of publications worldwide. Family psychology is particularly useful to understand the emotional and psychological well-being of Latinxs given the cultural importance of *familia* (family). The privileging of the family unit as the most important social organization for Latinxs has its roots in both Indigenous and Spanish cultural legacies (Flores, 2013). The models presented in this book have generated best practices for the treatment of Latinx families with problems rooted in their social location and migration legacies as well as intergenerational trauma related to historical experiences with conquest and domination and the sequelae of more recent social, political, and intrafamily violence both in the United States and abroad.

As McGoldrick has noted, to understand individual human beings we must comprehend them in the context of their family, which is situated within a community that is part of the larger society. In addition, it is also critical to examine the history of individuals and determine how past experiences may have impacted their current family formation and individual psychology as well as the influence of history and intergenerational legacies on the development of contemporary individual and family problems. For Latinx, as will be discussed later, the family may stretch across borders, form part of transnational

---

3   The American Family Therapy Academy, the American Family Therapy Association, the International Family Therapy Association, and dozens of state family therapy associations, for example.

communities, and intersect dominant and nondominant societies. Clearly, such positionality increases the complexity of the lived experience of Chicanx and Latinx families.

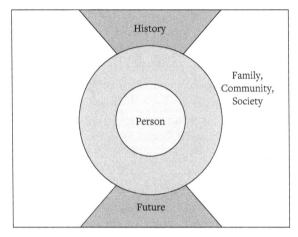

FIG. 1.1 Context for Understanding People

Monica McGoldrick, "Context for Understanding People," Context and Connections: Transforming Life Narratives: Workshop Presentation in Venice, Italy. Copyright © 2008 by Monica McGoldrick. Reprinted with permission.

Life Cycle Perspective

Family theorists McGoldrick, Carter, and Garcia Preto (2011) propose that families must be studied not only in terms of their social class, culture, and ethnicity but also with regard to the particular challenges presented by their individual and family stage of life. A **life cycle** perspective is utilized in this book because the strengths and challenges individuals and families face depend on their age and overall health (both individual and systemic). Such a perspective also considers the particular tasks families must negotiate as they transition from one stage of family life to another (Flores, 2013). These authors originally outlined stages of family formation, beginning with coupling or marriage, followed by parenting (from babies through adolescents), and concluding with launching adult children. However, as European Americans began to postpone marriage and parenting, the authors added the stage of independence, or single adults living apart from their parents. Likewise, as the **baby boomer** generation began to age, the stage of retirement or senior years was added (McGoldrick et al., 2005). Clearly, not all families follow a linear developmental path, and among Latinxs leaving home or launching may not be a cultural ideal, and raising grandchildren or continuing to live in extended family households may be a common pattern. Although limited by differences based on social class and culture and ethnicity, the life cycle perspective sheds light on the challenges families may face at various points in their formation. Likewise, such a perspective takes into consideration how the stresses of daily living, economic problems, chronic illness, death of a family member, migration, separation or divorce, and for Latinxs unauthorized status and the threat of detection and deportation can disrupt the normative processes of family life.

Family theorists suggest that mastering the skills and milestones of each life cycle stage allows individuals within families, and the family system as a whole, to successfully move from one stage of development to the next. Conversely, failure to master the skills necessary in each stage may result in relational difficulties and greater challenges in future transitions. Family life cycle theory suggests that successful transitioning may also help to prevent disease and emotional or stress-related disorders (McGoldrick et al., 2005). Others posit that difficulties or unsuccessful negotiation of life cycle stages may create patterns that are repeated invisibly or unconsciously across generations. For example, early or unplanned pregnancy resulting in a marriage may challenge the partners to solidify their couple relationship prior to raising children and my contribute to subsequent separation or divorce as the couple was not able to build a solid foundation before facing the tasks of parenting small or adolescent offspring (Flores, 2005; Flores-Ortiz, 1999). Often it is not until children are born that couples become aware of their expectations about each other in the rearing of children or of the cultural values that inform their parenting practices. If the couple is unable to resolve their conflicts, the relationship may dissolve. Such a family pattern of divorce may be replicated in subsequent generations.

The **caste/class system** that evolved as a result of the conquest of the Americas and the subsequent miscegenation of the population also must be considered in trying to understand the marriage and partnering patterns of U.S. Latinxs and immigrants from the Americas. Of equal importance is the consideration of how adaptation to the U.S. context and patterns of acculturation also may nuance the family life cycle of Latinx (Bernal & Flores-Ortiz, 1984). In sum, to fully understand the ways in which Latinx form families it is crucial to be familiar with the sociocultural and political context in which Latinx families are embedded and the ways in which such context impacts the family's life cycle.

Latinx Families: Structure and Functioning

Much has been written about Latinx families from a sociological, anthropological, and psychological perspective. However, early writings tended to stereotype and overgeneralize from anecdotal or limited samples (e.g., Lewis 1961; Madsen, 1964) creating a unidimensional view of Mexican families, which was generalized to other Latinx groups. Many early studies of Mexican families were conducted by European American researchers who had limited cultural knowledge of the groups under study. Such researchers also utilized the European American family as the norm to which Mexican and Chicanx families were compared. The "idealized" Latinx family that emerges in these studies is one that reflects a patriarchal structure, wherein the male head of household reigns supreme and women are depicted as docile and submissive. In such families, males are socialized to be the providers and women the nurturers. While patriarchal arrangements are not unique to traditional families from collectivist cultures, early studies presented them as the prototype for Latinx family organization. Latinx families were often described as having rigid gender roles, hierarchical, and male privileged. There was little discussion of how social class, generational status in the United States, or other demographic factors could account for or influence such apparent family organization (Bernal & Flores-Ortiz, 1984).

In his early writings, Salvador Minuchin (1967; 1974) argued that socioeconomically disadvantaged, multigenerational African American and Puerto Rican families should not be labeled dysfunctional simply because their family structure did not reflect the White middle class ideal of a (heterosexual) couple with two children. Instead, the difficulties these families faced were rooted in long-standing social and economic inequities. Solutions to their problems often could be found by supporting their culturally nuanced structure and organization, for example grandmothers helping raise grandchildren so that women could work and help lift the family out of poverty.

It was not until the 1990's that more nuanced accounts of Latinx family life began to emerge in social science literature. For example, Norma Williams's (1990) study of Chicanx families in Texas was the first book to address the changing patterns in the conjugal and familial patterns of this population, which resulted in part from women's increased participation in the labor market. Williams argued that traditional patriarchal family arrangements were largely due to social class rather than a culturally based overvaluing of males and a devaluing of females. Moreover, she found that the type of work in which women engaged influenced their adherence to traditional gender roles. In her study, women who worked in the service industry or were blue collar workers continued to view work as supplemental to their roles as mothers and wives, which remained their primary source of identity. Professional women evidenced a more complex identity. In addition, Williams found that working-class women experienced less role strain than professional women, who tended to identify first as professional and then as wives or mothers. The rise of professional status among more educated Latinas and Chicanas contributed to relational tensions and psychological distress for many women. In her study of Chicanx families, Flores-Ortiz (1993) found that women who adhered to more traditional roles experienced more depression and anxiety than women who tried to balance their work and professional roles with their traditional roles. Yet women who adhered to more traditional roles reported greater marital satisfaction than did professional women.

While many Latinx may hold an idealized view of family life, social and economic realities, along with acculturation and the influence of modern life, may determine in part the structure of the families they ultimately form. As feminist family theorists have noted, expectations of women to fulfill spousal and maternal roles will also influence the negotiation of life cycle transitions in their and their family's life. Across the lifecycle Chicanas and Latinas often are expected to fulfill familial obligations that are gendered (daughter, friend, parent, spouse, cousin, **comadre**)[4] while men continue to be expected to be the primary economic support of the family. In more egalitarian relationships, women may expect (or demand) equal decision making and more collaborative parenting and home maintenance arrangements.

Elena Flores et al. (2004) examined the role of acculturation in the marital conflict experienced by Chicanx couples. They found that with increased acculturation these

---

4   Literally means comother. This is a form of fictive kin that develops when a woman becomes godmother or *madrina* to another's child. This cultural and/or religious pattern expands the family network from solely blood relations to nonconsanguineal kin. The masculine pronouns are *compadre* and *padrino*.

couples tended to express their conflict openly and directly. Male partners often experienced their female partners to be more hostile or aggressive than their mothers had been. The men felt unprepared to respond to overt conflict. The women's behavior was described as a source of emotional distress to both partners and a potential threat to the viability of the relationship. Clearly societal changes in the 20th and 21st century have challenged couples to form families that can best support the individual and collective needs of their members. As indicated earlier, the family theory models discussed in this book are useful in understanding the contemporary challenges faced by Latinx families, while avoiding overgeneralizations that essentialize and stereotype the diverse Latinx groups.

Relevant Political Issues

Central to understanding Latinx family well-being is awareness of their position within the United States. A key aspect of Latinx experience is the negotiation of their position as an ethnic minority, and in particular the ways in which the government and other ethnocultural groups perceive and treat them. Many Mexican origin people who reside in the southwest are descendants of the original inhabitants of the United States who became foreigners and second-class citizens after the Mexican American War and the Treaty of Guadalupe Hidalgo (Acuña, 2011). Other Latinx groups became U.S. citizens after the U.S. annexed Puerto Rico; yet others came to the United States as exiles or refugees subsequent to the Cuban Revolution and the civil war in El Salvador. More recent Central and South American immigrants have come to the United States for a variety of political, educational, and social reasons. Mexican migration since 1848 has been largely in search of work or family reunification. The diverse roots of Latinx migration and the longstanding presence of Mexicans in this country are unknown to many. Knowledge and awareness of this history is threatened by its exclusion from K–12 and postsecondary education, especially in states such as Arizona, which has banned the teaching of Chicanx and other ethnic studies and books that document the experiences of Latinx in the United States.

The United States has a history of ambivalent immigration policies toward Latinx and Mexicans in particular. During wars or economic booms, Mexicans have been sought or welcomed as guest workers (e.g., **the Bracero program**) only to be expelled when their labor was no longer needed or during economic downturns (Johnson, 2009). No comprehensive immigration reform has taken place since the amnesty program passed by Congress and signed into law by President Regan (the Immigration Reform and Control Act of 1986). This law legalized certain seasonal agricultural undocumented immigrants and adjusted the status of unauthorized immigrants who had entered the United States before January 1, 1982 and who had resided in the United States continuously since then. Such persons had the penalty of a fine, had to pay back taxes, and had to admit guilt of unlawful entry. In addition, to qualify immigrants were required to prove that they were not guilty of crimes, that they were in the country before January 1, 1982, and that they possessed minimal knowledge about U.S. history, government, and the English language. About three million unauthorized immigrants were granted legal status through this act (Johnson, 2004).

The Illegal Immigrant Reform and Immigrant Responsibility Act of 1996 (IIRIRA) passed by Congress and signed by President Clinton pertained to the conditions by which certain unauthorized immigrants could adjust their status through "cancellation of removal" proceedings. The law also made the process more stringent. The war on terror, subsequent to the September 11, 2001, attacks in New York City, resulted in border protection policies that disproportionately targeted Mexicans and those crossing the southern border. The USA PATRIOT Act signed into law by President George W. Bush on October 26, 2001, expanded the offenses for which a person could be deported from the United States. Furthermore, immigration enforcement powers went beyond the scope of the federal government and expanded to the state and local governments, many of which have passed legislation outlawing many essential aspects of everyday lives for those who reside in the country without status, including Arizona's SB1070 and Alabama's HB56, among others. With the election of Donald Trump, more draconian immigration policies were put in effect, resulting in deportations, limitations on asylum claims, and continued efforts to cancel the **Dream Act,** an executive order signed by President Obama to allow temporary residency to undocumented young people who were brought to the United States by their parents or who immigrated before age 18 (White House, 2012).

In addition, deportations of unauthorized immigrants, many with long-standing ties to the United States or who have U.S. resident or citizen spouses and children, have resulted in the formation of transnational families as families are torn apart and children are separated from one or both parents. Such deportations and the threat of family separation also have contributed to significant psychological distress among mixed-status families who remain in the United States. In 2008 alone, Immigration and Customs Enforcement apprehended 792,000 noncitizens, detained more than 397,000, and deported more than 259,000 (Dreby, 2012). In the years 2010 and 2011, more than 400,000 people were deported from the United States each year. Of those individuals deported within the first 6 months, 46,000 had U.S. citizen children who were either left behind or were forced to resettle in Mexico (Dreby, 2012). These figures do not include the even greater number of individuals who returned to their home country through a voluntary departure (476,000 in 2010 and 580,000 in 2009). According to Dreby (2012), prior to the 9/11 attacks, only 189,000 immigrants were deported annually; these deportations usually were the result of felony convictions or engagement in other criminal activity. Given the failure of Congress to enact immigration reform during the Obama presidency, thousands of Latinx families will continue to live under the threat of separation. The impact on children of living under such uncertainty has only begun to be studied recently (Suarez-Orozco et al., 2013). Likewise, the influx of children fleeing social violence in Central America and being detained, caged, and further traumatized by Trump immigration policies began to be documented only recently (PHR, 2019). Since March of 2020, Stephen Miller has used the COVID-19 pandemic as an excuse to invoke a 1940s-era public health law that the Trump administration "believes allows border officials to bypass asylum, immigration and anti-trafficking laws" due to supposed pandemic concerns (De Parle, 2019). As a result, unaccompanied minors to the United States are being denied access to asylum petitions and are deported back to their countries, irrespective of whether they had legitimate claims or relatives in the United States.

Thus, in addition to the micro- and macroaggressions Latinxs experience due to their "minority status" in the United States, many Latinxs also face discrimination based on the erroneous perception held by many that they are immigrant and likely unauthorized. The adverse consequences of discrimination on the physical health of Latinxs and other people of color have been well documented (Flores, 2013); the impact of such experiences on the family as a system is less documented in the family literature. In her nearly 40 years of clinical practice as a family therapist, Flores has seen directly how such negative experiences impact the functioning and mental health of family members. These experiences nuance her understanding of and approach to working with Latinx families.

As McGoldrick (1997) has noted, how well a family is organized and how well it functions can only be fully understood if we examine it with consideration of the geopolitical structure within which it exists. Likewise, the family's socioeconomic position within society and the values, practices, and traditions of its members must be understood. These values, practices, and traditions evolve from the family's cultural influence(s) and spiritual and religious beliefs. All of these factors contribute to the diversity of family life and nuance both the strengths and challenges faced by contemporary families.

Author Positionality

The writing of this book draws on the authors' experience as clinical and counseling psychologists. Author Flores has over 40 years of experience as a master's-level family therapist and over 30 years of experience as a doctoral-level trained family theorist and therapist. Over the years, she specialized in working with families and individuals affected by intergenerational trauma, which manifests as substance abuse, violence against the self and others, as well as mood and anxiety disorders. Author Flores also has taught systems therapy to graduate students in professional schools and developed a course that offers psychological perspectives on Chicanx and Latinx families. This book was written also drawing on her experience teaching that course for nearly 30 years in the department of Chicana and Chicano Studies at the University of California, Davis.

Author Flores is also an immigrant. Her first migration occurred before she was 1 year of age when her Costa Rican–born father who had migrated to Panama for work during the Second World War decided to return to his country. Her Panamanian mother became a **coaxed migrant**: She followed her husband to keep the family together. Eleven years later her father decided to join his brothers in the United States. Once again author Flores's mother followed her father "for her sake," so that she could grow up with both parents. Author Flores arrived in South Central Los Angeles on April 11, 1965, and experienced firsthand, along with her nuclear family, much of what she writes about in this book. Her own family's migration narrative is used to highlight certain concepts. In addition, author Flores incorporates case vignettes from her many years of practice to illustrate the challenges faced and successes attained by immigrant Latinxs and their U.S.-raised or -born offspring.

Professor Flores's mentee Mónica Torreiro-Casal holds a master's in marriage and family therapy with a Latinx mental health emphasis and a PhD in counseling psychology.

She has been teaching as a lecturer for the last 5 years at the Chicanx Studies Department at UC Davis. Mónica is an immigrant from the Northern part of Spain, Galicia. Mónica moved to the Netherlands with her Dutch partner after graduating from the University of Santiago de Compostela, Spain. In 2012 they moved to the United States following her partner's career and lived in the Bay Area in California and in Boston, Massachusetts. Mónica has worked as a multilingual clinician in the Netherlands and the United States with diverse groups and multiple clinical presentations. Mónica's clinical experiences include school counseling, domestic violence, university counseling, chemical dependency, LGBTQIA, and immigrant populations. Mónica incorporates her lived experiences in her classes and conducts research on immigration and mental health.

As authors, we are mindful that our cisgender, heterosexual, immigrant status may pose unconscious biases and may limit our understanding of the family experiences of third-generation and beyond Latinx and Chicanx families. Likewise, as therapists we are cognizant that our positionality is always a variable in the consulting room—we try to make it visible and name it. We are women, we are straight, we are feminists, and we are immigrants to the United States. We have consulted with colleagues and invited them to review relevant chapters to reduce bias, misunderstanding, and misrepresentation. We owe much to our students who in their diversity and optimism continue to be our teachers. We also are indebted to our therapy clients whose life stories enrich our understanding of the resilience of the human spirit and inform our work.

Organization of the Book

The book is divided into two parts; the first consists of three chapters. The first chapter introduces the reader to the pioneering work of Celia Falicov, noted family psychologist who developed the multicultural ecosystem comparative approach (MECA) (Falicov, 1998). Through the lenses of that model, we examine the social and cultural context of Latinx and Chicanx families. The second chapter foregrounds the influence of class, race, nativity, gender, and generational level on family structure and functioning, paying particular attention to the challenges of raising mixed race, bi- or multicultural children. Chapter 3 utilizes family systems theory and particular approaches (contextual/intergenerational, narrative, and just therapy) to investigate what constitutes a healthy, well-functioning Latinx family. Through the use of case vignettes, examples of diverse family structures are examined, such as blended, remarried, single-parent families, as well as families led by lesbian and gay parents. Readers are encouraged to examine their own families through the use of genealogy.

In the second part of the book, the challenges faced by Latinx families are examined, as well as the impact of intergenerational trauma on the lives of Latinx.

Chapter 4 begins with an examination of troublesome triangles and continues with understanding the myriad factors that result in substance misuse and abuse, and family violence, including child maltreatment, domestic violence, and sexual abuse. Chapter 5 offers an in-depth analysis on the impact of politics and policies on the formation of transnational families. Chapter 6 focuses on the psychological impact of being a **mixed-**

status family and on the impact on children and adults of family separation and offers an overview of the new diaspora: Central American refugees. Case vignettes are used to illustrate the challenges faced by mixed-status families and families torn apart by deportation. Chapter 7 addresses separation, divorce, and blended families. Chapter 8 examines the scant literature on Latinx LGBTQ couples and families. Throughout these chapters we offer psychoeducational strategies to heal and transform hurtful ways of being into supportive culturally rooted relational patterns in family life. Chapter 9 focuses on (re)building healthy families. The book concludes with a discussion of the challenges that continue to face Latinx families and offers community-based participatory action research strategies to promote family justice and well-being among rural and urban Latinx families.

Intended Audience

While this book was developed for undergraduate instruction, it also can be useful for graduate students and professionals in education, psychology, social work, and related fields who wish to increase their **cultural humility** in their work with diverse Latinx families. While the book does not provide a comprehensive review of all family theories that may be helpful to understand and support Latinx families, it provides a perspective rooted in respect for the diversity and complexity of Latinx families in the 21st century. This is not a handbook on how to do therapy or treat Latinx; however, knowledge of and sensitivity to the issues addressed in the book are essential elements for evidence-based therapy with Latinx families (Bernal & Domenech-Rodriguez, 2012).

This book is written with the hope that it can contribute to increased justice and fairness toward all families, irrespective of race, class, ethnicity, nativity, sexuality or status, by addressing the intersectionalities that nuance family formation and functioning.

KEY TERMS

Baby boomer: Refers in the to those individuals who were born between 1944 and 1964.

Bracero program: From the Spanish term *bracero*, meaning "manual laborer" or "one who works using his arms." The Bracero program grew out of a series of bilateral agreements between Mexico and the United States that allowed millions of Mexican men to come to the United States to work on, short-term primarily agricultural labor contracts. From 1942 to 1964, 4.6 million contracts were signed, with many individuals returning several times on different contracts, making it the largest U.S. contract labor program.

Caste/class system: Terms used to describe the structure of societies in which people do not typically move from one level of society to another.

Coaxed migrant: A person who migrates to another country after being persuaded or convinced to emigrate.

Comadre: Meaning godmother as part of the Catholic tradition of coparenting. The term is also used between close friends showing their special bond.

Cultural capital: The accumulation of knowledge, behaviors, and skills that a person can tap into to demonstrate cultural competence and social status.

Cultural humility: A process of reflection and life-long inquiry, involves self-awareness of personal and cultural biases as well as awareness and sensitivity to significant cultural issues of others.

Dream Act: Refers to the Development, Relief, and Education for Alien Minors Act. It is a United

States legislative proposal to grant temporary conditional residency, with the right to work, to qualifying immigrants who entered the United States as minors.

Health disparities: Refers to a higher burden of illness, injury, disability, or mortality experienced by one group relative to another. A health care disparity typically refers to differences between groups in health insurance coverage, access to and use of care, and quality of care.

Life cycle perspective: In developmental psychology it refers to different stages that an individual, couple, or family encounters in life.

Mixed-status families: Families whose members include people with different citizenship or immigration statuses. One example of a mixed-status family is one in which the parents are undocu-mented and the children are U.S.-born citizens. The number of mixed-status families is growing.

Structural integration: Entails the incorporation of immigrants into the core institutions of the host society, such as the labor market or the educational system.

Unauthorized status: Refers to immigrants without working permits who can't get family reunification or humanitarian protection to regulate their status. Even those who pay taxes, work hard, and contribute to their communities have no way to get papers in the United States.

Unauthorized immigrants: All foreign-born non-citizens who are not resident with visa status. Most unauthorized residents either entered the United States without inspection or were admitted temporarily and stayed past the date they were required to leave.

PART | I

1

Latinx Families in Context

"As a nation of immigrants, the United States has always faced the challenge of understanding and integrating racial and ethnic diversity. This challenge has never been greater than now." (Falicov, 1998, p. 5)

Latinx families in the United States constitute an ethnic/racial/cultural mosaic that reflects the multiple migrations of Europeans to the American Continent, as well as the cultural exchange between pre-Colombian cultures and those of Asia and Africa. Likewise, the more recent migrations of Latinxs from South, Central, and North America and intermarriage with other racial and ethnic groups have led to a U.S.-based Latinx population that is racially and ethnically diverse.

While the U.S. Census categorizes Latinx as either White or Black, the majority of Latinx in the United States are *mestizos* (Spanish and Amerindian) and have historical connection to Africans, Asians, and Middle Eastern people. According to noted author and diplomat Carlos Fuentes (1999), to understand contemporary Latinx one needs to comprehend the multicultural and multiracial context of Spain at the time of the conquest and the already complex ethnic/racial world of Indigenous America. Race and ethnicity are interwoven into the identity of Latinx. Moreover, due to the caste and class system that evolved in the Americas post conquest, race and color have complicated the identity formation of Latinx as well as their family relations where oftentimes family members may be privileged or problematized because of their skin color or phenotype (Quintana & Scull, 2009).[1]

---

1 For example, terms of endearment used among Latinxs reflect this racialized identity. The use of *huera*, meaning blonde or light-skinned or *prieta*, darker skinned, are common among Mexicans and others who use their national equivalent to describe the skin color and racial features of family members. From an early age, children learn that skin color and phenotype matters. Quintana and Scull (2009) note that "Latino children develop ethnic identifications and identities under challenging circumstances" (p. 82), partly because parents often "ethnically socialize their children in indirect ways" (pp. 81–82), for example by the use of racial descriptors, such as "India" (meaning dark-skinned like an Indigenous person) or *huera*.

The largest Latinx group in the United States is of Mexican origin, either by nativity or migration. However, the 20th century saw large migrations of individuals and families from Cuba, El Salvador, Honduras, Argentina, Colombia, and Venezuela (U.S. Census Bureau, 2014). These migrations were largely the result of political instability or economic crisis in the country of origin. The influx of other immigrant groups from Latin America has resulted in a more complex national identity for the children of immigrants who intermarry or partner with individuals from differential national origins. Furthermore, while many U.S.-born or raised Latinx may use a term that implies ethnic/racial/cultural homogeneity, such as Latinx or Hispanic, most Latinx continue to identify with their national origins or those of their parents (Bernal & Flores-Ortiz, 1984) or choose identifiers that further nuance their ethnic and racial complexity, such as Blackxican to refer to African American and Mexican parentage (Flores, 2006).

To fully understand the context of Latinx families in the United States necessitates inquiring about their national origins, ethnic identification, generational status in the United States[2] and various other factors that nuance the context and experience of Latinxs, particularly their **ecological niche** within the larger U.S. society, the family's journey of migration and culture change, and their family organization and life cycle. Without such an extensive analysis, the diversity of the Latinx experience cannot be fully grasped.

The Multicultural Ecosystemic Comparative Approach (MECA)

Developed by psychologist Celia Falicov in the 1980s as a result of her own experiences as an immigrant to the United States and as a psychologist treating Latinx families and individuals from diverse origins, the MECA model offers a culturally sensitive approach to understanding the lived experience of, and the challenges faced by, these families. Falicov (1998) argues that focusing exclusively on a group's "cultural context" can essentialize, oversimplify, and lead to erroneous and stereotypic depictions of a group. A multicultural perspective, in contrast, recognizes the complexity of Latinx experience and identities. By **ecosystemic**, Falicov (1998) refers to the "unique combination of multiple contexts and partial perspectives that defines each family's culture" (p. 15). She refers to these contexts and perspectives as the family's ecological niche.

Falicov offers four generic domains of analysis in her model; the first addresses the journey of migration and the culture changes that result from migration. The second, the ecological context, examines "diversity in where and how the family lives and fits in the broader environment" (Falicov, 1988, p. 17), paying particular attention to the

---

2 Immigrants are generally referred to as first generation, with their offspring considered second generation and the grandchildren third generation, and so forth. Many Mexican-origin individuals in the Southwest have roots prior to the Treaty of Guadalupe Hidalgo and may not identify as either Mexican or Latino but rather as New Mexican, for example, or as Spanish or Spanish descent. The Chicano Movement of the 1960s (see Acuña, 2007) raised the consciousness of many U.S.-Mexican–origin people and led to the adoption of the terms *Chicano* and *Chicana* to represent either Mexican origins or political identification with the struggle for justice of Mexican-origin persons in the United States.

intersectionalities of Latinx experience, the race, ethnicity, class, religious, spiritual, and educational communities within which families live and interact. This dimension also examines the explanatory models of health and illness held by diverse Latinx groups. The third generic domain examines the family organizations of Latinx and how cultural values influence diverse family formations. Lastly, the fourth domain focuses on the life cycle of families and how the family's culture patterns or influences developmental milestones.

> "The process of leaving one's home country and encountering a new one constitutes an overlapping of events, developmental changes, and existential tasks that render a'very unique phenomenology of migration.'" (Falicov, 1998, p. 46)

Journey of Migration and Culture Change

Latinx exists as a result of the contact of distinct cultural groups at the time of the conquest. Thus, migration is not only central to the psyche of Latinx but a key factor in how family life is constituted, whether the migration occurred yesterday or many generations before. Migration is a process of relocation that includes both a physical and psychological experience. Latinx share many similarities with U.S. immigrants from other parts of the world in terms of the process of migration but diverge often in terms of the reception or degree of welcoming experienced from the host or dominant cultures.

Falicov proposes that both sociological and psychological adaptation post migration is influenced by the changes in **meaning systems**. She utilized the metaphor of rooting and uprooting to describe these changes in meaning in response to physical, social, and cultural uprooting. She describes physical uprooting as learning to live without the familiar sounds and sights, smells, and faces of home. When her parents migrated from Panama to Costa Rica, author Flores missed the sound of the ocean as she fell asleep; she longed for the smell of the Caribbean, the gentle breeze of the ocean air. She had no recollection of the place of her birth after her first migration at 1 year of age. But author Flores's senses remembered, and missed, the physical geography of the town where she was born. These memories returned in dreams in her adulthood, after having migrated north once again, even farther from the place of her birth (see Flores-Ortiz, 2001b).

The extent to which immigrants can recreate home in the new context or find elements of home will facilitate their adaptation. For many immigrants, being able to cook familiar foods is essential; not finding the necessary ingredients to do so may trigger a crisis. Living in the San Fernando Valley of California in the late 1960s, before the Latinx population grew in significant numbers, author Flores's father had to drive her mother to east Los Angeles so she could find the roots, vegetables, and cuts of meat with which she was familiar and the butchers and produce vendors who could speak to her in Spanish. Having left her older children and extended family behind in her native Panama, her mother clung to her language and familiar foods as her life raft. Her Sunday dinners consisted of *arroz con gandules, ropa vieja, patacones*, or *plátanos fritos*. She kept Panama alive through her cooking. Author Flores's second-generation Honduran son-in-law prepares traditional Afro-Caribbean Honduran dishes his parents taught him to cook. His wife cooks Mexican, Panamanian, Costa Rican, Honduran, and Tex-Mex foods with the same ease she prepares pasta and hamburgers. At various times on any given week, the sounds and smells of their current home transport author Flores back to the "home" where her spirit feels most at ease. Many immigrant Latinx live in two or more psychological spaces; their offspring sometimes feel that they don't belong either "here" or "there" but instead inhabit "cultural borderlands" or the interstices of cultures (Anzaldua, 1987; Falicov, 1998). Such psychological homelessness (Hardy & Laszloffy, 2005) can impact adversely both their own emotional well-being and that of the families they form.

In addition to physical uprooting, Falicov (1998) also notes that social uprooting "compounds the sense of physical alienation and intrapsychic confusion" (p. 53) resulting from migration. Social marginality and social isolation, which many immigrants face, exacerbate such distress and may evolve into mental health problems of anxiety and depression (Flores, 2013), as well as impact U.S.-born children, particularly if the family's economic status results in settlement in under-resourced communities ridden with crime and despair where education is poor and upward mobility is difficult to attain. In addition to recreating home through foods, decorations, and so on, immigrants often need to have contact with conationals, listen to news "from home," watch TV programs, and engage in activities that were performed in their country, such as playing soccer and *ballet folklorico*, attending religious festivals, and celebrating national holidays. Immigrants may also introduce their children to these practices to minimize the impact of their social uprooting and to root the children in their cultures of origin.

In author Flores's family when she was growing up, the women gathered for coffee and gossip every afternoon at 3. Since her migration to the United States at age 13, author Flores has missed being part of that ritual and finds the afternoon a time of longing, where she needs to spend quiet time and has caffeine. After 55 years in the United States, author Flores still feels the impact of the physical and social uprooting caused by her parents' migration to the United States. As her mother aged and after her father died, her mother longed to return to die in her homeland. Author Flores granted her that wish, stirring up more feelings in her of social and physical uprooting, as her mother and father had been the links and anchors to her geographic past. As discussed later, painful events such as the loss of a family member at particular stages of the family life cycle may lead to emotional distress or family crisis as the wounds caused by migration are reopened.

Immigrants often arrive with a preconception of what the new country will offer. Sometimes the "American dream," the belief that economic prosperity will be easier to attain in the United States and that adaptation will not be so difficult, influences these expectations. The reality of life in the United States may lead to disappointment and result in crisis, which can manifest as anxiety or depression (Falicov, 1989; Flores, 2013; Flores et al., 2019; Sluzki, 1979). Such cultural uprooting may also lead to family polarization as children grow up and become socialized in a bi- or multicultural context as a result of exposure to other cultures (Falicov, 1989). Parents may fear that their children will be lost to them if they acculturate too much to the U.S. ways of being (Flores, 2005).

According to Falicov, immigrants create a story of their migration, a migration narrative that helps them maintain psychological and cultural continuity and gives meaning to their experience in the new social context. These narratives often influence how family life is organized and how the family story and the cultural values of the parents are transmitted to the young. As a result, understanding the impact of migration on the family by its members, as well as professionals who work with families (teachers, psychologists, social workers, etc.), is facilitated by eliciting the family's migration narrative.

Another Argentinian family theorist, psychiatrist Carlos Sluzki, offered a model to understand how family dysfunction can develop by analyzing the process of migration of any given family. Sluzki proposes that migration entails stages with concomitant challenges and crises. There are five stages: The first is the preparatory stage; the second entails the actual migration, the third is the period of overcompensation, the fourth deals with the decompensation or crisis, and the last addresses the intergenerational phenomena that can affect future generations.

Preparatory Stage

Key considerations in the preparatory stage include the degree of planning prior to migration. Part of the analysis entails determining who decided that a migration would occur, the reasons for it, who is chosen to stay behind, and how the decisions are communicated, or not, to members of the family. This is often the time when particular roles are assigned to family members. Clearly, the extent to which there is preparation, information about the receiving community, and possibilities of employment will largely influence how the other stages of migration are experienced or negotiated.

Actual Migration

The family narrative often provides an account of what happened during the migration, with details of how the journey began, how long it lasted, and who helped along the way. The movie *My Family/Mi Familia*[3] provides the story of a young rural Mexican immigrant, Jose Sanchez, and his journey north, as well as the fate of his U.S.-born children and wife. In the movie, upon arrival to the United States, Jose tells the only person who might know of him that he walked all the way from central Mexico to East Los Angeles. He creates a narrative full of adventure that was part myth, part reality. Many immigrants, particularly those from Mexico and Central America, often face unspeakable horrors, trauma, and even death in their efforts to enter the United States without inspection.[4] Such histories often result in secrets and silences meant to spare future generations the burden of suffering experienced by the immigrants. Shame of one's origins and of unauthorized border crossings may also lead to the creation of alternative stories that hide elements of the actual migration. However, as will be discussed in later chapters, such silences and secrets may appear in subsequent generations as legacies and invisible loyalties (Boszormenyi-Nagy & Spark, 1984).

---

3   Directed, written, and produced by Gregory Nava and Anna Thomas, and starring Jimmy Smits, Edward James Olmos, Esai Morales, Constance Marie, and Jennifer Lopez, *Mi Familia/My Family* (1995), offers a poignant view of the multigenerational legacies of migration and the complicated efforts to find a sense of belonging in an often hostile environment.

4   See for example, *Enrique's Journey* by Sonia Nazario (2006). Nazario documents the harrowing journey of a young boy left in Honduras by his mother as he travels through Central America and Mexico atop train cars (la bestia/the beast) as he attempts to reach her and find both the mother he longed for as a child and the promise of a better life for his own partner and child left behind.

Period of Overcompensation

The first few weeks and months after migration are characterized by the immigrants' efforts to settle and survive. The primary tasks consist of instrumental activities: finding work, housing, and schools. The central focus is on survival and resettlement. There is generally a moratorium on feelings, as these may interfere with the tasks necessary to settle and reorganize life in a new context. The extent to which the immigrant has family or social networks that support it during this stage, the easier it will be to settle. However, many immigrants spend decades trying to root themselves and become economically sound, not able (or willing) to send for family members, and thus create de facto transnational families. Particularly those who work seasonally in agriculture, as day laborers or in the service sector or construction, may only earn enough to subsist and send remittances to their family "back home." Eventually however, for all immigrants a period of decompensation or crisis will occur.

Period of Decompensation or Crisis

When his wife Maria, a U.S. citizen, is deported as a result of a workplace raid, Jose Sanchez is left to care for his young son and daughter only with the help of his long lost relative *El Californio*. This begins a personal process of decompensation for Jose and sets the stage for a family crisis that will continue for generations. His second son Chucho is born in Mexico and nearly drowns during his mother's efforts to return home. Chucho personifies the child of immigrants who rejects both his parents' culture and that of the dominant culture that rejects him. Chucho becomes the identified patient in his family, the child who embodies the conflicts of biculturality and resorts to delinquent and self-injurious behaviors to call attention to the family's losses and the failure of the American dream. To understand family dysfunction, as will be discussed in later chapters, it is important to clarify when the period of decompensation began for a family, what triggered it, how long it has lasted, and who in the family has become the **mourner**, the **under-aculturator**, the one whose behavior calls attention to losses related to migration. Many families spend years and in some cases multiple generations in a state of crisis. Open recognition of the changes in meaning systems that led to the crisis and uncovering the migration narrative can be a beginning step in healing the family's spiritual and emotional wounds in the second and third generation and beyond.

Transgenerational Phenomena

Sluzki (1979) posits that the issues not resolved by the migrating generation will be manifested in the children. As did Chucho in the film *Mi Familia*, some second- or third-generation offspring of immigrants will reject the culture of the parents and the values that to them seem antiquated or not useful in the U.S. context. These cultural cut-offs may in turn result in feelings of marginality, substance misuse, and other forms of individual and family problems (Cervantes, 2004). In addition, intergenerational and/or gender conflicts may ensue as some family members with greater exposure to the dominant culture(s) may acculturate at a much faster rate and appear to shift their loyalty to the

United States rather than the country of origin. Women may enter the labor force and develop their own economic viability, and thereby a shift in power relations may occur in the relationship that can threaten males who hold more traditional values (Flores-Ortiz, 1997b). Individuals within families may experience difficulties in making commitments (jobs, schools, relationships), particularly if the immigrant parents maintained the dream of returning to the country of origin and did not support the cultural adaptation of their offspring to the United States. Often these offspring of immigrants describe their life as waiting for a return to somewhere unknown or unfamiliar to them, which precluded their setting roots in the country of their birth: *No somos ni de* aquí, *ni de allá* (we are neither from here nor from there) (Flores, 2013).

What Sluzki posits and many mental health professionals observe is that migration-related legacies, whether historical or contemporary, may transform into family dysfunction(s). In addition, according to family theory scholars (Falicov, 1989; Sluzki, 1979), the subsequent adaptation of individuals and families will depend partly on whether the migration was forced (that is, in response to political, social, or natural crisis), coaxed (as when one spouse follows the other who migrated previously or children migrate to join their parents), or voluntary. In the latter, the departure is fueled by a desire to seek better economic opportunities or adventure, or to follow a historical legacy of migration (see Flores et. al., 2019). Furthermore, within families roles are assigned pre and post migration. Such role assignments may be somewhat unconscious or invisible to the family. These roles initially may serve adaptive functions for the family, but overtime may contribute to dysfunction or individual and family distress.

Sluzki identifies four roles commonly assigned in immigrant families pre and post migration: the **bridge**, the **mourner**, the **under-acculturator,** and the **over-acculturator**. For example, a family member or friend who migrated previously may become the **bridge** for subsequent migrations. This individual may become the hero or villain of the migration narrative; he or she can be blamed for later family problems or credited for the family success. A family may have more than one bridge, or various members may become bridges to others at various points in the family life cycle. Sometimes children of immigrants become bridges by connecting the family to the United States or back to the country of origin, as is the case with children or grandchildren of Cuban immigrants who have reconnected to Cuba.[5] In the film *Mi Familia*, Toni, one of Jose and Maria's daughters, becomes a nun and later leaves the convent and becomes an immigrants' rights activist. In her own way she becomes a bridge that connects the past and the present of the Sanchez family.

In author Flores's family, a paternal uncle left home as a young man to seek adventure in Venezuela, as well as to leave a conflicted relationship with his father. From Venezuela he went to the United States. Many years later, he returned to Costa Rica with pockets full of dollars and tales about life in Hollywood, California. Within a few months, most of the young men in the neighborhood had left for the United States. This uncle encouraged and finally convinced author Flores's father to migrate to Los Angeles, California, as well. This uncle was her family's bridge to the United States.

---

5   See Ruth Behar's edited anthology *Bridges to Cuba*, which chronicles with poems, stories, and essays Cuban Americans' intellectual connection to their homeland.

The **mourners** in a family are expected to remain connected to the country of origin. They may be expected to hold the memories, write letters, contact the family left behind, or maintain cultural ties, continuing to speak the language and embodying the culture in some way. These family members, as did Jose's daughter who owned a Mexican restaurant and nurtured everyone with food, keep the culture of origin alive, although sometimes in frozen ways[6] (Flores-Ortiz, 1993). Very often the mourner in the immigrant generation will be female. Overtime, they may be **frozen** in the role and become symptomatic (experience depression, for example).

The **under-acculturator** is the U.S.-born or raised child of immigrants who also is expected to remain loyal to the culture of origin. Often this entails rejecting the new cultural context. If they do, they are less likely to have a successful adaptation and may experience marginalization from both cultures, as did Chucho first and then Jimmy in *Mi Familia*. In the second generation under-acculturators may become challenged by alcohol and other drug abuse or delinquency (Cervantes & Felix-Ortiz, 2004). Other family members may hold ambivalent feelings toward them, admiration if they maintain cultural ties, and shame that they are not "making it" in the new cultural milieu. As do the mourners in immigrant families, the under-acculturators embody the unresolved issues of the immigrants, and through their dysfunction or suffering remind the family of the losses endured or resulting from the migration.

Every immigrant family may have several bridges, mourners, and under-acculturators. The same individual may shift roles over the family life cycle. While mourners and under-acculturators may preserve directly or indirectly the family's ties to the ancestral culture, the **over-acculturator** is expected to actualize the family's "American dream." They often become the interpreters of the culture and translators of language for the family. Generally it is the older child who occupies this role. In some families it is the youngest child who attempts to actualize the family's American dream. In the film *Mi Familia*, Paco, the narrator, and Bill (who was baptized Guillermo but Anglicized his name to minimize his Mexicannesss) occupy these roles. Paco does this while maintaining a bicultural identity; Bill tries to assimilate and appears ashamed of his Mexican roots. As is the case with under-acculturators, the family may hold ambivalent feelings of pride and shame toward them; some may call them *vendido/as* (sell-outs or White-washed).

The MECA model also sheds light on the challenges of children of immigrants by underscoring the importance of understanding the processes of acculturation, transculturation, hybridity, and biculturality.

---

6 Author Flores coined the term *frozen* to refer to the ways in which families adhere to the dominant culture values that inform their development, whether or not these are useful or applicable in the new social context. It is as if the family or individual took a snapshot of their life before migration and tries to recreate in the new context. This may work for them as it provides cultural continuity. However, for their offspring frozen cultural values may result in adoption of stereotypic views of their culture, particularly since these may be reinforced in the media, or rejection of aspects of their parents' culture that in turn can lead to intergenerational conflicts.

Acculturation

This is a controversial and extensively studied construct, which refers to an individual or group's ability to adapt to the new context and adopt cultural values, ideals, traditions, and practices while retaining aspects of the culture of origin. The process is multidimensional and situational and depends on the degree of cultural and social capital the immigrant family can provide its members (Padilla, 1980). Family members who speak English and have higher education will have an easier time adjusting to the U.S. context, finding work, and/or continuing with their education than those who do not know the language or have employment skills not highly valued by U.S. society, such as agricultural work. Research findings (Cuellar et al., 2004) suggest that behaviors, attitudes, and practices acculturate at a faster rate than values and traditions with resulting dissonance between behaviors and underlying values. Moreover, core values, such as *familismo* (familism), may not acculturate while others adapt to new environments.

In studying the level of acculturation of a family and its influence on family structure and functioning it is important to distinguish between *cultural ideals* and *cultural realities*. While a couple may desire to create a traditional family where the woman stays home to raise her children (cultural ideal), the economic and social reality they face demands that both partners work. The cultural reality may create distress for the couple, as they encounter dissonance between the cultural ideal and their inability to fulfill it. Such distress can be compounded if the extended family and larger society do not support the idea and reality of working mothers or devalue their contributions. It is common for family members to have different levels of acculturation, which can also contribute to conflict and misunderstanding within and across generations of the same family. It is also common for families to become more traditional as they get older or at particular points in the family life cycle. For example, Chicanx parents may adopt a permissive parenting style when their children are young in order to foster independence, free will, and warmer relationships with their children than they had with their own, more **authoritarian** parents. However, as their children enter adolescence, the parents may fall back on more **authoritative** discipline to counter the "over-permissiveness" they see in their youngsters' behavior, which the parents may begin to label as lack of respect. This can be very confusing to the children and distressing to all involved. Therefore, in studying acculturation it is important to examine what changes in families and what stays the same, both in terms of ideals and realities. While attitudes and behaviors may become more modern, core values may remain fairly traditional.[7]

In contrast to acculturation, **assimilation** requires acceptance by the "host" or dominant culture; thus, English-speaking, fair-skinned Latinxs may have an easier time being accepted by other groups in the United States than more Indigenous-looking or darker-skinned Latinx. In their efforts to assimilate, to "try to pass" for Anglos by changing their name or identifying with a "Spanish" identity, individuals or groups make efforts to surrender their psychological loyalty and adherence to the culture of origin and join the new culture. Individuals who are similar to the dominant group (in terms of race, class, language, culture, religion, politics, etc.) are more likely to assimilate. In *Mi Familia*,

---

7   Core values and traditional and contemporary value orientations and how these affect family life are discussed in more detail in Chapter 2.

Guillermo, despite his phenotype, attempts to assimilate by changing his name to Bill, speaking English, and planning to marry a European American woman. As a college-educated attorney, he tries to fit in by downplaying his Mexicanness. Such efforts sometimes are the result of the discrimination individuals face due to their ethnic or racial identity (Falicov, 1989). Many Mexican Americans who grew up in the 1940s and 1950s intentionally did not teach their children Spanish to protect them from the pervasive discrimination Mexican-origin people experienced in the southwestern United States. Many of the children and grandchildren of these Mexican Americans in turn participated and provided leadership in the Chicano movement of the 1960s, which called attention to, and worked to rectify, the injustices faced by previous generations (Zavella, 2001a).

It is important to keep in mind that acculturation and assimilation are distinct processes and that assimilation is not the end result of acculturation. Both are strategies for survival among immigrants and for developing a sense of belonging for the children of immigrants. LaFramboise et al., (1993) among other theorists, points to the limitations of linear models of cultural adaptation and suggests instead alternation models, which posit that individuals can have a sense of belonging in two cultures without compromising their sense of belonging to either (Falicov, 1989). Individuals can be bicultural when they alternate or integrate two languages or cultures. These individuals may utilize different cultural values, perform behavior, and reflect attitudes of either or both cultures depending on the social context, life stage, and so on. Bicultural individuals tend to function equally well in both cultures, unlike monocultural individuals who function best in only one context or marginalized individuals who function well in neither, as Chucho in *Mi Familia*, for example.

Hybridization

Hybridization refers to the blending, rather than alternating, of cultural meanings that is often seen among children of immigrants. According to Falicov (1989), hybridization may "occur in cultural situations in which traditions are not quite past and modernity is not yet wholly present" (p. 74). This process implies a "sort of cognitive cultural know-how" of knowing intuitively or learning with purpose when a particular cultural code is appropriate to one setting versus another. For example, a highly educated woman who is assertive at work and who demands egalitarianism in her intimate relationships may become more solicitous and deferential when interacting with her immigrant parents or grandparents. Hybrid families may have a larger cultural repertoire to respond to dilemmas of family life than families who adhere strictly to traditional values or who, in their efforts to assimilate, try to divest themselves of the values of the culture of origin (Falicov, 1989).

Transculturation

Transculturation recognizes that cultural adaptation is not a linear process. Individuals and families may cross borders linguistically, psychologically, and physically. This may be easier for some Latinx groups, for instance Puerto Ricans who are U.S. citizens and Mexicans due to the geographic proximity of Mexico. Individuals and families often navigate multiple cultural spaces. Moreover, what migrants bring along and leave behind has implications for post-migration adjustment. What comes in the luggage (factual and imaginary), the cultural and social capital, of a migrant often determines their ability to acculturate or transculturate. For U.S.-born or raised offspring, cultural alternation may be necessary. For some, the ability to cross linguistic and literal borders is essential for sound mental health. When families experience conflict, it is helpful to assess to what extent acculturation, transculturation, or alternating cultural practices may be present and contribute to the family distress. Likewise, within these practices resilience and solutions to family dilemmas may be found (Falicov, 1998).

In summary, migrations are massive ecological transitions in time and space that may be filled with loss and disarray, resulting in long-term implications for the migrants and future generations. Involuntary, forced, or coerced migrations may increase vulnerabilities to physical and mental distress as well as family dysfunction. However, migration also creates opportunities for change and adaptation. The family's migration narrative may elucidate the sources of resilience in the family as well as the origins of present-day problems.

Ecological Context

Among the various Latinx groups, similarities may exist in terms of language, cultural values, and religion, but differences also may exist depending on country of origin, reason for migration, and U.S. social and political attitudes toward their particular group, as well as the value and cultural changes that accompany migration. Rumbaut (1994) offers a model of segmented adaptation that is helpful in understanding how migration and its sequelae affect family life. He argues that adjustment to a new context is not a unilinear or unidirectional process. Instead, his theory focuses on three issues when seeking to understand where immigrants settle and how well they fare: first, the nature of migration to the host country (forced or voluntary); second, the initial resources that immigrants bring (education and job skills, social networks); and third, the social context that greets immigrants in the host culture (positive, negative, or ambivalent) (Portes & Borocz, 1989). For example, early waves of Cuban immigrants who were fleeing the Cuban revolution were generally welcomed to the United States and afforded exile status, which included government assistance to reestablish themselves. These Cubans were mostly educated, White, and members of the professional classes. In contrast, exiles that came in in the late 1980s through the Mariel boatlift were less educated and younger, and about 20% were Black. *Marielitos*, as other Cubans and Latinxs named them, who did not have family members in the United States who could vouch for them, faced detention for many months and many ultimately became part of the Cuban underclass of South Florida. Others adjusted and integrated into the larger Cuban community (Skop, 2001).

From a sociological perspective, three factors are critical to immigrant adjustment. Essential among these is the cultural and social capital an immigrant brings; the more resources an immigrant has, such as high level of education and occupational skills, the more they will be able to meet the challenges encountered post migration. A second factor is the variety and kind of government programs available to immigrants, or what Portes and Borocz (1989) term "the context of reception" by the host government. These are also key to the adjustment process. In the case of the first wave of Cuban immigrants of the 1950s, the support included financial assistance and educational programs (Skop, 2001). This level of government reception, as Skop has noted, is quite distinct from the minimal assistance offered to labor migrants. Instead they are often demonized, criminalized, and blamed for economic problems in the United States. A third factor that predicts the immigrants' structural integration is the degree of solidarity and sense of community with compatriots already in the United States. Clearly family and social networks will also facilitate immigrant adjustments. As has been evident in the increased anti-immigrant sentiments of the late 20th century, not all established Mexican American or Latinx compatriots are welcoming of newer unauthorized immigrants from Central America or Mexico. In fact, many politically conservative Latinx groups argue against immigration reform and endorse stricter border enforcement (Southern Poverty Law Center, 2014).

Skop proposes that "place of incorporation" is a fourth element necessary in the segmented adaptation framework. Where immigrants ultimately settle may reflect the degree of sociocultural and economic incorporation of the particular group. Many scholars argue that ethnicity and ethnic identification may exert some influence in residential location. Ethnic enclaves remain, but many Latinxs live in integrated neighborhoods in urban, suburban, and rural areas of the United States. Although 2 decades ago most Latinx lived in rural or semi-rural communities, since the 2000 census, Latinxs predominantly are urban dwellers. Moreover, Skop argues that ethnic communities may be symbolically constructed and not necessarily located within a particular geographic space. For example, Mexican immigrants from Michoacán may continue to identify with their *Michoacano* roots and town of origin despite living in racially and ethnically integrated urban centers in the United States. While their identity is nuanced by U.S. experience, they may remain connected psychologically to their "hometown"; they may evidence transcultural or hybrid cultural practices. Such identification may continue into the second and third generation, even when U.S.-born children have not ever lived or visited their parents' or grandparents' *rancho* or town.

In summary, Latinx families in the United States vary according to socioeconomic status, geographical location, and country of origin. Their **ecological niche** is partly determined by their **intersectional identities**. Likewise, the journey of migration and culture change and the degree of structural integration of immigrant groups has implications for Latinx family organization.

Family Organization

As suggested by sociologists, family structure often is determined by location, work (migrant, seasonal, blue and white collar, professional) and kinship or social ties that were preexistent to the migration. The basic social unit idealized by many Latinx is the extended family, which may include three or four generations as well as horizontal relationships among siblings, cousins (even twice or thrice removed) (Falicov, 1989). Such preference reflects the core value of *familismo* (familism), defined as a strong orientation and commitment toward the family. *Familismo* is not intrinsic to Latinx families; rather it is characteristic of collectivist cultures.[8] *Familismo* is also connected to a high value on

---

8 Collectivistic cultures emphasize the needs and goals of the group as a whole over the needs and wishes of each individual. In such cultures, relationships with other members of the group and the interconnectedness between people play a central role in each person's identity. As a result, values of respect, interdependence, humility, saving face, and personalism are valued more than independence and individualism.

(heterosexual) marriage, childbearing, and responsibility toward siblings. *Familismo* is also accompanied with prescribed duties, including loyalty, and interconnection to family members in both the nuclear and extended family. The ideology of *familismo* extends beyond blood relations to include fictive kin (individuals not related by blood but who have the status of family), which may include extended families of several generations and godparents (*compadres*), in-laws, and close friends (Falicov, 1989; Flores, 2005).

While the cultural ideal reflects the collectivist value of an extended, close-knit, interdependent family organization, post-migration realities result in more diverse family structures. In many cases, the ideal of an extended family system has been replaced by single-parent families, nuclear family households, and "alternative families" (e.g., single adults living together, gay and lesbian couples, common law arrangements, several families living together to share costs) (Flores, 2005). As Minuchin (1974) argued several decades ago, the organization of a family must be understood in terms of the factors that help shape it, in particular the economic realities of the family. Likewise, nativity, generational status, and the social position of the family may influence its structure and organization.[9]

As Falicov (1998) points out, regardless of the household composition, a central organizing principle of Latinx families is the concept of connectedness and the importance ascribed to family bonds. Such connectedness is evident in family rituals, such as baptisms, *quinceañeras*,[10] and other family gatherings. In addition, families who espouse *familismo* expect frequent contact through visits or phone calls to parents, elders in the family, and godparents. Participation in family events and gatherings is valued and expected as well. The failure to meet such expectations, due to migration or economic realities that preclude leisure time activities, can be a source of family conflict. In author Flores's own extended family a great deal of resentment was built because she could not attend family gatherings when she was away at school. After some time, she was no longer invited to baby showers or the birthday parties of her cousin's children. The assumption was that she was "too busy for family affairs." Some family members saw her as too acculturated and cautioned others in the family that the pursuit of higher education eroded family bonds. On more than one occasion, author Flores's parents received sympathy for their lot—having a highly educated professional daughter—which in their eyes changed her. She was seen as no longer prioritizing family activities. As will be discussed in later chapters, the appearance that family connection is not as important as *it should be* for children of immigrants can be a source of distress and conflict for both parents and adult children.

The value of family connection is transmitted to family members by modeling devotion to parents, particularly in their older years, participation in family rituals, and inculcating in the children another important value for Latinx, **personalismo** , which is defined as the concern for the well-being of others and the ethical stance that conflict should be avoided to save face and maintain harmony in family relations. The central element of

---

9   A more detailed analysis of family structure and organization will be provided in later chapters.

10 The *quinceañera* or *quince* is the celebration of a girl's 15th birthday, which historically signaled her entry into womanhood. Among wealthy Mexican families it served as an introduction to society, akin to the cotillion. In the 19th and early 20th centuries, the *quince* was used to present the young woman to society and announce her availability for marriage. In the United States, the *quince* may have more of a religious or cultural meaning and not be associated with readiness for marriage. See Cantu and Najera-Ramirez (2002).

personalismo is emotional resonance and personal involvement with family encounters (Falicov, 1998). These values are related to the concept of familial self, a sense of self that includes one's close relationships as part of who one is (Falicov, 1989). *Tu eres mi otro yo* (you are my other self) is an indigenous Meso American value commonly held among Chicanxs of varying generations (Tello, 2008). This value reflects the notion of the familial self. Another saying in Spanish, *hoy por ti, mañana por mí*, also illustrates this concept. Inherent in the belief that today I do for you because tomorrow you will do for me is the value of interconnectedness and the reciprocity that is expected in family relationships and with fictive kin. The familial self is balanced by the private self, which may be more bounded and more difficult to access in order to maintain relational order. Highly familistic individuals may keep their feelings to themselves and avoid direct confrontations or direct expression of disagreement to protect the feelings of the other and thereby maintain harmony. The feelings may be expressed indirectly or shared with a third party who can try to convey the information without hurting the feelings of the person responsible for the concerns of the aggrieved. Such style of communication may become problematic when family members of different generations or partners from different cultural backgrounds or levels of acculturation do not share the "cultural rules" that govern such interactions.

When U.S.-raised or born children appear to prioritize their private self over the familial self, the immigrant parents may perceive their children as disrespectful, uncaring, or selfish. When one of author Flores's therapy clients, an immigrant woman from Nicaragua, told her mother that she was not willing to expose her daughter to her step-father's drinking and verbal abusiveness, her mother cried in despair, "You don't love me; you are going to kill me with your selfishness." Although the client understood how her mother would interpret her boundary setting as uncaring, she still felt the hurt of her mother's words and experienced significant guilt. Although this interaction is reflective of problematic family dynamics (which will be described in later chapters), it also highlights the differences that emerge between generations in how *personalismo* and *familismo* are lived and negotiated between first- and second-generation Chicanxs and Latinxs.

Since immigrant and second-generation Latinxs often inhabit two psychological spaces (United States and country of origin), their family structure and organization may reflect hybridity or different cultural patterns at various points in the life cycle. For example, a young couple may want to live independently of their parents. When a child is born, they may wish to live in closer proximity to their parents for emotional and logistical support. The grandparents may expect to be very involved with the grandchildren and may suffer if distance or conflict separates them. Latinx adults are expected to take care of aging parents; inability to do so will cause significant emotional distress. Families who adhere to the traditional value of interconnectedness often will rally around family members in need to provide emotional, financial, or logistical support and thereby reduce stress or the burden of caregiving (Flores, 2008).

Given the diversity of Latinxs, it is important to determine how cultural values, their socioeconomic status, nativity, and generation have influenced and shaped their family structure and organization. Equally important is the recognition that the ecological niche occupied by Latinx may be different across generations as some family members may experience upward mobility through education, work or marriage, while others may not, and yet some may face greater economic stress and poverty than did the immigrant generation. Another important aspect to consider is the family life cycle.

Family Life Cycle

From a developmental perspective families are systems that evolve over time. Families, as individuals, go through stages of development. The family life cycle is based on the assumption that individuals continue to marry and form nuclear families. However, it is important to consider cultural influences and how these modify the life cycle. According to McGoldrick (2011) each stage of the family life cycle has tasks and challenges that must be negotiated in order for the family to successfully navigate successive stages. If challenges are not successfully met, subsequent stages may be compromised or the family may dissolve.

The single adult living independently of their parents is a stage added in the late 20th century as increasingly middle-class young adults postponed marriage in order to pursue higher education or to work. The primary task of this stage is to establish economic and emotional independence from parents. The challenge, particularly during economic downturns and high unemployment, is to become or remain economically independent from parents. In Latinx families, as will be discussed in Chapter 2, the independence of late adolescent and young adult children may not be as valued as it is in other ethnic groups. Thus, efforts to move out and become "independent" may be viewed as disloyal or a break from the relational connection to the family that is expected by the immigrant or less acculturated parents. In such families, this stage may be postponed until marriage, the time when it is culturally accepted among traditional Latinxs for children to move out. Author Flores's father used to say that women should leave home either in a white dress or in a coffin. She found an acceptable alternative for an immigrant family; she left home to pursue an education. It was still a time fraught with anxiety for her mother, who became depressed as she found herself more socially isolated and experiencing a role shift and a drastic change in her cultural meaning system. Who was she, if her daughter was not there for her "to mother?"

The second stage of family formation is expected to occur through **marriage**, especially among Latinxs who hold traditional values.[11] The primary task for the newly married couple is to establish boundaries around the new relationship as separate from the families of origin and to balance loyalties between the new family and the family to which they belong (family of origin). There are a number of challenges a newly married couple may encounter: meddlesome in-laws; cultural, religious, or ethnic differences that interfere with the formation of the new family; financial problems; and the possibility of moving away from the parents, which can constitute another migration for the couple or their respective families. Leaving home may trigger memories of earlier migrations and their attendant crises, challenges, or traumas, creating distress for all involved. There are a number of crises the newly married couple may encounter, including not having had

---

11 This is a middle-class value in Latin America, as many couples form unions rather than marry. In the U.S. context "living together" prior to or instead of marriage has become more common among working-class origin Latinx). However, the cultural ideal of having both a civil and religious marriage is still held by many Latinx.

permission to marry the partner, conflicts with family of origin, or marriage due to an unplanned pregnancy. According to family theorists, these circumstances may signal future trouble for the couple as they may render more difficult the successful negotiation of subsequent life cycle stages.

The *birth of the first child* is a significant developmental milestone for any couple. Among some Latinxs, despite being married, a separate family unit may not be recognized until children are born. Couples without children of their own may not be viewed as separate or independent by their traditional parents. The principal task of this stage is to solidify the marriage before having children in order to withstand the challenge of including new family members and to balance preestablished roles to include parenting. Multiple challenges need to be negotiated: differences in ideas about parenting, negotiation of equitable distribution of workload, and balancing the marital, parental, and worker roles. A number of crises may ensue: difficulty balancing multiple roles, difficulty including the child into the couple dyad, or including the partner when the focus is on parenting a small child. Differences in parenting ideals or practices between the family of origin and the new parents may result in the perception (or reality) that grandparents are meddlesome, particularly when grandparents convey the attitude that they know best or try to take over parental duties, which is more likely to happen in multigenerational households (Falicov, 1998). Differences in the degree of *familismo* between partners may increase the tension if one partner desires a greater involvement of grandparents, while the other prefers stronger boundaries between them and the in-laws. Clearly the more children a couple has, or the closer the age of the offspring, the greater the number of adjustments and challenges the couple may face. In more traditional families, the involvement of extended family in childrearing and the help of older children in raising younger ones may reduce the stress faced by the couple who has to parent and to work for a living.

The next significant developmental milestone occurs when *children begin school*. In many families this stage begins much earlier, when babies begin day care. For the parents, especially the mother, this is the beginning of separation from the child, which may occur when the infant is only a few weeks old. This can be a very challenging time for women who work. Significant stress may accompany efforts to balance the parenting and worker roles, return to work (if either parent stayed home), and extended family and partner expectations. A long-term consequence of developmental crisis during this stage can be attachment problems and/or separation anxiety in either the child or the parent or couple conflicts resulting from women feeling overburdened because household tasks are not shared to their satisfaction or their partner's.

Adolescence is a challenging time for most parents. The primary tasks of this developmental stage include allowing increasing independence of the adolescent child while maintaining rules but increasing flexibility. Latinx parents are described as authoritarian or authoritative (Flores, 2005); such parenting practices at times make it difficult to balance cultural expectations nuanced by the parents' own socialization with the demands of modernity. Additional challenges include negotiating differences between partners regarding appropriate levels of independence. Crises may occur when these differences cannot be bridged, resulting in marital discord, adolescent behavioral problems, or conflict between grandparents and parents. In some cases, the adolescent may become the identified patient if the couple is in crisis. The youth may "act out" in order to bring the parents together and rally around their child's "problem" and thereby prevent a separation (Bernal & Flores-Ortiz, 1991).

In the ***launching stage*** the primary task of parents is to prepare the adolescent to leave home. As stated, in some Latinx families, leaving home is not a cultural ideal. Thus, parents may not be prepared for letting their youth leave for college, to move out on their own to seek work, or to leave with roommates or intimate partners outside of marriage. Additional challenges may result with regard to disagreements between the parents as to how and when a child can and should leave home. After the last child is launched, the couple needs to find each other again and reestablish a relationship that may have been neglected due to the demands of parenting and balancing multiple roles. Among some Latinx, the importance accorded to children and child-rearing is far greater than maintaining a close intimate relationship. Contemporary couples may maintain greater balance between the couple and parenting roles and thus experience less "empty nest" than more traditional couples. For those whose primary role was child-rearing, the anticipation of the empty nest may lead to symptoms of depression and reopen the wounds related to the losses of migration, or the appearance of dysfunctional patterns that attempt to keep the child from leaving. In turn, such family crises can result in the pseudo independence of a child, through teen pregnancy or behavioral or mental health problems (Bernal & Flores-Ortiz, 1990; Falicov, 1989).

Recently the ***boomerang stage*** has been added to the life cycle theory to incorporate the return of adult children to the parents' home, alone or with their own nuclear families (Rasheed & Rasheed, 2011). The challenges inherent in this stage have to do with renegotiating personal and collective space and rebalancing roles. In author Flores's own personal situation, her married daughter, her husband, and two daughters returned to live with her after living in another state for 2 years. Their household transformed in a short 5 years from that of a divorced woman living alone to an extended family of a young married couple living with their three children, her daughter's stepson, and the author. Included in the negotiations was allocation of space, relationship boundaries, shared expenses, and decision making regarding the children. Whether they should or could move in with her was never an issue for author Flores. Her son-in-law had concerns about her living alone, post-divorce. He wanted to move in to support and protect her. In author Flores' view, her home was the family home to which her daughter and her family could return anytime, as could her son should he ever need to. Despite author Flores having spent most of her life in the United States and her daughter and son-in-law being second generation, highly educated, and otherwise acculturated, they hold on to strong familistic values. Their working-class origins may be a contributing factor to the maintenance of those values.

The last stage of the family life cycle is referred to as the ***empty nest***, when children have left home and the challenge for the couple is to renew the marriage or partnership without children, rebalance roles, and include grandchildren if present. Among many Latinx, the empty nest never truly occurs, as they are expected culturally to continue the connection to their adult children and become involved with their grandchildren, or in some instances continue to support adult children who by reason of economics or psychosocial issues cannot become fully independent (Cervantes & Félix-Ortiz, 2004). This stage often coincides with middle age and the midlife crisis of one or both partners; if the couple has not maintained their marital relationship, divorce or separation may occur. As stated, among traditional Latinx this crisis is less likely to happen if the couple adheres to traditional cultural roles and their familial self is more dominant than their independent self.

Also included more recently, the ***aging family members stage*** addresses the challenges of providing for older parents while still raising children or supporting adult children. Latinx families and other collectivist groups may experience less dissonance with the need to form multigenerational households to address the realities of the aging of grandparents and the need to become their caregivers (see Flores, 2008). The tasks and challenges of this stage entail dealing with the involvement of grandchildren and partners of adult children, as well as facing the health crisis of old age while striving to maintain their dignity and independence. Author Flores's mother lived with her nuclear family after her father died. Author Flores and her children took care of her until she decided to go to her country to die. There her son took care of her and author Flores traveled frequently to see her and supported her and her son financially during the last 10 years of her mother's life. Author Flores's children expect that they will have to do the same for their father and mother, despite her protestations that they do not have to. The cultural values of *familismo* have been passed down to the next generation through modeling, more than as an explicitly stated expectation.

The life cycle model has been critiqued because it reflects the realities of middle-class European American families to a greater degree than the context of working-class and ethnic minority groups. The model also assumes a linear progression and pathologizes those who do not follow the stages sequentially.[12] The model also is not sensitive to the particular challenges of immigrant families. Clearly the life cycle is more complicated when divorce and remarriage occurs along the way creating a blended family, as we discuss in Chapter 7. However, the model is helpful in understanding at what points families may face developmental challenges or crises that need attention in order to function to the benefit of all its members. Particular challenges may result from pregnancy before marriage, as the couple may not have time to solidify the couple subsystem before a child arrives; therefore, they must negotiate two stages simultaneously. In cultures where child-rearing is more important than the couple relationship, the couple may continually struggle with balancing parental and marital roles. In such cases, women may be dissatisfied with the marriage and become symptomatic (Flores-Ortiz, 1993; Hirsch, 2003).

The life cycle model points to particular times where crises may occur. Couples face a greater risk of separation or divorce during the second stage if they cannot balance family-of-origin obligations with the new family unit, or during adolescence when normative changes overstress a couple without a strong foundation, or during empty nest stage when the couple may see no reason to stay together once the children are grown (Carter & McGoldrick, 1988). For some immigrants, this stage may result in men wanting to return to their country of origin, whereas women may wish to remain closer to the children. Thus, this stage may also result in the formation of transnational families, which will be discussed in Chapter 5.

For Latinx families, migration and the process of acculturation may lead to crisis points as well, as the families need to negotiate "cultural borderlands," the zones of similarity

---

12   The applicability of the model to blended or step-families and LGBTQ families has received some investigation (Rasheed et al., 2010).

and differences between and within cultures (Falicov, 1998). In addition, as stated earlier in this chapter, the need to negotiate or modify cultural meaning systems and cultural expectations, which can be disrupted by migration, may complicate the family life cycle. Acculturation implies adoption of new behaviors, attitudes, and sometimes values that can cause conflict within the family. For effective clinical work with Latinx families, it is critical to explore and understand how nativity, migration, social class and other intersectionalities may nuance family adaptation and negotiation of life cycle stages.

This chapter has provided an overview of the MECA model, highlighting the influence of migration and related legacies, social context, and the family life cycle on the formation of Chicanx and Latinx families. Chapter 2 offers a more detailed analysis of the influence of values, race, culture, gender, and class on the functioning of diverse Latinx families.

HOMEWORK ASSIGNMENT

1. Reflecting on Sluki's model of migration and family life, in what stage do you think your parents, siblings, grandparents, and you are at the present time? Provide examples.
2. In terms of the family life cycle, at what stage of family development is your nuclear family (parents and siblings) at the present time?
3. What do you think are the major challenges your family has faced relative to the family migration cycle?
4. What is your role in your family, thinking about it in terms of Sluzki's model?

KEY TERMS

Adolescence: A transitional stage of physical and psychological development that generally occurs during the period from puberty to legal adulthood. Adolescence is usually associated with the teenage years, but its physical, psychological, or cultural expressions may begin earlier and end later.

Aging family members stage: During the retirement phase of the family life cycle individuals witness many changes such as becoming grandparents and seeing children marry or divorce.

Alternation: Refers to cultural alternation and those individuals who are able to gain competence within two cultures without losing their cultural identity or having to choose one culture over the other.

Assimilation: The process in which a minority group or culture comes to resemble a dominant group or assume the values, behaviors, and beliefs of another group.

Authoritarian: A parenting style characterized by high demands and low responsiveness. Parents with an authoritarian style have very high expectations of their children yet provide very little in the way of feedback and nurturance. Mistakes tend to be punished harshly.

Authoritative: A parenting style characterized by high responsiveness and high demands. Authoritative parents are responsive to the child's emotional needs while having high standards. They set limits and are very consistent in enforcing boundaries.

The bridge: Based on migration patterns this is the first family member or friend who migrates and helps others to migrate after them.

Boomerang stage: Refers to an adult who has moved back home to live with parents after a period of living independently. Frequently used in the press, this term is sometimes applied to individuals but also describes a generational shift, referred to as the boomerang generation.

Coaxed: Gently and persistently persuaded to do something.

Cultural borderlands: Viewed as a psychological space in which border-crossers struggle with their bicultural or multicultural identities. In this borderland individuals decide how much they want to identify with their cultures of origin or of adoption.

Cultural cut-offs: Experienced by immigrants who left behind their countries of origin and who have less access to their cultural practices and traditions.

Ecological niche: The role and position a species has in its environment; how it meets its needs for food and shelter, how it survives, and how it reproduces. A species's niche includes all of its interactions with the biotic and abiotic factors of its environment.

Ecosystemic: An approach to therapy that emphasizes the interaction between the individual or family and larger social contexts, such as schools, workplaces, and social agencies.

Empty nest: A household consisting only of a parent or parents whose children have grown up and left home.

Explanatory models: In psychology those help determine if what is being observed might be explained by a currently existing theory.

Familismo: Cultural value among Latinx; refers to the importance of strong family loyalty, closeness, and getting along with and contributing to the well-being of the nuclear family, extended family, and kinship networks.

Fictive kin: A term used by anthropologists and ethnographers to describe forms of kinship or social ties that are based on neither consanguineal (blood ties) nor affinal (by marriage) ties. It contrasts with true kinship ties.

Frozen: In cultural terms it refers to those immigrants who maintain and adhere to the traditions, values, and customs from their country of origin as how they were when they left.

The identified patient: A clinical term often heard in family therapy discussion. It describes one family member in a dysfunctional family who expresses the family's authentic inner conflicts.

Intersectional identities: Including gender, race, ethnicity, class, and sexuality. Some individuals prefer to use the plural word *identities*, emphasizing that identity is fluid and shifts throughout one's life.

Launching stage: Starts when the first child leaves home and ends with the empty nest. New members are added into the family through children's relationships.

Marriage: Also called matrimony or wedlock, is a culturally recognized union between people, called spouses, that establishes rights and obligations between them, as well as between them and their children and between them and their in-laws.

Meaning systems: A branch of both theoretical psychology and applied psychology that studies human behavior and experience in complex systems. Groups and individuals are considered systems in homeostasis or balance.

Mourner: Refers to the family member in a family of immigrants who maintains cultural practices and traditions.

Over-acculturator: Refers to a member in a family of immigrants born in the new country who shows less loyalty to culture and traditions.

Personalismo: Cultural construct among Latinx that emphasizes the importance of relationships, warmth, and kindness among individuals but also refers to the unconditional recognition of the essential value of each individual rather than from their social status or from their professional accomplishments.

Psychological homelessness: A lack of a sense of worth, purpose, and belonging in an individual.

Segmented adaptation: Suggests how immigrant groups get incorporated into different segments of society.

Transnational families: Those families whose members are separated physically between two or more nation-states but maintain close ties and relationships. Transnational families must also cope with family separation and associated difficulties.

Under-acculturator: Refers to a member in a family of immigrants born in the new country who remains loyal to cultural practices and traditions.

2

The Influence of Cultural Values, Race, and Class on Family Functioning

Introduction

Mexican American and Latinx families have been studied since the 1950s by sociologists, anthropologists, and psychologists (Peñalosa, 1968). Early accounts of family life tended to rely primarily on cultural deficit models of analysis that were grounded on comparisons of these families to an idealized "European American norm." Literature from psychology tended to exclude a more nuanced analysis of the influence of structural integration or lack thereof (Falicov, 1998, 2013) on the ways in which families were organized and functioned. Sociological and anthropological studies also essentialized Latinx culture, as if it were monolithic, thereby creating stereotypic accounts of Mexican American and Latinx family life.[1] In general, family problems were seen to result from the culture of the family or their lack of assimilation to or adoption of presumably more functional European American family patterns. It was not until the late 1960s and early 1970s that Chicanx and Latinx scholars began to study families through broader lenses (Keefe & Padilla, 1987; Minuchin et al., 1967). These authors argued that Chicanx and Latinx cultural values were not the root cause of family problems; instead it was the family's experiences with discrimination and inequality that often resulted in family problems.

In the 1980s with the emergence of family psychology and a shift toward a broader analysis of the family as a system that operates within and is influenced by a larger social context, more attention began to be paid to the role of socioeconomic class on family functioning. However, it was not until the mid 1980s and the work of McGoldrick, Giordano, and Garcia Preto (2005) and Falicov (1998), among others, that Latinx families began to be studied holistically, paying attention to the influence of ethnicity, race, class, and gender on how families form and function. While foregrounding the position of Latinxs within the larger U.S. society, Falicov (1998) and Bernal and Flores Ortiz (1982, 1984) and

---

1   See for example Lewis (1961) and Madsen (1964).

Bernal et al., (1986) also argue that understanding Latinx values is crucial to the analysis of how Latinxs construct the idea of family and give meaning to the experience of family life.

This chapter examines the role of cultural values in the formation and functioning of families at various points in the family life cycle. The ways in which the family's intersectionalities (ethnicity/race/class/sexuality) also influence family organization and functioning is examined through case vignettes as well. The importance of gender and the gendering of family members is considered, particularly as it relates to the negotiation of power and the performance of roles within the family.

Role of Cultural Values in Latinx Family Life

The family became the central social unit of Latinx during the colonial period; Spaniards and other Europeans brought to the Americas a value system that privileged a patriarchal and patrilineal family organization. During this period, a caste system based on nativity, indigeneity, color, and gender also influenced family formation (Fuentes, 1999). Spanish nobility held the highest social position with the Indigenous holding the bottom of the social class (Johnson & Henderson, 2002). To preserve racial purity and ensure control of the "landholdings" the Spanish crown established laws that only recognized legitimate children who were born within the marriage of two Spaniards. The offspring of Spaniards and Native women, whether born of rape or voluntary union, were not considered legal heirs. Thus, the importance of legal Catholic marriages was used to maintain the caste/class system.

The history of colonization in Latin America left a legacy of racism and discrimination based on color, phenotype, and an idealization of the White European, particularly with regard to standards of beauty. Many families who aspired to raise their social status discouraged their offspring from mixing with darker-skinned individuals or those whose features suggested Indigenous or African ancestry. "Passing" for White was desired by many. Within the U.S. context, darker skin also rendered Latinx immigrants and those born in the United States more at risk for discrimination. At various points in U.S. history (see Acuña, 2007), open discrimination against Mexicans was legal in southern states, including Texas. For many Mexican origin families, experiences of racism influenced the raising of their children, whether or not cultural values and practices were passed down to the next generation, and even whether Spanish was taught (see Zavella, 2001a). Thus, to truly understand Latinx family dynamics, including racial identification, recognition of or adherence to the ancestral cultures and language, the family's history of oppression must be considered.

During the colonial period to ensure the power of the crown, a set of values became reified, among them familism—the expectation of loyalty to the social group connected by blood and kinship ties—and respect to authority, elders, and people of a higher class. These values were instilled through education and religion. Identity was linked to a familial self and family name, which in turn situated the individual within a family group linked to a particular class. Men held the power and the privilege and were expected to form a family and produce heirs. They were not expected to be monogamous but to be discreet. Patriarchal privilege included the right to have as many women as they chose. *Machismo* emerged as a set of rules of conduct for men that included chivalry, honor, responsibility toward the crown, the church, and blood kin. Virility was also valued, often resulting in the pattern of forming *casas grandes* and *casas chicas* (Paz, 2003). The former, literally "the big house," was the family home where the wife and legitimate children lived. The latter referred to the home where a man's mistress and illegitimate children were housed. A "good man" provided for all his women and children and generally was admired for his landholdings and his progeny. Spanish women, on the other hand, were expected to be faithful as a way to ensure racial purity and preserve the family name. Religion was used to strengthen the expectation of sexual purity. Girls were expected to be like the Virgin Mary: pure, virginal, devoted, and pious. Their role was to protect the family name, support the husband, as well as raise children who would honor their father. A virgin-whore dichotomy was created that was also racialized. Being a legitimate wife, *la señora*, was the highest aspiration a woman was expected to have (Flores, 2013; Hurtado, 2003). All other women a husband might have, *las otras*, the others, had no value; they were cast as whores who did not threaten the *señoras'* status because they were not the legal wives nor "ladies." The sexuality of "good women" was to be controlled by their fathers, brothers, and husbands. The others were cast as wanton, licentious, and immoral. Given their lack of morals, they could be used by men of higher status at will. Indigenous men, who had suffered the indignity and trauma of conquest and who carried legacies of oppression, were punished if they so much as looked at a White man's woman. According to psychoanalytic Mexican writers (Diaz-Guerrero, 1956; Paz, 2003) this historical context gave rise to the dark side of Machismo—men who both loved and hated women, who blamed women for their own *mestizaje*, and who engaged in hypermasculine behaviors (fighting, womanizing, drinking) to mask their trauma, their grief, and their feelings of inferiority.

The colonization of Indigenous people in the Americas left a legacy of cultural hybridity, intergenerational trauma, and the potential for troubled intimate relationships (Flores & Valdez Curiel, 2009). Within the Spanish caste/class system, those born in Spain had highest value, followed by *criollos,* Spaniards born in the Americas. *Mestizos*, those of Indigenous and Spanish descent, were generally illegitimate and marginalized, as were Mulattos (Spanish-African descendants), Africans, and Indigenous inhabitants of the colonies. Colorism, the value ascribed to people based on their skin color, and phenotype became important markers for social desirability or marginalization. The value of **respect** also became important; it was demanded of those in a lower social location and expected of children and spouses and extended family members. Social approval and social desirability were important to maintain one's social location and codes of interpersonal conduct—personalism—to ensure protection of the family name was developed and taught. The concept of *el que dirán* (What will people say?) became an important element of parenting. However, these Spanish values were also influenced by the Indigenous value system of collaboration, mutuality, and interpersonal accountability. Personalism also entails regard for the well-being of others and indirectness in confrontation and communication in order to not offend, to "save face." The value system during the colonial period in the Americas was transmitted by education, religion, parenting, and *dichos*, sayings. For example, *Hoy por ti y mañana por mi* (Today I do for you; tomorrow you do for me) is reflective of the mutuality that informs personalism (Flores, 2005).

Prior to the conquest, the primary social group had been the clan; children were raised communally and their identity was connected to the land and the ancestors (Flores, 2013). Parents and community elders were expected to root the children into the values of the group and help identify the child's destiny (Flores, 2013; Tello, 2008). These values were maintained to varying degrees during the colonial period due to the marginalization of the Indigenous and the *mestizo*; however, enculturation to "Spanish ways" was carried out through Christianization efforts. What emerged over time in the Americas was a hybrid culture that valued family connections, in part because often the family was the only source of support, yet maintained some Indigenous values, including collectivism and social accountability.

In the study of families, values can be viewed as mirrors of the culture; they can be traditional, transitional, or contemporary. Values also can be viewed as idealized, ideal, and enacted. Idealized values refer to the cultural scripts of how things "should be." Ideal values refer to conduct and behaviors the family and/or individuals aspire to or prefer; enacted values are what people actually perform (Bernal & Alvarez, 1983).

Among Latinx, idealized values include virginity before marriage and fidelity thereafter for women, but not necessarily for men. Other idealized values are respect for elders, solidarity (*compañerismo*), cooperation, and collectivism. With increasing acculturation and modernization, individuals' behaviors mirror idealized values less and less. Moreover, in modern times Latinx families continue to reflect hybrid cultural influences. Familism, personalism, and respect are cultural ideals. Respect for elders, those in authority, and extended kin are central to Latinx parenting (Flores, 2005); interpersonal accountability, social desirability, and protection of the family name are still highly valued. The degree of adherence to these cultural ideals varies depending on the family's and individual's level of acculturation to non-Latinx cultures, exposure to other cultural values, and parenting practices.

Adherence to traditional values also may be influenced by the family's relationship to the means of production. At any given time, values and social class interact to influence specific family behaviors, attitudes, or practices (Bernal & Alvarez, 1983).

TABLE 2.1 Social Class and Cultural Values in Family Life

		Traditional	Transitional	Contemporary
Urban families	Wealthy			
	Middle class			
	Working class			
Rural families	Large landowners			
	Small farmers			
	Migrant farmers			

Adapted from: "Cultural Perspectives in Family Therapy," *Cultural Perspectives in Family Therapy*, pp. 38. Copyright © 1983 by Aspen Publishers.

Idealized values refer to the cultural scripts of how things "should be" (Falicov, 1998, 2013; Flores, 2013), for example the enculturation of female children to be modest, loyal, and pure in order to marry well. Ideal values refer to conduct and behaviors the family and/or individuals aspire to or prefer; for example "a well-educated child" is one who is obedient to parents and other family members and is respectful, humble, and deferential. An ideal man is one who is honest, hardworking, responsible, chivalrous, and loyal (Flores, 2013). Enacted values are what people actually perform.

Among Latinxs, idealized values include virginity before marriage and fidelity thereafter for women, but not necessarily for men. Other idealized values are respect for elders, solidarity (compañerismo), cooperation, and collectivism. Ramirez (1967, 1969), among others, posits that values often are at the core of people's behaviors and less likely to change *initially* due to contact with other cultures. Attitudes and behaviors may change more rapidly to facilitate adaptation, particularly among immigrant adolescents and children. With increasing acculturation and modernization, individuals' behaviors may mirror idealized values less and less, often resulting in conflict between parents and children, as demonstrated in the case study that follows.

The Lopez Family

Jose and Elena Lopez were referred to therapy after Elena slapped Judy, their 15-year-old daughter, and the school became concerned when Judy told her teacher about it. It was not the first time Elena and her daughter had engaged in a loud altercation. According to Elena, since age 13 Judy had become *malcriada e irrespetuosa* (bad mannered and disrespectful). Elena described her eldest child as a loving, kind, *considerate* girl until age 13; overnight, it seemed, she had become "willful and disrespectful." Judy stated that her mother was rigid, authoritarian, uptight, and disrespectful. The conflict that led to the referral began when Elena told Judy to change clothes. According to Elena, her daughter was dressing inappropriately: Her shorts were too short and her shirt showed too much cleavage. When Judy refused to change, Elena "lost it" and told her daughter she looked like a slut (*pareces una puta*). In response, Judy called her mother a bitch, and, horrified, Elena slapped her.

José indicated that he did not know what to do. It seemed to him that his wife had overreacted but agreed that Judy had become a stranger to him as well. His sweet little girl had become an angry, disrespectful teen. Their two younger children, an 11-year-old boy and a 5-year-old girl, were terrified by the hostile climate in the home.

José was a second-generation Chicano; Elena had immigrated to the United States as an adolescent. Both held strong familistic values; however, José appeared to be more flexible in his parenting style. He believed that Judy should have more independence than did his wife. His wife was raised by traditional parents and stated that she had difficulty adjusting to the United States when she first arrived. Her parents lived as if they had never left rural Michoacán; they were strict and Elena did not date until she started working after graduating high school. Elena did not challenge her parents' ways and was comfortable growing up in a primarily immigrant Mexican community. José had met Elena at the grocery store where she worked, and he often shopped when he visited his parents in "the barrio." Traditional parents raised him, but as a male he had been granted a lot of freedom. He went to college and became an architect. He had paid off his parents' home when he obtained his first job and had later bought himself a home in an ethnically diverse suburb. When he asked Elena out, she told him he would have to come ask permission of her parents. He thought that was "cute" and agreed. When he told his mother, she was happy that he was interested in someone *de buena familia*. His mother equated traditionalism with being a good family—one who raises proper well-mannered and modest daughters.

José went to visit Elena's parents, accompanied by his mother, to ask permission to date Elena. The two families soon became friends, and within 1 year, José and Elena had married both legally and in the church, as was the Mexican tradition. Elena was 20 and José 25 years old when they married. Elena worked until Judy was born and then remained home raising the children. She was a loving and devoted mother and wife. They tried to raise their children with traditional values of familism and respect. They visited each other's parents on Sunday after church, and although they had a diverse group of friends, Elena felt more comfortable with other Mexican women and felt a bit out of place with the more educated couples in José's social network. The couple spoke Spanish at home, as Elena did not fully master English in school and was more comfortable speaking Spanish. José was more fluent in English than Spanish, so he often "slipped" into speaking English with the children. Judy was bilingual but preferred to speak English. This was a source of contention between her and her mother. Elena felt hurt that her daughter spoke less and less Spanish and often answered her in English. Elena felt disrespected.

As Judy entered adolescence, both parents felt ill equipped to parent a girl who was influenced by U.S. culture more than their own Mexican ways. Elena was particularly concerned about her daughter's sexuality and tried to control it, as her parents had controlled and protected her own. However, Judy was not as docile as Elena had been. Judy was offended that her mother had called her a slut, when she was a "good girl." The family had reached an impasse.

The "problem" in this family can be understood as reflective of cultural differences. Elena espoused traditional cultural values, largely idealized, and had difficulty supporting Judy's biculturality. She relied on cultural scripts learned in the home—the dichotomization of good versus bad females—and feared that her daughter would be judged as "bad" due to her style of dress. Judy, whose primary exposure to Latinx and Mexican culture was through the media and immediate family, was presented with objectified sexualized images of Latinas. She did not feel she was dressing inappropriately; rather, she was dressing like all her other Latina friends. She did not see her disagreement with her mother as disrespectful; instead, she was attempting to express her views and exercise her own agency. José felt torn; he wanted to support his wife's parenting views but felt she was too strict. He loved Judy and admired her "spunk" but could not let her disrespect his wife.

What often leads to this type of problem is lack of communication about underlying values. Parents often do not realize that cultural values have to be taught; they are not assimilated by osmosis. Moreover, U.S.-born and/or -raised children are exposed to multiple cultural influences. They also must negotiate more complex identities than did their immigrant parents. In family therapy, José and Elena were invited to discuss their underlying value systems and expectations as well as the concerns they had regarding

Judy's place in the world as a female and as a Mexican origin woman. In turn, Judy was able to ask questions of her parents and negotiate age-appropriate activities. They all worked on improving communication. The parents were largely unaware of the sociocultural demands and the degree of marginalization their daughter faced on a daily basis. Judy did not know her parents as people informed by the cultural values of their families of origin. Conversations about these issues and foregrounding the family's history and current social context helped the parents and Judy negotiate the normative challenges of adolescence. The mother-daughter relationship took some time to heal, but eventually both came to understand and respect their uniqueness and similarities.

At various points in the family life cycle different levels of adherence to traditional values may create conflict. For newly formed couples, balancing the social, individual, and family self and loyalty expectations from the family of origin may create stress. Traditional Latinx families tend to be child centered; that is, parenting may take a more prominent role than the couple relationship. If Latinas and Latinos with different levels of adherence to this value coparent, one may feel neglected if the mother focuses more on being a mother than being a wife. If women try to balance both roles, more traditional family members may criticize her as selfish or chastise her for not being sufficiently self-sacrificing.

A devoted mother who focused primarily on parenting raised author Flores. Her father, who lost his mother at a young age, supported her mother's focus on being a mother but found sexual partners outside the marriage. As a function of acculturation and education, and of migrating to the United States in her youth, author Flores's values became transitional. She balanced parenting with education, work, and marriage. As is the case with many Latinas, trying to fulfill multiple roles and obligations was a challenge and often fraught with stress. Author Flores was able to fulfill her academic desires and career aspirations because her mother helped her raise her children. Both of her parents filled in whenever she was too busy (Flores, 1998). Author Flores's daughter demonstrates a more contemporary value system: She is a caring mother and wife who works and takes time for herself. She juggles her multiple obligations and roles with greater ease than her mother ever did. She is reflective of more contemporary values—highly familistic with a strong familial and individual self. Moreover, as did her mother before her, author Flores supports her daughter and her husband's parenting of their children. In this way she also fulfills her own cultural script of being a good grandmother. However, the fulfillment of this role is nuanced by author Flores's privilege; as an academic, she has the time to help out her daughter given her flexible work schedule.

Social Class

Historically, family organization and the enactment of gender roles was influenced, if not determined, by the family's relationship with the means of production. Agricultural families included small and large landowners, peasants, itinerant workers, and migrant workers. In rural settings these are still the predominant classes; these families tended to be larger, extended, with more children, and dependent on the seasonal nature of agriculture. For example, families who experienced the *tiempo muerto*, the time of year when there is no cultivation of crops, also could face the migration of males and young adults who follow other crops (Bernal & Alvarez, 1983). In these families gender roles may be more flexible. While the male head of household may hold most of the decision-making power while he is at home, once he leaves the woman emerges as head of household and exercises greater authority. Some women refer to this as "borrowed power" (Flores & Valdez-Curiel, 2009). When the man returns, she needs to cede the power. In such families, male and female children may be exposed to shared power and less strict division of labor along gender lines.

The Industrial Revolution brought about mass migrations and a shift from agricultural economies to wage labor; in turn, families became less extended, with fewer children, and often with more rigid sex roles. Likewise, the Industrial Revolution gave rise to a class structure that was not necessarily land based, but rather on the accumulation of wealth. The upper class enjoyed wealth, while the middle class strove to attain it and the working class worked to survive; their production increased the wealth of the upper classes (Bernal & Alvarez, 1983). The upper class enjoyed leisure time and the privilege of their social position. Gender roles tended to be more fluid while still showing traditional practices and expectations. Many of the roles and tasks typically ascribed to women—taking care of children, cooking, cleaning, and so forth—were performed by maids who were women from the lower classes, thereby freeing up the time of wealthy women to pursue education or leisure activities. The middle class typically consisted of women and men who worked and raised families with the aid of extended family members or older children who helped with parenting and domestic chores. The poor remained poor and strove to survive economically and to raise children, often in adverse conditions that limited education and upward mobility.

In most of Latin America the class divisions that were created during the colonial period remain. Industrialization and neoliberal policies have created greater economic disparities, resulting in domestic and international migrations, both unauthorized and authorized, as people pursue greater economic opportunities. Likewise, political instability and repression in many Latin American countries as a result of military dictatorships, civil wars, and U.S. intervention also have destabilized economies and contributed to migration to the United States (Falicov, 2013).

In the late 20th century, economic shifts in the United States gave rise to the working poor and, as a result of the welfare system, a nonworking class. Many Latinx families fall into the category of the working poor. Their values often reflect the importance of hard work and education as a way out of poverty, yet their social position and limited structural integration (Rumbaut, 1994) prevents many of their children to attain the American dream of upward mobility. Farm work remains a large source of employment for immigrant Mexicans; blue-collar jobs in construction and manufacturing are also prevalent among Latinx, as are service jobs: housekeeping, maintenance, and landscaping/gardening. Few Latinos hold managerial or professional jobs. Therefore, Latinx are overrepresented among the working poor (55% versus 36% of all working adults; 2015–2017 average), while Whites are underrepresented (25% versus 39% of all working adults) (Public Policy Institute of California (PPIC), 2019).

The relationship of socioeconomic status to health outcomes has become painfully evident during the COVID-19 pandemic, as the majority of Latinx hold jobs considered essential in the service sector, sanitary workers, hospitality staff, and janitorial services, among others. They cannot shelter at home. Instead they must work. As a result, they have been exposed to the virus and constitute a large percentage of COVID-19-related deaths in New York and California. Latinx in New York have a 2.6 times higher death than the rate for Whites. In California, where Latinx are 36% of the population, they are 39% of the deaths (APM Research Lab, 2020).

Likewise, increased poverty and "economic downturns" have resulted in homeless families and family systems that "break down," resulting in dysfunction in the form of individual and family social and mental health problems. Latinx children in foster care have increased significantly in the past decade (Casey Family, 2010); this is indicative of a substantial breakdown in the family's ability to parent and protect its children, a core cultural value (Flores, 2013).

Families may share more similarities with others of the same class level from different ethnic or racial groups than with families of the same ethnicity of higher or lower class. Irrespective of the class position Latinx families occupy, core cultural values may influence patterns of interaction and determine what is considered important. The enactment of core values, however, will be influenced by the intersection of class and culture (Bernal & Alvarez, 1983; Falicov, 1998). At any given time, families can be "plotted" in terms of class and culture, thus producing great within–ethnic group diversity. As stated earlier, according to Williams (1990), with increasing upward mobility, the gender and family roles of Chicanxs change significantly. Women for example, may define themselves more in terms of their professional than family role. Stress related to internal conflict regarding cultural loyalty and adherence to traditional values may accompany such shifts in identi-fication and variation in the performance of gender roles (Flores-Ortiz, 1993).

All these factors are influenced by generational and acculturation level. More recent immigrants, particularly from rural areas of Mexico and Central America, may hold more traditional values. Their children, born or raised in the United States may evidence transitional values in the second generation and beyond; those who have attained higher education and social status may also hold more contemporary values, which primarily nuance gender relations, power dynamics within the family, and sexuality (Flores, 1993; Flores & Valdez Curiel, 2009). In the Lopez family discussed earlier, the husband's edu-cation and career opportunities positioned them in the middle class. The family took vacations, owned a home, and appeared to enjoy the benefits of their social class. Yet in the home Elena tried to create traditional family life; she stayed home and raised chil-dren. She helped them with homework, prepared all the meals, and while her husband "helped" she was still primarily responsible for household management. They parented their children together; however, Elena held more traditional views of parenting. She was authoritative; she believed children should not question their parents' dictums and should display respect. Elena expected Judy to be modest, collaborative, and kind. When Judy entered adolescence and began to express her own views and imitate her peer's style of dress, Judy became authoritarian. Conflict arose between them. In this family the class position influenced some of their behaviors, but the mother's value system remained traditional while Judy's showed transitional values, as did her father's. Elena worried her daughter's behavioral changes were nuanced by her anxieties about Judy's nascent sexuality. Elena "heard tapes in [her] head" of her mother's admonitions about a girl's proper conduct—how she should act, dress, and talk—to gain and maintain respect from men. Elena worried that her daughter's appearance and style, which to her was provocative and inappropriate, would draw the attention of men with bad intentions who would perceive her daughter as wanton and cheap. Elena was unconsciously influenced by the *puta thing* (Souza, 2001), the fear of *el que dirán*, that her daughter would be criticized and harmed by a misperception of who she was. When Judy called her a bitch, Elena was so offended she responded with aggression, something she had never done before and regretted immediately.

As the parents externalized their internal value system, their three children began to understand their parents' position on many issues and comprehend how cultural values, and their parents' own upbringing, influenced their expectations of how their offspring should behave. Judy came to see her mother as a woman who held traditional Mexican values that often clashed with U.S. adolescent views of what was appropriate behavior and dress. Judy's ethnic identity was not fully solidified (Hurtado & Gurin, 2004). Her peer group was mixed, Latina and European American; she preferred to speak English, and while speaking Spanish with her maternal grandparents, she did not identify as Mexican but as Latina, although she did not have a clear sense of what that meant. She stated that she was not White and did not feel fully accepted by White peers. Thus, she socialized mostly with other second-generation Latinas, some of whom were of Mexican origin. Until the family therapy sessions, she had not given much thought to what it meant to identify as Latina or how her parents' culture and upbringing had affected her own sense of self and ethnic identity.

The intersection of race and class can create significant crisis points for families, as seen in the following vignette.

Lola and Luis were White Cuban exiles who migrated to California after a few years living in Florida. When Luis obtained a better job in the San Francisco Bay Area, the family relocated. In Cuba, Lola and Luis's families had been financially secure. However, after the Revolution, their parents fled, fearing that their children would be indoctrinated as communists. Lola and Luis were raised in South Florida and lived among other exiles who viewed their migration to the United States as temporary. As a result, both were raised with traditional values and the expectation that once Fidel Castro fell, the families would return to Cuba and assume their proper place in society. When Lola and Luis partnered, they vowed to raise their children with "Cuban values." The family was referred to therapy when their 14-year-old daughter, Elizabet, told her teacher that her mother had slapped her. After a social worker visited the home, she concluded that the family would benefit from counseling. Lola initially did not want to see a psychologist and insisted that the problem was Elizabet's lack of respect. However, in order not to lose custody of her daughter, she needed to agree to treatment.

During the course of the first interview, Lola argued that Elizabet deserved to be slapped, as she had behaved inappropriately. After significant prodding, Lola disclosed that she had caught her daughter kissing a boy outside the door of the home. Elizabet added that the problem was not the kiss; the problem was that her boyfriend was Black. Lola vehemently denied that she was racist but insisted that a proper young lady does not kiss anyone where people can see her. Elizabet insisted that had the boy been White, her mother "would not have lost her shit." Luis seemed particularly annoyed by the discussion and also argued that race had nothing to do with it. The young man, he argued, dressed like a thug with sagging pants, and neither he nor his wife knew the parents; therefore, they could not assess whether he was of good moral character. Elizabet was incensed by her parents' stereotypic views. Although both Lola and Luis denied being racist, they readily admitted that they would never approve of a young man from a lower social status. Furthermore, they assumed that the young man was of low socioeconomic status because he was Black. The parents admitted that inside their home they lived as if they had never left Cuba but accepted that Elizabet had to negotiate a fairly different social context. However, while at home she was expected to act "like a proper Cuban girl." Luis worked and had contact with individuals from many cultures. Lola, however, rarely left home and only socialized with a few White Latinas, mostly exiles from Chile and Argentina, she had met. She did not socialize with Mexicans or Central Americans, as she perceived them to be poor or working class. She argued that they had nothing in common. Elizabet was an early adolescent who rejected what she perceived to be "old school" values and racist and classist attitudes held by her parents. Although the focus of treatment had to be improved parent-child relationship in order to prevent child maltreatment, the parents' values and expectations had to be understood and stereotypic notions had to be challenged. These are difficult but essential conversations in working with Latinx families.

Parenting

Latinx parenting practices are described as largely authoritative (Flores, 2005); the children are rooted into the value system of the parents by example and by explicit and implicit expectations. Often through sayings or *dichos* parental messages are conveyed regarding the way to remain on the good path and become a productive citizen. Tello (2008) argues that in pre-Colombian times parenting was the responsibility of the community and the family. Children were to be rooted into their clan and actively taught the values of the people through example and stories. Through colonization and in more recent times, parenting has become increasingly the responsibility of the nuclear family, which often must root the child to the family's culture while the schools acculturate to the dominant culture.

The Lopez family raised their children with largely traditional values that were reflected in how they lived, their high degree of contact with their families of origin, their church participation, and the expectation that family loyalty and respect were fundamental. Although they lived in the suburbs, they visited the grandparents who had remained in ethnic enclaves, or *barrios*. José had tried to move his parents closer to their home, but his father and mother preferred to stay "*entre Mexicanos.*" José's father had experienced a great deal of racism and discrimination when he first came to the United States as a *bracero*. He did not want to reexperience that marginalization by moving into a more affluent, predominantly White neighborhood. He liked walking to the *mercado* and chatting with older immigrant men. His wife also preferred to remain in her *barrio*, where she knew the people and had lady friends on whom she could rely for social support.

José and Elena modeled for their children respect for their parents, concern for their well-being, and loyalty. At the same time, they modeled traditional gender roles within the home. José was not waited on by the women to the same degree as his father, but he also benefited from the male privilege traditional Mexican culture afforded men. He was the provider; consequently, he did not have to help out much at home. Judy and her younger sister had already noticed, and denounced, that their younger brother had less chores assigned to him than they did. Judy felt it was unfair that by virtue of her gender and of being the eldest she should be responsible for most of the chores. Her mother insisted that it was important for her daughter to learn how to run a home, cook, clean, and be of service to her husband. Elena became upset when Judy challenged these home practices, which Judy considered sexist. Elena viewed her daughter's disagreement as disrespect; Judy saw her complaints as legitimate.

Authoritarian parenting practices are characterized by rigid rules, typically along gender lines, and offer little room for negotiation. Children are to be seen and not heard. In these families patriarchal practices are more stringent. Sometimes men eat first, children second, and women last; women wait on the men and boys hand and foot, from mothers to wives and daughters. In traditional and transitional families, boys tend to have less responsibility with home chores; often they are expected to help their fathers with more masculine chores (e.g., washing cars, yard work, etc.), reflecting the view that the home is women's turf and the outside world is the realm of men (Flores, 2005).

More acculturated and higher-status families may practice more contemporary values and exercise less traditional gender role assignments. Their parenting practices may be seen as more egalitarian or democratic (Flores, 2005). Boys and girls are taught basic family values and their gender role expectations may be more age dependent than based on cultural ideals of how men and women *should* act or behave. Among our working class–origin college students, traditional masculine values of being responsible, respectful, and loyal remain deeply ingrained despite U.S. nativity and higher education. The women often hold more contemporary values regarding gender roles and simultaneously hold highly familistic views. Often the women experience internal conflict if their behavioral patterns do not match the underlying value system inculcated by the parents (Flores, 2013).

In general, immigrant parents find it more challenging to parent U.S.-born or -raised children since these are exposed to the cultures of the school and the peer system; over-time these cultural influences may appear to take over the values taught or expected at home. Some parents feel that they are losing control of or influence over their children and may become more authoritarian in order to feel they are doing a good enough job of preparing their children to follow the good path. Others seek ways to support their children's biculturality, while others feel overwhelmed and become permissive, as they perceive it to be less stressful than trying to maintain traditional values in a social context perceived not to support their efforts. In general, Latinx parenting practices vary by class, nativity, level of education, and acculturation. However, the fundamental values of respect, familism, and personalism remain to varying degrees across generations of Latinx families.

Coupling

Cultural values and social class also influence how couples form and negotiate their intimate relationships. Patriarchal notions of power and privilege influence heterosexual couple relationships among Latinx. The stereotypical description of traditional Latinx couples is that of a submissive, docile wife and an overbearing, controlling *macho*. While such relationships do exist, the partnering of Latinx males and females is far more complex and largely influenced by class, education, the value system of the partners, and the larger social context in which they live and love.

Latinx adults tend to marry and stay married. In 2012 there were 11.6 million Latino households. Of these 62.3% were married couple households. Over 60% of Latinx married couples had children under 18 living in the home; 65.7% of Latinx children lived with both parents. Only about 28,000 children lived with only their father and about 131,000 lived only with their grandparents (U.S. Census Bureau, 2012). Latinx have had lower divorce rates than other ethnic groups and tend to marry other Latinx with greater prevalence than they marry European Americans or other ethnic or racial groups.

Latinx families generally expect their children to marry and form their own families. In Latin America women tend to marry young, unless they pursue an education. Typically by age 23 it is expected that women be married. A common expression is that women over 23 who are unmarried *las dejó el tren*; that is, the train left without them. The fear of many parents is that the older the woman, the less likely she will be to marry. The underlying concern is that a woman *needs* the protection of a man who will support her financially and emotionally. Without such a man, she will then be left *para vestir santos*, to dress the saints in church. The preference has been that women partner with older males who will have had time to obtain an education or stable employment and therefore be ready to settle down and provide for their family. Marriage, both legal and by the church, is expected among the economically privileged and more religious families. A common pattern among those with lower education or social status is to form unions outside of marriage. Among the more acculturated and educated Latinx, living together is seen as an alternative or precursor to marriage while higher education is pursued. Traditional parents will often "look the other way" and pretend that their daughters are not participating in premarital sex or unions, reflecting underlying cultural values and concerns about appearance, *el que dirán*, and protecting the family's reputation.

Family theory suggests that the more support a couple receives from their families of origin, the easier the transition to married life will be. The more disapproval or conflict the union generates among extended family members, the more difficult it will be for the partners to negotiate the transition to married life. Cultural value differences may present particular challenges. The Lopez couple found support for their union. Both Elena and José had immigrant parents who held traditional views. José's mother was relieved that her son was marrying "a good girl." Elena's parents were pleased that she was going to marry an educated man, a son of Mexicans, whom they assumed held similar familistic values. Although José was more acculturated than Elena, they shared highly familistic views. They had more diverse views of parenting, but José enjoyed and benefited from Elena's traditional attitudes toward home life. She did not expect him to do much work around the house. When he "helped," she was appreciative. However, she believed that running the home was her duty, which she performed with great pride and love. José stated that he enjoyed that privilege, although he would have been perfectly happy with helping more. Elena did not want him in the kitchen. She considered that woman's work. Judy was beginning to resent that she was expected to become equally skilled in household tasks, for which she had no passion. She grudgingly did chores, not to learn how to do them to her mother's standards, but to prevent conflict with her mother. She argued that she did not see any point to learning to iron or do laundry well, as she planned to become educated and "send her clothes out." Elena heard those statements as a devaluing of her beliefs. She felt she was failing at raising a daughter who would make someone a good wife.

Until very recent times Latinx cultures pathologized homosexual and lesbian unions. Although laws and policies have changed in the past few years, popular views remain mixed. Most families hold heteronormative ideals and struggle with accepting children who are queer. Many parents prefer the "don't ask, don't tell" approach to their children's sexuality. Forming couple relationships within this larger sociocultural context adds multiple layers of complexity (Espin, 2012).

Mariluz and Eva

Mariluz, a South American immigrant, fled her country during a dark period of political repression. She had been a college student at the time and had to seek political asylum in the United States after her brother was kidnapped and murdered by the military. In the United States she became an attorney and human rights activist. She married and had two children. However, she "always knew" she was attracted to women but tried to repress her feelings given her refugee status and the multiple traumas she had endured. She stated that she could not imagine having to deal with any more persecution. At a political rally she met Eva. Mariluz was 35; Eva was 28. A child of Mexican immigrants and a politically active queer feminist Chicana, Eva was Mariluz's role model of a well-integrated identity. They became friends. Eva had grown up in a large extended family that held very traditional values. Mariluz was estranged from her Italian American husband but considered herself "very married."

Initially Eva was unaware that Mariluz was falling in love with her. Eva stated that she had never wanted to become involved with anyone who was ambivalent about her sexuality. From early childhood Eva knew she was lesbian. She came out to her parents in adolescence; they initially rejected her largely due to their conservative religious views. Eva struggled to complete high school as an emancipated minor and earned a scholarship to attend college. She became an activist in college and "came out to the world." In college she found a supportive community of Chicanas who were feminist and accepting of queer sisters. She worked for a community-based organization that advocated for women and immigrants' rights. Her life was full, she stated, and did not need the drama that a relationship with Mariluz might bring.

The two women formed a strong friendship based on their shared political views and activism. Eva became enamored of Mariluz's children, who were 11 and 13 when they met. They began to spend more and more time together as family. One day Dolores, Mariluz's 13-year-old daughter, asked Eva if she was going to be her mother's new partner. Eva was confused by the question. Dolores looked at her "straight in the eye" and told her it was obvious the two were in love. Eva was shocked, and relieved, that the truth had been said out loud. Eva and Mariluz realized they were in love and wanted to be together. Full of fear and trepidation they spoke to Danilo, the 11-year-old boy who tried to make sense of the changes about to happen in their life. Both children were supportive. Eva, who had never wanted to own property, bought a flat and had Mariluz and the children move in with her. Mariluz was living in a home bought by her husband. When Mariluz told her husband that she was filing for divorce, he promised to fight her for custody to protect his children from "her deviancy."

Mariluz's mother wept when her daughter told her she was moving in with Eva and that they were going to be a family. However, her mother already had lost her only son to a military dictatorship and was not willing to lose her daughter as well. Consequently, she asked her daughter for time to get used to this new reality. Eventually, she became Mariluz and Eva's most ardent supporter, testifying in court on their behalf during the protracted custody battle that ensued. Having been rejected by her family once before, Eva did not reach out to her parents when Mariluz's estranged husband began to threaten and harass her. However, when Eva's three brothers found out that a man was threatening their sister, they came to her defense and support. One of Eva's brothers was a police officer in another county; he asked his colleagues to pay this man a visit. The harassment ceased. Eva's mother could not acknowledge that her daughter was in an intimate relationship with another woman but welcomed Dolores and Danilo into her family. Over time the children "won her over" and she began to call them her grandchildren.

The early stages of couple formation were challenging for Mariluz and Eva due to the pervasive homophobia they encountered in the legal system. Despite being an attorney, Mariluz had difficulty finding a compassionate attorney who was willing to represent her. Her estranged husband was part of a well-established and affluent family with political contacts. They were willing to spend whatever amount of money was necessary to remove the children from Mariluz's custody. The treatment of Mariluz by her former in-laws became increasingly hostile with open racist attacks against her former status as a political refugee and as a Latina. They labeled her as an ungrateful woman who had used their son to get residency (which was untrue) and had had "anchor children" to remain in the United States. Their vitriolic attacks were inflamed by the anti-immigrant fervor of the early 21st century. In addition, they argued that two lesbians would pervert their grandchildren. Moreover, while they had tolerated Mariluz's Latinidad, as she was light-skinned and highly educated, they were incensed that Mariluz was leaving their son for "a low-class dark-skinned Mexican."

Eva and Mariluz spent thousands of dollars in legal fees and "experts" who could testify in court, evaluate the children, do family studies, and so forth. The children had to enter therapy to deal with the conflict, and the mothers began couple therapy to deal with the stress on their relationship. Mariluz was granted a divorce, but the custody agreement was not reached for 2 more years. The father obtained 50% custody and often violated the visitation agreements, dragged Mariluz to court on multiple occasions, and falsely accused them of child abuse until Dorothy refused to visit him anymore. Dorothy confided that her father raged against Mariluz and Eva and frequently threatened to take the children to Italy and never return. Danilo was particularly affected by his father's rage. He decided to go live with his father when he was 13 in hopes that this would appease him. It did not. Danilo then went to live with his paternal grandparents for 2 years and eventually returned to Mariluz and Eva. He remained in therapy for years to deal with the trauma caused by his father's anger and his grandparents' racism.

In couple therapy Mariluz expressed her feelings of guilt; she was plagued by "should's": She should have suppressed her feelings and her love for Eva for the sake of the children;

she should have anticipated her ex-husband's rancor and her former in-laws' response to the situation; she should have sacrificed her desires for the sake of the children. She found it ironic that she had fled a military regime to fall prey to an intimate terrorist who tried to destroy her, compromised their children's mental health, and damaged her relationship with Eva. Eva, on the other hand, was unwavering in her support for Mariluz and reiterated that although she had anticipated the drama, the sorrow was worth it. She had found her soulmate and no threats from any man or his well-heeled family would break their bond. Her motto in life, Eva stated, was to push forward against all odds, *contra viento y marea*, doing what was necessary to protect her family and her marriage.

Seven years after the divorce, Mariluz's former husband, who was then in his mid 40s, married a 20-year-old woman and started a new family. He stopped harassing Mariluz and stopped seeing their children. Dorothy and Danilo, then respectively a young adult and a late adolescent, had to return to therapy to deal with their father's abandonment and to make sense of why he had done such damage to them. In 2012 Eva and Mariluz celebrated 20 years together; they married legally in early 2014 and now live peacefully, without drama, continuing their fight for social justice.

Mariluz and Eva were able to withstand the assaults to their relationship and their own integrity because they had shared values of family, loyalty, commitment, and a profound love and respect for each other. Perhaps if they had not had such passion for social justice they might not have been able to remain together in the face of such attacks. Despite their differences in nativity and social class, particularly in their families of origin, they were able to create *familia* and transcend the challenges they faced.

Gender Roles: Power and Sexuality

In the context of a patriarchal culture, traditional gender values and roles emerged, which mirrored those that are *complementary*. The man *should* be the *head* of the family and the woman the *heart*; the value of a man is based on how well his family runs (how disciplined the children are and how supportive his wife is). If each observes the respective role, he will be respected (if not feared) and she will be revered. This complementarity also is nuanced by *machismo* and *Marianismo*. *Machismo* is the code of conduct of a man and a direct legacy of Spanish conquest and its sequelae (Paz, 2003); it entails men being physically strong, potentially virile, indomitable in character, and stoic. The better man is the man who can drink the most, defend himself the best, dominate his wife (even using physical force if necessary, command the respect of the children, have more sexual relationships, and engender more sons (Falicov, 1998). This cultural archetype may be attenuated by socioeconomic changes, education, and/or migration (see Flores et al., 2019).

At the core of the archetype is the expectation that a man should please women and behave like a gentleman. An important part of being a good *macho* is being devoted to women in his biological family, his mother above all others. Mexican movie stars of the 1950s, most notably Pedro Infante, embody this cultural ideal. Contemporary Chicano and Latino men may hold some aspects of the ideal consciously or unconsciously yet strive for more egalitarian relationships with women.

The counterpart of machismo, *Marianismo*, refers to the docile, self-sacrificing ideal of good womanhood. The term literally means "cult and emulation of the virgin Mary."

A traditional socialization script calls for loyalty to family, especially men, over-valuing of sons, protection of spouses, and absolute respect for and obedience of parental authority. While education and migration may reduce adherence to a strict practice of this role, it may be a core value that surfaces at various points in the life cycle. In addition to *Marianismo*, *hembrismo* refers to the qualities of strength, endurance, courage, perseverance, and bravery embodied by some women. The strength of Latinas in the face of adversity is admired as long as the moral codes imposed on them are not violated.

Hembrismo may operate in the work sphere while *Marianismo* is practiced at home.

Clearly, balancing cultural expectations in the face of cultural change can be very stressful for both men and women (Flores-Ortiz, 1993).

Power, or the ability to exercise agency, make decisions affecting the self and other(s), will be determined partly by the degree of adherence to traditional values. In traditional couples, men decide over the family but women exert authority over the domestic sphere.

Women can exercise their power as long as it does not *directly* challenge or sabotage males' authority. Women often use indirect power, subtlety and persuasion; thus, it may appear to outsiders that they lack power in the relationship when in fact they may hold significant power. In egalitarian relationships, it is presumed that couples *discuss, hear each other's opinions, and jointly decide.*

In summary, in traditional Latinx families gender roles tend to be shaped by class and patriarchal notions of who should do what. Women's identities are nuanced by the value of familism and the expectation that a woman is the heart of the home and family. Women often are socialized with the image of the Virgin Mary as the guide for their behavior. Purity, docility, sacrifice, and service to others represent "the good woman." Deviation from those traits may be viewed as selfish. Men are to be the protectors and providers for the family. More modern ideas and attitudes about shared responsibility in the management of the home and the raising of children are associated with higher social status and greater educational access. In most of Latin America, however, traditional values regarding gender continue to influence how men and women live their lives.

Power is often negotiated between partners on the basis of home/work responsibilities and income earned. In more modern couples, important decisions are made jointly, and power is shared. Conflict can arise in couples when each holds a different view and value regarding gender roles and decision-making power (Flores, 2005; Flores-Ortiz et al., 2002). Elena and José were able to coparent and create a fairly harmonious family because they had similar familistic views; although José was more egalitarian in his gender role views, he was willing to enjoy the privilege accorded by his wife's more traditional gender role views. He was not oppressive, and she enjoyed taking care of her family by being at home and assuming most of the home duties, which she had begun to teach her daughters, but not her son. In this way, she was perpetuating a more traditional role assignment to her children based on gender.

Julian and Emma

Julian and Emma met in college; she was a second-generation Chicana who considered herself feminist. Noelia, a single mother, an immigrant from El Salvador, raised Julian. As the eldest child of a single parent, Julian learned from an early age that he had to help out. He learned to cook by age 8; he did laundry by age 11 and was fairly good at house cleaning since he joined his mother on the weekends when she cleaned other people's homes. However, his mother often would tell him that he should marry a traditional woman who would take care of him. He did not give much thought to his mother's "advice" until he and Emma moved in together in their last year of college. Suddenly, Julian realized that he was expecting Emma to cook, clean, and take care of him. Emma was shocked, since he had seemed quite independent and capable of doing these things for himself. When Noelia came to visit, Emma noticed that she seemed to disapprove of their lifestyle. Noelia commented that the apartment could be cleaner and told Emma how Julian liked his shirts ironed. Emma was furious. She and Julian began to argue and considered separating.

Julian realized that although he had been actively involved in domestic duties since early childhood, he had done so out of necessity, not because these chores "belonged" to him. When he did housework, he was helping his mother or Emma. He believed these activities were indeed women's work. Emma expected and encouraged "an attitude adjustment" to preserve their relationship.

Emmanuel and Leila

Not all men raised by single women learn domestic duties or have more egalitarian ideas about gender and gender roles. Emmanuel was the eldest of four; his father left the family when he was 10. Thereafter, the family faced significant economic adversity. His mother worked two jobs. His sister Lucy took over the household duties and Emmanuel was elevated to "man of the house." He was not expected to do housework but to help with the discipline of the younger children. In adolescence, Emmanuel began to come home late and act "like a man." His mother gave him a great deal of latitude, as she was raised traditionally and was passing on those practices to her children, both out of necessity as well as tradition. When Emmanuel met Leila, a third-generation Chicana, he liked her independence, as she also worked and went to school at the local junior college. However, when she became pregnant, their relationship problems began. Emmanuel had lacked an appropriate role model of responsible masculinity. He did not know how to be a father or a partner. Leila insisted he "step up" or else. He went to work to support them but insisted that she do all of the housework, which she found to be unfair since she had to nurse an infant and tend to her baby's needs. They lived together for a few months; however, each returned to live with their respective parents because Emmanuel was not ready to be a husband/father and was in danger of repeating his father's pattern of abandonment. He seemed unable, and unwilling, to negotiate their conflicts. They had been unprepared to assume the parenting role. Although he remained involved minimally with his son's upbringing and paid child support, his relationship with Leila ended. He subsequently partnered with a more traditional woman who "made no demands" on him.

Sexuality

The American Psychological Association (2010) defines sexuality as encompassing a person's sex, gender identity and expression, and sexual orientation. Thus, in most families, boys and girls are socialized according to their gender and taught family and culturally expected ways to express their gender identity. Most cultures and families rely on heteronormative assumptions about "proper behavior" and privilege a heterosexual orientation. In traditional Latino families the expectation is that girls will remain virgins until marriage while boys should gain sexual experience prior to settling down (Hurtado, 2003). The general assumption has been that men have greater sexual desires and needs than women. Women who are more sexual are likely to be labeled as wanton, licentious, and promiscuous. Those with more transitional and contemporary value orientations are less likely to hold the double standard regarding sexuality. Nevertheless, most Chicana scholars of sexuality find that even highly educated Latinas and Chicanas often hold conflicting and stressful views regarding their sexuality and the right to enjoying their sexual lives (Castañeda, 2013; Flores, 2013; Hurtado, 2003).

Sousa (2002) posits that the gender socialization of Latinas supports the dichotomization of women into good and bad objects. With the implicit and explicit threat of being labeled *puta*, Latina girls are encouraged to disconnect from their bodies, suppress and repress their sexuality, and problematize their desires. Latinas' concern with sexuality begins in childhood and continues throughout their life cycle (Flores 2013). Sexual identity is an integral part of healthy identity formation (Hurtado & Gurin, 2004; Castañeda & Zavella, 2003). However, the sexuality of young Latinas is problematized and associated with their reproductive patterns. Worries about teen pregnancy tend to be a concern of both parents and social scientists who view Latinas' high fertility rates (when compared to European American women) as problematic, irrespective of whether it is for the young woman. Latino boys tend to engage in sexual behavior earlier than girls; however, there is less concern in the family and among social scientists about this pattern, except for worries about sexually transmitted infections and overall health (Aguirre Molina & Betancourt, 2010).

According to Chicana lesbian writers (Anzaldúa, 1987; Perez, 1991, 1993; Trujillo, 2003, among others) it is the perception that queer Latinas are less constrained by traditional gender sexuality that makes them so dangerous to patriarchy. However, Espín (2013) and Hurtado (2003) find that regardless of their sexual orientation, Latinas continue to struggle with gender socialization and patriarchal cultural expectations about women's proper behavior and expressions of their sexuality. The role of sexuality in family life is discussed in greater detail in Chapter 8.

As a result of the COVID-19 pandemic and the shelter-in-place order, many of our students had to return home, as dormitories closed and other essential campus services were not available to them. Teaching transitioned to online and Web-based instruction. Many of our Latinx students began to confide that in addition to lack of proper space to connect to their coursework due to limited Wi-Fi availability and limited privacy, they also began to encounter parental and other family expectations to help out more, to seek employment due to parental unemployment, and to assume their precollege role within the family. Many of our female students complained that parents adhered to traditional gender roles and wanted them to behave according to those roles. Many of the women complained about relatives' sexist, racist, or homophobic comments and struggled to remain silent, given their more progressive views, largely acquired while away at college. They noted that their brothers were accorded more freedom and had less conflict with "being themselves" while at home than they did.

Chapter Summary

In this chapter we examined the influence of historical legacies from the colonial period on the construction of race, class, gender, and sexuality. Contemporary Latinx families in the United States may have different degrees of adherence to traditional, transitional, or contemporary values as a function of their generation, level of acculturation and structural integration, as well as the family's contact with conationals. To understand Latinx and Chicanx families their history and diversity must be taken into account. Our case examples show how culture, race, class, and experiences of discrimination may nuance family functioning and structure. Health professionals must be aware of Latinx diversity and experience to fully understand the importance of family for individuals and the challenges faced and resources available to families.

Beginning to Theorize One's Family

In order to fully understand Latinx families it is critical to analyze them in context (see Figure 1.1 in Chapter 1) and to view them as a system of people connected by blood, history, experience, love, marriage, friendship, and so on. In addition, consideration must be given to the historical events that have shaped each family over time. Multigenerational patterns and legacies become visible through the use of genealogy (McGoldrick et al., 2008). A vertical and horizontal analysis of each family helps understand the present—the family's social location (socioeconomic status (SES), educational levels of its members, employment patterns and status) as well as the influence of history on current generations and family patterns.

HOMEWORK ASSIGNMENT

1. Reflecting on your family in the present, determine their social location (SES, educational level, employment status).
2. Reflect on your family history:
   o What do you know?
   o How long has your family been in the United States?
   o Who came first (or who came first to them)?
   o What is the racial/ethnic composition of the family?
   o Where are the silences?
   o What are the secrets?

3. Reflect on the values held by your family:
    o Which values are more traditional?
    o Which values appear to be in transition?
    o Which values could be considered contemporary?
4. How are gender roles assigned and negotiated in your family?
    o What are the gender roles evident in your family?
    o Who does what?
    o Who decides what?
5. To what extent are your gender values reflective of your family's cultural ideals?
    o How have gender roles changed or evolved over the years?
    o What accounts for the changes in gender roles?
    o In what ways has your family's history of migration impacted or changed gender roles?
    o Who holds the power?
    o How is power negotiated between partners?
6. To what degree, if at all, are or were your sexuality and sexual identification supported, ignored, or silenced by your family?

KEY TERMS

El que dirán: "What they will say"; refers to moral concerns about individuals' behaviors and what others may think about them. In the context of Latinx families, individuals' behaviors may have an impact on what others may think of them as a unit.

Hembrismo: Term used as alternative to *Marianismo* and in opposition to *machismo* to claim women's roles as broader than the loving, caring, and self-sacrificed image expected of Latinx women following traditional roles.

Idealized values: Expectations in the family context of an individual's behavior based on family values and roles.

Machismo: Refers to the expectation for men to show exaggerated masculinity and a strong sense of masculine pride. It is also associated with a man's responsibility to provide for, protect, and defend his family. It is considered a cultural Latinx construct.

Marginalization: The social disadvantage and relegation to the fringe of society of individuals. It is used across disciplines including education, sociology, psychology, politics, and economics

Marianismo: Refers to the expectation that women live as the Virgin Mary in the Catholic tradition did. Women are expected to be submissive to men and meet their every need in a passive and unassertive manner. They are loving, caring, docile, and completely devoted to their roles as wives, mothers, and life bearers. To accomplish this, women must renounce their own needs, acting in a spiritual and immaculate manner.

Respect: In the context of Latinx culture it refers to the cultural value manifested in several domains and relationships. For children respect or *respeto* includes obedience to authority, deference, decorum, and public behavior.

3

Family Functioning Through Cultural Lenses

Introduction

Families can be viewed as systems evolving over time as their members pass through and negotiate the various life cycle stages and developmental milestones. As stated earlier, Latinx families must be viewed contextually. McGoldrick and Hardy (2008) propose that families are embedded within a geopolitical structure; the policies that derive from that structure influence how well the family functions within society. Likewise, family functioning is determined in part by the family's value system and by the ethnicity, race, and class of its members, which positions it within a particular ecological niche (Falicov, 1998). The gender and sexual orientation of family members also influences its functioning. The family and its members' religion or spiritual practices also will nuance how family members relate to one another and to the outside world.

This chapter examines family functioning among Latinxs while describing three major family theories that have been useful in the evaluation and treatment of Latinx clients. First, a brief overview of family systems theory is presented and is followed by a more detailed description of contextual intergeneration, relational justice, and narrative approaches. Lastly, the use of genealogy to appreciate family uniqueness and identify patterns of resilience and dysfunction is reviewed in some detail. The overarching questions inherent in this chapter are "What constitutes well-being in *Latinx* families? What factors contribute to fairness and justice and unfairness and injustice in Latinx family relations?"

Family Systems Theory

Murray Bowen (1978) suggested that individuals couldn't be understood in isolation from one another, but rather as a part of their family. He posited that families are systems of interconnected and interdependent individuals, none of whom can be understood in isolation from the system. Furthermore, Bowen viewed the family as an emotional unit.

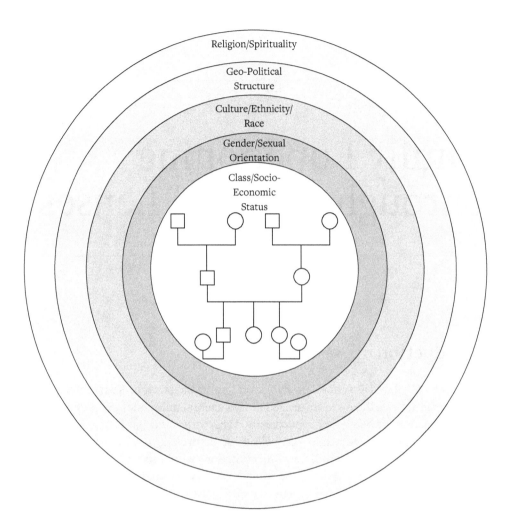

FIG. 3.1 The Genogram in Multiple Contexts

Monica McGoldrick, "Genogram 1.3: The Genogram in Multiple Contexts," Context and Connections: Transforming Life Narratives: Workshop Presentation in Venice, Italy. Copyright © 2008 by Monica McGoldrick. Reprinted with permission.

That is, the emotional state of one member reverberated throughout the system and affected the other family members.

Bowen also introduced a number of important concepts that were further developed by other theorists. He highlighted the importance of **differentiation of the self** from parents and other family members; otherwise **emotional fusion** might occur, resulting in adult psychopathology. Clearly differentiation is a Western concept inherent in individualistic cultures. Families from collectivist cultures might not emphasize individuation; instead they may promote emotional interdependence (Bernal & Flores-Ortiz, 1991). Bowen also introduced the notion of **family triangles**, that is alliances or coalitions between two family members and the exclusion of a third. For example, a mother and son might form a tight coalition to the exclusion of the father. Such a coalition might become dysfunctional over time, fostering emotional fusion between mother and son and lack of differentiation of the son from his mother. In his early writings Minuchin (1974) argued that not all triangles are problematic. For example, among socioeconomically disadvantaged families, Puerto Ricans and other Latinx, as well as African Americans, intergenerational households and intergenerational triangles (grandmother-mother-grandchild) could be functional and in fact necessary for family survival.

Although he considered the nuclear family, that is the family created by the partnering or marriage of two adults, to be most important in the shaping of children, Bowen also recognized the contributions of the extended family, both as a resource and as a source of intergenerational dysfunction, particularly if individuals were not sufficiently differentiated. He noted that couple conflict and the symptoms in a spouse or child all could be understood as emerging from the family emotional system while being influenced by the **multigenerational transmission process**. This is the process whereby the relational anxieties and problems of previous generations are passed down to subsequent ones, particularly if there was insufficient differentiation. This concept was an important contribution that underscored the importance of considering and studying the family's history to comprehend (and treat) the problems nuclear families might develop (see Flores-Ortiz & Bernal, 1991).

Bowen argued that the triangles and anxieties of previous generations were passed down to subsequent ones and thus could contribute to the development of family problems. Bowen also coined the term **family projection process** to describe how children develop symptoms when they get caught up in the previous generation's anxiety about relationships. For example, a child may develop a school phobia when the parents' marital conflicts escalate as a result of one family's disapproval of the marriage and their efforts to sabotage the union; the parents must then "work together" to help their child and shift the focus away from their marital distress. The parents "projected" their anxiety about possible separation onto the child, who in turn "is afraid" to leave the parents and go to school. In effect, within systems theory children are considered the emotional barometers of the family. Well-adjusted children are indicative of a family system that is functioning well. Children who manifest emotional problems may be mirroring distress, most likely in the parental subsystem, but that could be the result of intergenerational conflicts or lack of differentiation of one partner from their family of origin.

Bowen also introduced the concept of **emotional cutoffs**, the efforts by family members to try to escape emotional fusion in a family (Bowen, 1978). Cutoffs can be attained by physical and emotional separation or distance and are distinct from efforts at separating from the family in young adulthood in order to attain greater independence. Bowen also noted the importance of **sibling positions** within a family. Likewise, the emotional climate and context of the family at the time of the child's birth might influence their position and role within the family. The replacement child, after the death of a loved one for example, might be at risk for developing separation problems, emotional fusion, and adult mental health problems.

In traditional Latinx families the firstborn male tends to hold a very privileged position; he is often a coparent with the mother if the father is absent or disengaged. The younger siblings are to respect him and seek his approval and advice. If all family members share that value, sibling relationships may be smooth. If the parent overburdens the son, he may rebel. If he is parentified, he is expected to fill the emotional needs of his mother, which he may be ill equipped to do. He may become symptomatic or pseudo individuate; that is, he could act as if he were an adult (by engaging in drinking and stereotypic male behaviors) while remaining economically and emotionally dependent on the mother. A cultural pattern could then become problematic and contribute to mental health problems in the son, the mother, or the siblings.

Bowen's early theories influenced the development of family psychology (Guerin, 1976). Other important concepts in family theory address the structure of the family (nuclear, extended, blended) and the subsystems within the larger system (see Carter & McGoldrick, 2010; Guerin, 1996; Minuchin, 1974). The executive subsystem would include the parents as architects of the family and decision makers. The sibling subsystem would consist of the children. Family boundaries, the degree to which family members understand their place, their roles, and the expectations of them held by other family members are also important. Well-defined but permeable boundaries with clear lines of communication are considered optimal. Families with excessive closeness and diffuse boundaries are considered enmeshed. In these families rules and roles may be unclear, and "emotional fusion" is more likely to happen.

Because interdependence and reciprocity are cultural values among Latinxs, emotional closeness is expected. Families may appear enmeshed to those who hold more individualistic values. This may be particularly the case in multigenerational households, where grandparents and parents collaboratively raise children, older children perform some executive functions, and smaller children may appear to have a closer emotional bond with a sibling or grandparent than a parent who is away at work most of the time. On the other hand, disengaged families are those where the boundaries are so strict there may be reduced emotional closeness and minimal communication and exchange between subsystems. In such families there may be an expectation that children leave home at age 18 and become financially and emotionally independent from the parents. This may be a cultural ideal in some families but appear dysfunctional to other, more collectivist groups. Clearly boundaries are important and contribute to family functioning if there is communication and clear expectations and roles. However, cultural values and class position, as well as family history and intergenerational patterns, will also influence the structure and functioning of the family.

From a family systems perspective, a well-functioning family is one with a clear hierarchy—the parents constitute the executive subsystem, with clear communication between them and the children. Every family member is aware of the rules and norms of the family. The parents facilitate the children's transition through their developmental stages while mindful of their own life cycle, both as individuals and as members of a family. Boundaries are permeable such that children have access to the parents and there is emotional closeness without fusion or enmeshment.

Latinx families who hold traditional values may appear less differentiated and more enmeshed than middle-class European American families. Communication patterns may be less direct and clear; in many families triangulated conversations are more common. That is, to maintain balance and harmony, direct confrontations are avoided and indirect messages are more common. For example, a mother may tell a child that a particular behavior displeased the father. The child then is expected to correct the behavior for the sake of family harmony. Within a monocultural context this pattern may work, but, as will be seen in later chapters, within a multicultural context an adolescent may opt for ignoring the advice since it did not come directly from the father; this can be viewed as disrespect by both parents (as seen in Jose and Elena's difficulties with Judy).

From a family system's perspective, a well-functioning Latinx family is one with clear and permeable boundaries, emotional closeness within and across generations of the family, and where the values of respect, personalism, collaboration, and solidarity are enacted (Falicov, 2013). Nativity, generational level, religious affiliation, class, and level of acculturation will determine the extent to which these values are adhered to or expected from the parents and grandparents. Likewise, economic concerns, lack of structural integration, and experiences of discrimination may interfere with the family's ability to function well, as we will discuss in the next chapter.

A contemporary of Bowen, Ivan Boszormenyi-Nagy, who was also a psychiatrist, developed a family therapy theory that has been used extensively to understand and treat Latinx families with a variety of problems, including substance abuse and intrafamily violence (see Bernal & Flores-Ortiz, 1991; Bernal et al., 1986, 1990; Flores-Ortiz, 1991).

Contextual Intergenerational Family Theory

This model highlights the importance of studying families in context and across generations. The model consists of four dimensions of analysis: historical realities or facts, individual psychology, systemic issues, and relational justice.

Historical Realities or Facts

This dimension deals with the facts, history, and legacies of an individual that are generally unchangeable, for example sex at birth, gender, ability, birth order, race, and ethnicity. In the case of Latinxs, important attention must be paid as well to the family's history of migration and the transgenerational legacies such migrations create. In addition, the circumstances surrounding birth and early development of family members also may contribute to particular patterns of functioning. A premature baby, for example, may become an overprotected child, especially if they are the firstborn and there is a family history of infant mortality and a privileging of firstborn males.

Individual Psychology

Unlike other family theories that focus exclusively on the nuclear family and family interactions, this model also privileges the individual psychology of family members. It is critically important to ascertain the meaning an individual gives to their historical facts and legacies. What does it mean to be a second-generation Chicanx born into a working-class family of Mexican immigrants who have struggled unsuccessfully to attain the American dream? How does that historical reality affect self-esteem, ego strength, coping style, and so on? How do they see the legacies of their parents' migration affecting them, if at all? Likewise, what are the identity issues (race, ethnicity, sexuality, politics, etc.) each family member must negotiate and how do such issues affect the family as a system? How do the life cycle stage and degree of dependence/interdependence of family members influence or affect the family as a whole? What are the challenges and opportunities each family member faces as a result of their nativity, generational status, gender, sexual orientation, class position, and so forth?

Systemic Issues

In addition to individual psychology issues, this model also examines both family of origin and nuclear family arrangements. Specifically, the type of family structure that is created, the degree of functioning, life cycle stage of the families of origin, and procreation all must be examined. In particular, a systemic analysis views the family life cycle as key to understanding the problems that develop at particular points in time (Carter & McGoldrick, 2010). For example, immigrant Latinx parents may experience anxiety and other psychological distress when their first child wants to leave for college. This is a normative part of the launching stage (see Chapter 1) and although desired by many parents, for immigrant parents separation from a child may reopen the wounds created by migration-related losses. The fear of separating from the child may result in depression or anxiety in a parent and adversely impact the emotional well-being of the entire family.[1]

Likewise, the family roles, rules, and norms must be understood within an ecological context of class, race, nativity, and overall social position. As Minuchin et al. (1967) noted, families often organize on the basis of need, forming triads across generations to raise children and support one another. Such arrangements, which do not mirror the middle-class organization of an executive and sibling subsystem separate from the family of origin, are not inherently dysfunctional. Instead, if the women collaborate and the rules and roles are clear, multigenerational households and arrangements can be functional.

As stated earlier, some family theories posit that clear, distinct but permeable boundaries are optimal for family functioning. Boszormenyi-Nagy argued that equally important is the degree of cohesion, closeness, and interdependence of a family, *if* it reflects their cultural values system. Families should not be compared to a social science European American ideal of functioning without consideration of their ethnicity, race, and class. Furthermore, determination of the cutoffs, enmeshment, or disengagement of a family also must be culturally informed (Bernal et al., 1986; McGoldrick & Hardy, 2008). As stated earlier, some Latinx families may appear enmeshed because of the high degree of extended and nuclear family interaction and interdependence that is valued and performed.

Relational Justice

Boszormenyi-Nagy believed that *trust*, *loyalty*, and *mutual support* or *reciprocity* are the key elements that underlie family relationships and hold families together. Symptoms develop when a lack of caring and accountability result in a breakdown of trust in relationships (Nichols & Schwartz, 1998). Boszormenyi-Nagy referred to these elements as relational justice. Ethical, fair, and just family relationships form healthy children and adults who are loyal and trustworthy.

---

1   For an excellent depiction of this crisis, see *Real Women Have Curves*, a 2002 film with America Ferreira depicting the struggles of a working-class Los Angeles–based Chicano family when their high-achieving daughter wants to go to college on the East Coast.

Family relationships occur within a context of give and take. Central to relational ethics is the concept of balance. Balance, reciprocity, and an oscillating balance between give and take characterize ethical relations. Giving to others vertically (parent to child, adult to parent) earns credits or merits. Those who receive become indebted and must give vertically to balance the relational ledger over generations (children grow to become providers of their parents and so forth). Adults cannot collect from children or peers that which they did not receive from their parents, as this is unethical and unfair, resulting in what Tello (2008) terms *cargas* (burdens) for the children, their potential parentification, and conflict in couple relationships.

An oscillating balance also exists between giving and receiving vertically (between parents and children, grandparents and parents, extended family members and younger generations) and horizontally, among peers and siblings. If there is reciprocity in the giving and receiving, individuals maintain balance between merits earned by giving and the debits resulting from receiving. These merits and debits are earned both vertically and horizontally. Injustice occurs when there is exploitation or lack of reciprocity in family relationships.

Boszoremni-Nagy introduced other important concepts, including the degree of *entitlement*, the inherent right to fair treatment held by family members, which could be constructive or destructive. A loving caring environment fosters a sense of entitlement that is balanced. Parents owe their children care, love, and nurturing. Early bonding and fair parenting practices lead children to develop **constructive entitlement**. They grow up believing that they deserve to be treated fairly and will treat others ethically; in turn, as adults they will be accountable in their interpersonal relationships, particularly with intimate partners and children.

Exploitation, deprivation, and maltreatment foster **destructive entitlement**, the ethical position that the world owes one what the parents did not or could not provide, resulting in a chip-on-the-shoulder attitude. A child who is not cared for by their caregivers will grow into adulthood seeking such caring from partners who cannot fill the void left by parental neglect. Such early wounds also may result in self-destructive behavioral patterns (to be discussed in later chapters). Destructively entitled people attempt to collect from others what they did not receive and what they cannot give. Destructive entitlement is often at the root of couple problems and abusive parenting.

Furthermore, within families relationships are rooted in **visible and invisible loyalties**.

Families have rules about giving and receiving, which shape loyalties vertically and horizontally. Visible loyalties are those that are explicit and congruent. Visible loyalties foster balance and are grounded in reciprocity because trust and reciprocity constitute the fabric of connection among individuals. When relationships are fair and balanced, loyalty considerations are visible. Loyalty is expected visibly within families, particularly those rooted in collectivist values. Children are taught directly and by example the importance of loyalty to the parents, grandparents, and siblings as well as extended family members. This loyalty comes from trust and fairness in relationships. On the other hand, invisible loyalties develop out of injustice.

Invisible loyalties are characterized by covert expectations and incongruent messages. They result from exploitation, imbalance, and lack of reciprocity. Invisible loyalties may be at the root of individual and family dysfunction. A child who is maltreated will experience soul wounding and develop deep emotional scars. Their love for the parent who was not trustworthy or accountable will be entangled with feelings of rejection, abandonment, and pain. They may feel a compulsion to exonerate the poor parenting received by being a less than accountable and trustworthy individual in both vertical and horizontal relationships. In this way the adult who was a maltreated child or who experienced any form of relational injustice becomes invisibly loyal to their progenitors and is likely to replicate those patterns in subsequent intimate relationships. Can I be a better parent than my own parent was? Through individual and family dysfunction we exonerate our progenitors and fulfill legacies of earlier generations (Bernal & Flores-Ortiz, 1991).

Contextual intergenerational family therapy has been used successfully with Latinxs whose emotional wounds manifest as addiction, depression, and family violence (Bernal & Flores-Ortiz, 1991; Bernal et al., 1986; Flores-Ortiz, 1993, 1996, 1999a, b, c). This model has been particularly effective because of its consideration of the multiple dimensions of family life, including the family's historical realities or facts. Such an analysis is critical to understand Latinx families of varying generations and levels of acculturation, as well as their degree of structural integration.

Narrative- and Justice-Based Approaches

The context of social and therapeutic problems is critical to their resolution, and many of them stem from historical and structural injustice … contextual issues of cultural, gender, and socioeconomic equity as providing important insights into authentic notions of social inclusion and well-being, and encourage[] therapists, service providers, researchers, and policy makers to take responsibility to ensure that these injustices are addressed, and become part of the public discourse about the sources and solutions of endemic social problems.

(Waldegrave et al., 2009, p. 85).

In the mid to late 20th century two mental health professionals from Australia and New Zealand, David Epston and Michael White, began to offer workshops on a different form of treatment of individuals and families in distress (Beels, 2009). They "decentered" the role of the master therapist and instead focused on collaboration with clients and organizations. Their ideas, which have developed and expanded globally, gave birth to what others have labeled narrative therapy. What was unique to the West about this approach is that it suggested that therapy itself could be oppressive if practiced from the perspective that a "master," a trained and certified "expert," had the solutions to others' problems. Both psychoanalysis and family therapy had converted "problems" into pathologies and people with problems into patients who *were* pathological. Family therapists often spoke of "dysfunctional families," suggesting that the family was sick, much as psychoanalysis had viewed the person as sick. White and Epston argued that the problem was not in the person; thus, the person was not the problem. The problem *was* the problem. Moreover, their approach resonated with many Latinxs because of its emphasis on understanding the stories and narratives that influence and shape people's lives. Both White and Epston worked with marginalized and disenfranchised communities, including Aborigines, Maoris, and Samoans as well as White Australians and New Zealanders, not as experts but as consultants who had to be accountable to these communities because of their class, race, gender, and sexual privilege (Beels, 2009; Waldegrave et al., 2009). They stated that a "critique and deconstruction of institutional power in our public, private, and voluntary services is encouraged in a manner that honors diversity and enables sensitive therapy, other forms of service delivery and policy making that genuinely reflect the range of cultural, gender, and socioeconomic experiences of citizens" (Waldegrave et al., 2009, p. 85).

Just Therapy

Developed by staff at the Dulwich Family Center in New Zealand, this model is grounded on the belief that human problems are related to situations of injustice, particularly marginalization of groups on the basis of race, gender, ethnicity, sexual orientation, ability, and so on. Furthermore, histories of colonization, miscegenation, oppression, sexism, and racism foster multigenerational legacies of pain and disenfranchisement. These legacies influence how people understand or "story" their lives; narratives of empowerment and disempowerment can underlie people's problems. People in marginalized communities may "internalize" isms and create stories about themselves and their people which may reduce agency and efficacy and foster psychological "homelessness" (Hardy & Laszloffy, 2005). As will be discussed later, these grand narratives can influence the way people live their lives. Healing entails restoring one's life to increase agency, ability, and self-worth. Such healing can happen optimally within family and community. Waldegrave et al. (2009) argue that we need to listen to each other's stories and help each other create more positive narratives to counter the dominant discourse that engenders or supports any form of oppression.

Narrative Therapy

At the core of narrative theory is that people's lives are multistoried. No single story of life can be free of ambiguity or contradiction. No self-narrative can handle all the contingencies of life. The role of therapy is to bring these alternate stories out of the shadows and to elevate them so that they play a far more central role in the shaping of people's lives (White & Epston, 1990).

Among the basic concepts of narrative theory is that of the *saturated story*, which other methods of treatment labeled "the presenting problem." The therapist facilitates the deconstruction of the saturated story by posing questions, which *externalize* the problem. For example, Latinx couples often present with stories embedded within multiple stories. These stories often reflect the stories and narratives of others who are important to their life (e.g., extended family members, in-laws, neighbors) or historical issues of justice/injustice. The central idea is that the couple (or the individual or family) does not own the story; instead, the story owns them: It has taken charge of their life. The narrative therapist poses questions to help externalize the problem in order to deconstruct it and reconstruct it. It is important to be aware of cultural/familial embedded stories that oppress (e.g., *el que dirán*, the concern with what others will think, which is a common worry among more traditional Latinxs). Elena, for example, worried about what others might think about Judy, which in turn would be a reflection of her "bad parenting." Elena did not own the story of being a good parent. A grand narrative about proper sexuality and women's conduct, a legacy of the colonial period, owned her perception of her parenting. A therapeutic shift would be to ask, *Como lo diré o como lo diríamos* (How would I or how would we say it?). In this way the individual, couple, or family owns the story. In other words, might Elena consider her daughter's behavior as reflecting her efforts to fit in with her peers, not as a sign of disrespect or rejection of Mexican culture?

In working with couples the therapist might ask *how the problem is shaping or affecting the couple's life*. Through questioning the consideration for alternative stories is generated and the couple begins to develop an alternative story so that unique outcomes can be possible. For example, a therapist might ask, "*Señor, cuando dejó usted de ser esposo para convertirse en problema?*" (Sir, when did you stop being a husband to become a problem?) (Flores et al., 2014). What couples and families often bring to therapy is the "gift," or the saturated story, which often reflects cultural grand narratives or the legacies/grand narratives of the parents, for example migration stories, family stories, stories of political oppression/trauma/torture; stories of biculturality and lack of belonging (*no ser "ni de aquí ni de allá*, to not feel that one is from "here" or "there").

In working with Latinx families who are Spanish speaking an important question is whether stories written in one language can be restoried in another. We often ask clients, *Cuando usted llora en qué idioma llora, en Inglés o en Español?* (When you cry, in which language do you cry?). With couples, if the nature of his problem is in one language and his partner's in another, how can they restory a mutually satisfying and respectful narrative?

For Latinxs whose grand narratives are of abandonment, the therapist needs to consider the following questions: How are we as children impacted by parental loss or abandonment through death, separation, divorce, or dysfunction in the parent? What is the dominant story for an individual who has suffered such loss? How can such narratives be restoried?

How is the experience of being an unauthorized immigrant story my life in the United States? How can the challenge of returning to the homeland without having fulfilled the American Dream construct dominant stories for the offspring of other family members?

When adults are not accountable due to their own saturated stories, dysfunction, illness, or responses to structural forces (e.g., migrations to improve the family circumstances), children *may* grow up with a diminished sense of value. The dominant story may be "I am not important enough to be loved, for my parent to stay, to take care of me." This dominant story may lead to feelings of disentitlement or destructive entitlement, as articulated by Boszormenyi-Nagy and Spark (1984).

Likewise, physical and sexual victimization in childhood creates a negative script for adult intimate relationships. The sequelae are fear and disconnection from body, mind, or spirit. Post-traumatic stress disorder is the equivalent of *espanto* or soul loss in the Indigenous emic system (Flores, 2013). Healing from such victimization entails reconnecting mind/body/spirit, holding perpetrators accountable, and forgiving oneself (see Flores-Ortiz, 1998, 1999a).

Restorying cultural narratives about alcohol and other drugs requires an understanding of the historical legacies of colonization and the use of alcohol by the conquerors to subdue the Indigenous. There are roles in the culture: *el tecato, el vato loco, el hijo de la chingada, el pobre, y el pelado*, which evoke images of a castrated male who has no agency, a buffoon who covers his feelings of insecurity and self-hatred with grandiose masculinity and masks his pain with alcohol (Paz, 1970). *El hijo de la chingada* refers to the *mestizo*, "half-breed" product of Spanish conquest and colonization. *El pobre y el pelado* refer to members of the social underclass who may be poor but have dignity.

There is a link between dominant stories and alcohol and drug abuse that must be explored to understand the nature of addiction in Latinx families (to be discussed in subsequent chapters). Likewise, the cultural views about alcohol need to be deconstructed: Alcohol is central to having fun; the ability to hold one's liquor is a sign of masculinity (or of being a strong woman). How can these cultural notions be deconstructed and reconstructed to transform those roles and stories into more positive ones? The Family Center proposes that healing from substance misuse is like a journey from one identity to another: from victim to survivor to well-balanced whole person (Smith & Winslade, 1997). Healing is facilitated by promoting authentic connections and reconnections with the ancestral culture and worldview.

Narrative and just therapy approaches propose relational paradigm shifts and the coconstruction of justice based preferred relational stories. With regard to historical and intergenerational trauma as well as relational injustice, the collaborative team (client, family, community, therapist) works on transforming "victimhood" to survivorship; mindful of the external political context, the team cocreates a preferred story.

Transforming stories entails reconnecting to ancestral spirits and cultural stories before conquest and colonization; honoring the ancestors through constructive legacies; using humor and connection; and building healthy relationships and families and through activism, balance, and health (Waldegrave, 2003). Author Flores's work with Latinx students and clients over the years has utilized just therapy and narrative ideas to promote health and the rescripting of dominant stories that limited agency and perpetuated pain.

Genealogy as Method

McGoldrick and Gerson (1985) developed a systematic method of obtaining one's family history in order to identify behavioral patterns, repetitive histories of family problems (early death, divorce, migration), and the ways in which context (Figure 2.1) may have influenced the family development over time. The authors encourage the use of genealogy in family therapy. As a first step, one should identify relatives on both sides of the family, up to three or four generations or more, if possible. It is helpful to obtain basic information (date of birth, death, marriages, illnesses) and to identify ethnic, racial, and/or religious affiliation. Symbols are used as shorthand to determine the type of bond among family members; for example, married couples are connected with solid lines, unions (without marriage) with broken lines. In getting the family story, one can interview family members, particularly those who may be the family historian or genealogist.[2]

---

2 A useful resource is McGoldrick (1997) or the newer edition (2011). There are also a number of Web-based applications to develop a family tree.

When you interview your relatives, try to ascertain stories of migration, roles in that process (i.e., who was the bridge, mourner, etc.), even if you think migration is not relevant to your family. Listen for stories of cutoffs, disconnections from relatives, culture, language, and so on; ask about patterns of marriage, divorce, informal adoptions, and so on. Inquire about roles, patterns of communication, rules about family life, values and traditions, as well as illnesses, particularly chronic illnesses with a genetic component. Look for traumatic events, being mindful of "silences" around stories that may signal a reluctance to divulge information that may be too sensitive or a secret for someone else.

Once the information is obtained, the "family tree" can be drawn, using the symbols developed by McGoldrick and Gerson (1985) to denote conflict, overinvolvement, or disengagement in family relations. Once the tree is complete, one can begin to identify patterns. From these patterns, one can theorize about the genesis of particular family problems, sources of injustice, or saturated stories that have affected the family over time. Likewise, family resources, sources of connection, and resilience can be identified.

What Is a Healthy, Functional, Resilient *Latinx* Family?

Returning to the fundamental premise of family theory, a functional family is one that loves, nurtures, protects, and provides for its members. Among Latinxs, those fundamental mandates of family life are nuanced by historical legacies and histories that can both promote resilience and survival and potentiate problems if the social context does not support the family's culture and race. To determine how well a Latinx family is functioning, a thorough evaluation of its structure, patterns of communication, historical realities, and ecological niche is necessary. Furthermore, each family is unique and must be evaluated in terms of how it is fulfilling its commitment to its members, not compared against a European American middle-class family ideal that may no longer exist, even for European Americans, or an idealized Latinx family structure that may not be possible in the U.S. context post-migration.

At various times in the life cycle a family may face the challenge of illness, a premature birth, or the arrival of a child with special needs. The extent to which the couple and family can negotiate these challenges also may be influenced by their ideas about health, the meaning ascribed to the illness or different ability, their faith, and coping mechanisms, along with extended family and social support. Following we offer our perspective on two challenges Latinx couples may face. First, couples who are unable or who prefer not to have children, and second couples whose children have special needs.

Coping With Infertility

Latinxs, particularly Mexican-origin women, have a high fertility rate. Therefore, most couples assume that they will have children once they marry or partner. Given the high value ascribed to children and parenting among Latinxs who hold traditional values, difficulties in conceiving may create stress for couples and their extended families. The extant studies of infertility among Latinx couples find that immigrants to a greater degree than U.S.-born Latinx want to have children. Mexican-origin Hispanic immigrants have higher fertility rates than second-generation immigrants and native non-Hispanic Whites, with immigrants and Spanish speakers having a strong desire to bear sons or trying to have children until a son is born (Becker et al., 2006; Unger & Molina, 1999). However, the high fertility rate of Mexican-origin women has declined in the past decade for U.S.-born females, in particular those with higher levels of education (Alvira-Hammond, 2019).

Becker et al. (2006) argue that most infertile women and sterile men who have a strong desire to parent mourn the loss of the biological parent role. Moreover, for Latinxs the social costs of female infertility or male sterility may be higher, particularly for low-income immigrants given their gender roles and the cultural centrality of the parenthood role for men and women. Often the stress of infertility is compounded by the couple's parents and extended family who question, cajole, and offer natural remedies for the infertility.

Infertile couples may experience significant shame, guilt, and sadness about their inability to have children. Studies find that half as many Latinx women with fertility problems seek treatment and even fewer seek adoption services, even if they have a supportive partner. Socioeconomic and language barriers also must be considered as these also affect access to fertility treatments, many of which are not covered by insurance (Becker et al., 2006).

Adriana and Jose are both second generation Chicanx professionals. In her 20s, Adriana was diagnosed with lupus[3] and both she and her husband decided not to have children as a pregnancy would increase the risk of health complications for Adriana. While they both grieved the decision not to be able to have their own child, they also had to manage the distress of their parents who longed for a grandchild. Adriana was encouraged by extended family members to seek the help of traditional healers, *curanderas*, *sobadores* (massage therapists), and herbalists in the rural community in which the parents lived. The family was dumbfounded that Adriana and Jose preferred instead to utilize fertility treatments. After two failed in-vitro attempts, Adriana and Jose decided to adopt but had been unsuccessful in obtaining a child. They sought mental health treatment to deal with the grief of lost parenthood and to find ways to resolve the conflict with extended family who continued to pressure them "to try one more time."

Unlike Adriana and Jose, Joaquin and Yolanda were a couple in their 30s who grew up in very large families in rural Mexico and had migrated as adolescents to work in order to help out their parents and siblings. Both met while working in the fields and began to live together. Yolanda made it clear to Joaquin that she did not want to have children. She had helped raise seven younger siblings and did not want to spend her entire life changing diapers, feeding, and nurturing others. She wanted to work, improve her financial future by going to school, and eventually be able to leave her factory job. Joaquin worked in construction and did not feel it necessary to sire a child. He was one of 10 children, and although he did not have to parent them, he saw the burden such a large family was for the parents. They began to live together, and soon after they both began to receive messages from their families in Mexico that they needed to start having children, as Yolanda "was

3   Lupus is a chronic (long-term) disease that can cause inflammation and pain in any part of the body. It's an autoimmune disease; that is, the body system that usually fights infections attacks healthy tissue instead. Lupus can affect the skin, the joints, and internal organs, such as the kidneys and heart. There is no cure for lupus, but it can be managed with medication and stress reduction.

getting older." When Joaquin told his mother that they were not going to have children, his mother assumed that Yolanda was barren and encouraged her son to find another woman. Yolanda was furious but understood that for her in-laws their decision not to have children was felt as a devaluation of their choice to have so many children. Joaquin's mother worried that her son would not have anyone to take care of him when he was old. Joaquin gently noted that although she had borne 10 children, she was now alone as all offspring had left the rancho (rural town) and were either in the United States or in larger · cities. She too was alone. Nevertheless, his mother's hurtful statements temporarily created conflict between Yolanda and Joaquin, which threatened the relationship.

Family Resilience

Resilience is a dynamic and multidimensional process in which individuals experience positive outcomes despite their exposure to significant adversity (Masten, 1994, 2001). Research on resilience has been expanded, looking at the interplay and effect of neurobiological, psychosocial, and global influences on individuals' ability to overcome adversity, as well as how this interplay takes place within ethnocultural groups, such as Latinx youth (Kuperminc et al., 2009). In the context of families, different models on resilience have been developed, integrating life span and family perspectives (Hawley & DeHaan, 1996; Walsh, 1996), and some have specifically addressed family resilience among immigrant Latinx (Cardoso & Thompson, 2010), identifying four major domains that contribute to their resilience, such as individual characteristics, family strengths, cultural factors, and community support.

Family theoretical frameworks on resilience are of special interest when working with Latinx families since those contribute to a strengths-based psychological perspective on this population. We learn through these frameworks how families survive and thrive despite all the multiple challenges that they may experience. Indeed, Latinx families are exposed to multiple adversities and encounter multiple systemic barriers. The majority of Latinx families in the United States live in poverty, and many are transnational families; most of Latinx adults are immigrants with or without documents. Large numbers of these families live without health insurance, and many reside in neighborhoods with high rates of violence. They often face discrimination, institutional oppressions, and multiple attacks to their integrity and dignity. However, the largest demographic group among Latinxs in the United States are Mexican immigrants who live longer and present healthier outcomes; this is described as the Latinx paradox (Abraído-Lanza et al., 1999). These communities and families possess tools, which seem to contribute to these health outcomes and to their survival despite adversity. From a Latinx psychological perspective on resilience, cultural and social capital seem to be sources of psychological strength for Latinx immigrant communities. Indeed, several studies on Latinxs have identified cultural capital and its implications for positive mental health outcomes (Almedom, 2005; Valencia-Garcia et al., 2012). Further, cultural identity and cultural practices also seem to contribute to the well-being of Latinx: *la cultura cura* or culture cures (Tello, 1994). A Latinx/Chicanx theoretical framework on resilience is therefore embedded in legacies of wisdom transmitted through generations, in cultural meanings, in family rituals, and in the multiple layers that conform to the rich universe and idiosyncrasy of Latinx families.

This multiplicity as source of resilience is captured by Gloria Anzaldúa (1987) in her work on *mestizaje* or hybridity. She illuminates how multiple identities, languages, traditions, and the capacity of Latinx/Chicanx to adapt, to live within different spaces, and to resist through history contributes to their resilience.

Further, Yosso's (2005) community cultural wealth theory (CWT), which also aligns with a strengths-based perspective in the field of education, critically deconstructs "deficit" perspective theories (Garcia & Guerra, 2004) when addressing Latinx communities. Yosso (2005) describes an array of cultural skills and knowledge possessed by immigrants through six forms of capital, such as aspirational (hope for the future), navigational (strategies to resist and navigate systems), social (networks and community resources), familial (cultural knowledge nurture through the family), linguistic, and resistant capital (inner strengths, knowledge and skills to oppose oppression). Often college students in our classes share how *los consejos* or advice from parents and *dichos*, sayings such as *querer es poder* (where there is a will, there is a way) or words of encouragement, as *échale ganas* (do your best) or *ponte las pilas* (work hard), come to their minds during challenging times. This helps students connect with their families' wisdom and repertoire of strategies to overcome difficulties; it also connects them with their cultural heritage and the lessons learned at home, the pedagogies of the home (Bernal, 2001), which ultimately provide them with strategies of resistance. For instance, Rosa Manzo (2016) describes how migrant farmworker families may instill in their children the value of education through their example as hard workers; they may teach the value of getting an education by bringing their children to the fields and showing that they will not have to perform the same work if they get an academic degree.

In working with families from a clinical strengths-based perspective, the model developed by Bermudez and Mancini (2013), *familias fuertes* or strong families, addresses different domains of resilience and psychological strength in relation to their cultural and social capital. Those include their family belief systems and how they make meaning of adversity through spirituality utilizing *dichos* or sayings such as *así es la vida* (such is life) or *si Dios quiere* (God willing). Family belief systems also demonstrate how families manage a crisis; *no hay mal que por bien no venga* (there is always good that comes out of something bad). Their model includes the role of religion and spirituality as well religious practices as sources of strength or protective factors for many Latinx families. They also consider family rituals, celebrations, and values of being cooperative, helpful, respectful, and courteous to others whether they are family members or not. Rituals and manners or *educación* increase family members' sense of well-being and self-worth. Another area of strength that contributes to family resilience is the use of humor and teasing, *bromear*, which decreases anxiety and tension and increases positive feelings. Additionally, in working with Latinx families this model integrates a cultural genogram that traces history as a source of pride and *mestizo* heritage, including bicultural/bilingual or multicultural/multilingual identity and skills.

Conceptualizing Latinx families with clinical models, which not only acknowledges families' strengths but also utilizes their psychological tools or coping mechanisms, opens venues for families to connect with clinicians, educators, and other professionals and ultimately contributes to destigmatize mental health. For instance, author Torreiro-Casal, when giving workshops on mental health on migrant farm camps, uses strengths-based perspectives and honors their participants' wisdom, hospitality, and *humildad*. She goes to these spaces as a learner, listening to their knowledge of self-care practices, on what motivates them to resist the very hard-working conditions they encounter. They also share very powerful lessons of strength and resilience and how they manage to find ways to cope with adverse conditions, for instance by listening to music from their regions of origin in Mexico, using their sense of humor, keeping their cultural practices, and caring for and loving their children and families. Therefore, in working with college students from backgrounds of families who every day overcome very hard living conditions, author Torreiro-Casal is very conscious of their strengths and resilience, although the students often are not aware of these. In part because the majority of our first-generation college students share that they do not feel welcome in academic spaces, their resilience, their rich cultural and social capital, is not valued, acknowledged, and nurtured. Therefore, we as faculty ensure that our students' own cultural wealth is recognized, validated, and enhanced within and outside the classroom.

Children With Special Needs

Latinx families with children with special needs encounter multiple challenges, such as experiencing various barriers navigating unfamiliar systems and lack of support from institutions and providers. As author Flores (2013) reported, health disparities among Latinx families involve the delay of the necessary diagnosis and early intervention when young children evidence developmental delays or behavioral problems. Further, the lack of awareness or understanding of childhood disorders among Latinx parents, possible concerns about stigmatization, and unresponsive health care and school systems may contribute to underreporting and lack of adequate support for children with behavioral, emotional, or developmental problems. In our clinical experiences working with parents and children with disabilities, we found multiple cases that illustrate these health disparities. For instance, parents reported how they lacked access to appropriate care during pregnancy and postpartum follow-ups, and how their children did not receive adequate evaluations or basic tests, delaying their diagnosis and treatment. Parents also reported that they were not aware that their children were born with **down syndrome** or were children **on the autism spectrum** until they started to notice that something was different about their children. Additionally, some parents disclosed that often providers minimized their concerns or did not provide information, guidelines, or the necessary support to help with their children's needs. Thus, as author Flores (2013) indicates, a combination of lack of awareness or understanding of childhood disorders, concerns about stigmatization, and unresponsive health care and school systems may contribute to underreporting and lack of adequate support for children with behavioral, emotional, or developmental problems.

Indeed, schools represent for many Latinx families a venue to get support for their children, such as access to services, evaluations, and different programs to help with the cognitive, behavioral, linguistic, and academic development of children with disabilities. Latinx families often consider schools a safe place; families often feel supported by teachers and administrators, and they value and have *respeto* for them. They consider their children in *buenas manos* or good hands, especially they seem to feel more comfortable in those schools settings where they can communicate in their language of preference, where they see that those school members look like them, share common cultural values, or are willing to help them. However, often as clinicians we have observed that in many cases those in positions of power at schools, health facilities, or other institutions do not represent the populations they serve or lack cultural training to work with diverse populations. This lack of representation and lack of culturally trained providers has a direct impact on those families who often feel alienated from institutions and even more when they have to face the stigma of having children with special needs.

Author Torreiro-Casal worked at school settings as a counselor, conducting psychological assessments and advocating for children and families. She became familiar with the systemic issues experienced by those families and children when attending **IEP (individualized educational program)** meetings with students, parents, and families. Author Torreiro-Casal realized how intimidating and disempowering the experience is for many parents and, on the contrary, how powerful it is when teachers, therapists, principals, or other parties properly inform an advocate for families despite their ethnic and racial backgrounds. The same applies to family interactions with health providers, such as medical doctors, pediatricians, and counselors. In most cases, families are not aware of their children's rights for accommodation, services, possible referrals, and comprehensive assistance for their children. Often parents are asked to sign papers without being fully aware of the meaning of the evaluations and the implications, trusting that their children are in "good hands" at school settings. Unfortunately, many of these children never receive adequate support at critical moments in their development, suffering the consequences for the rest of their lives.

In addition to the systemic barriers and lack of access to services, Latinx parents' responses to having a child with special needs vary depending on the family's unique characteristics, including socioeconomic status, access to services, understanding of the child's special needs, and familiarity with the U.S. health care system. Initially, when confronted with their child's disability, parents may become overwhelmed and go through a period of grief, adjustment, and eventual adaptation (Flores, 2011). Hughes et al.'s (2008) study on Latinx parents and their adjustment to having a child with special needs found that most of the parents tried to treat their child like any other child, although they had to spend more time and energy on that child. Further, religion plays an important role and acts as a protective factor for families with children with disabilities. It provides a framework to give meaning to the experience of having a child with special needs, such as seeing the child with a disability as an opportunity given by God rather than a burden (Weisner et al., 1991). These interpretations embedded in religion were often shared in our clinical interactions with Latinx mothers who expressed that it was God's will to be a mother of a child with special needs or that only a few mothers have the strength to take care of children with disabilities. The case that follows illustrates some barriers faced by a migrant farmworker mother of a daughter with a disability.

Ana was born to a family from Sinaloa, who came to California every year to work as seasonal migrant farmworkers. Soon after Ana was born, her parents became permanent residents, and her older brother did not have to attend schools in Sinaloa and California anymore. Ana was born with a viral ear infection that causes hearing loss. However, their family was not aware of it until Celia, Ana's mother, started to notice that her daughter acted and responded differently than the other children. Celia requested a medical evaluation for her daughter, and she received the confirmation as she suspected that Ana was hard of hearing. It took Celia 2 years to find out that her daughter could benefit from ear implants that would allow her to develop hearing and language ability. However, that process was very long, and Celia felt lonely and not supported, encountering multiple linguistic and systemic barriers, such as insurance coverage. It was crucial to operate on Ana as soon as possible, and the family needed to stay in the United States. Celia invested time to get informed, seek services, and get the necessary support for her daughter. She suffered not only systemic barriers as a monolingual migrant woman but also the lack of support from her husband, who started to abuse her verbally and emotionally. Author Torreiro-Casal started working with Celia when Ana already had the implants and was attending a special education school for children with implants. Celia was delighted to have her daughter attend the school; she became a volunteer and regularly attended the meetings with other Latinx parents with children with similar presentations. However, the school and the school district had to determine if Ana would continue attending the special education school or attend another program at the school district with limited resources. Celia was overwhelmed and asked author Torreiro-Casal to help her with the IEP meeting to request the school district to continue supporting her daughter's education at the school she was attending. In her role as an advocate, author Torreiro-Casal consistently attended all the IEP meetings, reviewed all the evaluations, psychological assessments, goals, progress, and objectives and closely monitored letters of exchange and interactions with the school district and the schools, as well as coordinated work with other agencies and available resources. Celia's daughter is now able to speak in English and Spanish. Celia said that her daughter changed her life and made her grow as a human being, mother, and woman. In the community, Celia had her friends from *el campito* or a migrant farmer workers camp, who always had time to help a *comadre* with food, childcare, and advice. She also had help from school personnel who were sensitive to the needs of parents like Celia.

Author Flores also has worked with families who have children with special needs. In her experience, the parents' response to the birth of a special needs child often depends on their age, level of education, and, as noted, level of social support. Most often, they treat the child as if they were "normal" and do their best to support their child. The couple relationship often becomes unduly stressed, as the mother's focus shifts to the child. Husband/partners and other children may complain of feeling neglected and may become resentful of the child, which then leads to feelings of guilt. It is critical to attend to the needs of the parents and other children, as well as the child, to ensure that the family will remain cohesive and well.

In our work, regardless of the "problem" or challenge that brings a family to treatment, we find it helpful to assess the family's history of migration, unresolved issues related to that cultural change, degree of biculturality of its members, psychological rootedness, and justice and injustice in family relations and the dominant stories that may need to be transformed to create greater harmony and balance in family relations (see Bernal et al., 1986; Flores-Ortiz & Bernal, 1989; Flores-Ortiz, 1993, 1999b, 2005). Each family that seeks treatment should be compared against itself and its ideals and realities. In collaboration, challenging problems and grand narratives can be deconstructed and reconstructed to promote greater healing. However, the reality is that most of the work that author Flores and Torreiro-Casal have been doing is to advocate for these families and children who will hopefully become professionals to help their communities and others struggling to access services and educational opportunities. In the next few chapters, the most pressing problems faced by diverse groups of Latinx are discussed.

Summary

In this chapter we offer several models to evaluate the ways in which families are organized and function. We pay particular attention to normative changes families undergo, as well as particular challenges they may face if they have difficulty fulfilling the cultural and familial expectation to have children. Likewise, we examine the impact of the decision to not have children and the extended family's reaction to such a choice, particularly among more traditional parents. While having children with special needs may be very challenging to most parents, Latinx couples and families often find cultural ways of coping to ensure their child will have quality in life and succeed academically and socially whenever possible.

HOMEWORK ASSIGNMENT

1. Identify the dominant story that has influenced your academic trajectory.
2. Identify the facts of your family history that may affect you in visible and invisible ways (e.g., histories of migration, family instability, divorce, etc.)
3. Reflect on your family's value system. What values do you find useful and which may cause you stress at this point in your life?

KEY TERMS

Autism spectrum: A disorder related to brain development that impacts how a person perceives and socializes with others, causing problems in social interaction and communication. The disorder also includes limited and repetitive patterns of behavior.

Cargas: Burdens. In the context of a family these can be related to responsibilities, expectations, and support from individuals in a family. In the case of children these burdens could potentially be detrimental for their psychological well-being.

Down syndrome: A condition in which a person has an extra chromosome. Typically, a baby is born with 46 chromosomes.

Destructive entitlement: The development of symptomatic behaviors due to deficient caring and responsibility from parental figures. The child may develop resentment against parental figures and act out with destructive and abusive behavior toward other family members.

Differentiation of the self: In the field of psychology this involves being able to possess and identify your own thoughts and feelings and distinguish them from others. In the context of families, children learn in growing up to differentiate from their parents.

Emotional cutoffs: Describes people managing their unresolved emotional issues with parents, siblings, and other family members by reducing or totally cutting off emotional contact with them.

Enmeshed: Refers to families who don't have healthy boundaries. For instance, in an enmeshed family the boundary lines between mom's needs and child's needs become blurred together. Mom's emotions and needs became the priority, leaving you little space to understand the child's emotions and needs.

Entitlement: Entitlement in the family context refers to members' attitudes who appear to believe that they have rights to prioritize their needs above others.

Executive subsystem: Refers in systems theory to the parents in the family. Subsystems map the relationships between family members or between subsets of the family.

Family boundaries: Boundaries help children develop self-control, to be part of society and to feel cared for and safe. They also help parents look after themselves and other family members. Boundaries are guidelines between people about suitable behavior, responsibilities, and respect for people's individual characteristics.

Family projection process: Family patterns repeat through generations. Specific roles and triangles reappear. Examples are the scapegoat/superstar sibling dyad, depression, substance abuse, or a "big secret." Any family dynamic is subject to being reenacted.

Family triangles: A three-person relationship system. Triangles are formed when a two-person system is unstable and because it tolerates little tension before involving a third person.

Humildad: Or *modestia*, meaning humbleness, a value core to the Latinx connected to religious beliefs. Children are raised to be humble, lack arrogance, and never show off.

Individualized educational program (IEP): Helps kids with specific needs to succeed in school and describes the goals the team sets for a child during the school year, as well as any special support needed to help achieve them.

Invisible loyalties: In family theory these refer to loyalties, characteristics, and behaviors manifested in relationships with ourselves and others, which are passed down through generations unconsciously. For example, an individual who is hurt and frustrated by parental criticism growing up may harshly criticize others.

Multigenerational transmission processes: In the context of a family it implies the repetition of patterns and behaviors through generations consciously or unconsciously.

Narrative therapy: A method of therapy that separates a person from their problem. It encourages people to rely on their own skills to minimize problems that exist in their lives. Throughout life, personal experiences become personal stories.

Nuclear family: Elementary family or conjugal family consisting of two parents and their children. It is in contrast to a single-parent family, the larger extended family, and a family with more than two parents.**Parental child:** Or parentified child, this refers to those children who become the "parents" to their parents and younger siblings. They provide instrumental and psychological support to other family members and perform roles that are not developmentally expected from a child. The burdens that their parentified role implies can have psychological consequences for those children.

Permeable boundaries: Refers for instance to interactions between parents and children in the family context. Those are determined by age and role differences and are most often permeable as they share information, resources, chores, and other resources of value within the family.

Relational justice: Defined as the justice produced through cooperative behavior, agreement, negotiation, or dialogue among actors in a post-conflict situation.

Saturated story: The story that a client presents to a therapist in which the problem is so dominant that there at first appears little sign of any alternative story. The therapist, using a narrative therapy approach, will encourage the client to develop new and alternative stories to gain a sense of agency.

Sibling positions: The basic idea in psychological systems theories that people who grow up in the same sibling position predictably have important common characteristics. For example, oldest children tend to gravitate to leadership positions and youngest children often prefer to be followers.

Sibling subsystem: In systems theory, this refers to children in the family and their relationship dynamics.

Triangulated conversations: Triangulation is a manipulation tactic where one person will not communicate directly with another person, instead using a third person to relay communication to the second, thus forming a triangle.

Visible loyalties: The awareness in the family context of the interactions with other family members and their implications. The idea is to develop healthy boundaries, finding balance and reciprocity in our interactions with others.

PART | II

4

When Love Is Not Enough

Injustice in the Family

A well-functioning family is a system in balance that can negotiate transitions and resolve conflicts with fairness and consideration of the individual and collective needs of its members. Families are likely to face challenges at various points in the life cycle; family systems with good communication, shared values and goals, and permeable boundaries can successfully meet these challenges. A migration and separation from loved ones at any point in the life cycle can create significant challenges for families. As noted in earlier chapters, forming a new couple unit may be difficult if either partner feels overly loyal to their family of origin, has not attained enough emotional independence from that family, or if they face larger social, economic, or cultural pressures than they are equipped to handle, for example homophobia, racism, classism, sexism, or poverty. The arrival of the first child also can challenge a couple, particularly if they have different expectations and ideas about parenting, or if the in-laws desire more involvement than does either member of the couple. Likewise, balancing work/life can prove difficult for couples with varying degrees of adherence to traditional cultural values and gender norms.

In this chapter, we will explore some of the normative challenges families may face as well as the more serious problems contemporary Latinxs experience. These problems are situated within the frameworks offered by McGoldrick (see Figure 2.1) and Falicov (2014) and analyzed using the models reviewed in Chapter 3.

Troublesome Triangles

Minuchin (1974) developed structural family therapy as a method to address the challenges in family life that poverty, migration, and cultural change created for people. Although his early focus was on families with a schizophrenic child and families who lived in poverty, his ideas are applicable to many family systems. As stated in earlier chapters, families, as any organization or system, have structure. Traditional Latinx families are hierarchical, with adults occupying the decision and rule-making roles (executive functions); however, children also may share these functions, depending on age, birth order, and gender. For example, the parental child may help with chores and childrearing (Falicov, 1998). In systems with clear but permeable boundaries, every family member knows their role, the rules that apply to them, and what is expected. No single family member is or feels over-burdened by the expectations of others. In multigenerational households, grandparents or other extended family members may participate in some of the childrearing functions or take care of domestic duties. In well-functioning systems, members collaborate and support one another.

Problems arise when communication is not clear or when some members unwittingly or deliberately sabotage the authority of another. This may lead to the development of troublesome triangles, which can cause stress, conflict, and overtime result in more serious difficulties, as seen in the following vignette.

Doña Rosa, Maria, Pepe, and Susanita

Doña Rosa is an immigrant woman from El Salvador who raised two sons and a daughter alone, after her husband abandoned her. She migrated to the United States during the Civil War and worked as a cook in the San Francisco Bay Area to support her children. Her sons and daughter adored her for her sacrifice, her strength, and her good heart. Her daughter Maria married young, and both of her sons went off to college. Maria did not want her mother to live alone, worrying about her safety since Doña Rosa lived in a high crime area of Northern California. Doña Rosa, however, did not want to impose on the newly formed couple, especially because Pepe was Mexican origin and born in the United States. Doña Rosa worried that they might have different values and he might not want to have a *suegra*, mother-in-law, living in his home. However, when Maria became pregnant, her mother acquiesced and moved in to help. Initially, both Pepe and Maria appreciated Doña Rosa's cooking and cleaning. Pepe in particular enjoyed coming home to warm meals and a clean house. Initially the family functioned well; Doña Maria tried to be unobtrusive. When Susanita was born, things began to change. Both Maria and Pepe wanted to raise their children following the advice of the pediatrician and parent-ing books. Doña Rosa believed children should be carried all the time and fed when they cried and was appalled that the tiny baby was sleeping alone in a crib in a separate room. She kept her views to herself but indulged her granddaughter when no one was around to see her. On several occasions when Maria went to check on the baby at night, she found her mother asleep on the rocking chair holding the baby. Maria believed the baby should learn to "self-soothe" by being allowed to cry. Doña Rosa disagreed. Maria talked to her mother about her wishes on several occasions to no avail. Maria began to feel disrespected and sabotaged in her parenting by her mother. Doña Rosa was hurt that her daughter "did not trust" her parenting abilities and knowledge; moreover, she was only trying to help. Pepe felt caught between the two women and guilty that he had begun to resent his mother-in-law. The situation grew tense and Pepe suggested to Doña Rosa that she take a vacation and go visit her relatives in El Salvador. Doña Rosa felt she was being "kicked out"; she packed her bags, kissed the baby, and left without saying goodbye. Maria was furious about her mother's drama and Pepe felt guilty and ashamed.

After a few weeks, Maria realized how much help her mother had provided, as both she and her husband had to juggle work, childcare, and domestic chores and found they had no time for themselves. They both pleaded for Doña Rosa to return and negotiated some agreements about childcare. Maria and Pepe realized they were being a bit rigid with their ideas and Doña Rosa agreed to consult with them before doing things "her way." Things may not always work out so smoothly, however, and problems with *la suegra* can create irreparable damage to a new relationship.

Edward, Luisa, and Doña Esther

Edward, a 60-year-old divorced man met Luisa, a 49-year-old single woman, when he went to visit family in his native Honduras. Luisa was a single parent of an adult child and lived with her mother and stepfather. They began to date, and Edward decided to set up a household with her. He rented a spacious house, furnished it to her liking, and began to visit every few months once he retired. Edward planned to obtain a fiancé visit for Luisa in order to bring her to the United States; however, over the course of several visits he became concerned about her "overdependence" on her mother. Edward complained that Doña Esther would arrive unannounced at their home and decide what program should be watched on TV; she also told Edward that he should not drink because it was against her religious beliefs. Edward was incensed. No woman, not even his mother, had ever told him what to do once he became a man. When he told Luisa that she should set some limits on her mother, Luisa angrily refused and began to give him "the cold shoulder."

Edward felt that Doña Esther did not trust him and filled Luisa's head with jealous ideas about his relationship with his ex-wife, which was amicable. Edward knew he could not give Luisa an ultimatum and have her choose between her mother and him, but he was at his wit's end and considering ending the relationship unless things changed and Luisa became more differentiated from her mother.

Although Edward and Luisa came from similar cultural backgrounds, Edward had lived in the United States for most of his adult life, and although his ex-wife had been a very strong woman, he had been the one in charge. Edward also held very traditional ideas about men's position within the family. Luisa was his woman; he was supporting her and had created a home for both of them, which he visited regularly. He had formed a transnational relationship (to be discussed further in the next chapter) while he obtained a visa for her to come to the United States and decide whether she wanted to move there permanently with him. His plan was to spend part of the year in the United States until the violence in Honduras subsided and then he would retire there permanently. However, he was very attached to his grandchildren and did not foresee leaving the United States until the youngest, who was still a baby, was at least in elementary school. Luisa was not sure she wanted to leave her mother and join his family, which he had formed with "another woman." They had reached an impasse. Luisa felt she could not leave her mother for less than a sure thing; she did not trust that he would marry her. He was not sure he wanted to marry a woman so dependent on her mother. At his age, he stated, he just wanted to live and let live. When he was in the United States, Luisa called throughout the day wanting to know what he was doing and with whom. He felt suffocated. The troublesome triangle with Luisa's mother was threatening the viability of the relationship.

Problems that are rooted in cultural differences, communication difficulties, or relational impasses generally can be resolved utilizing most family therapy modalities, as long as these are culturally attuned. However, many of the more serious challenges Latinxs experience have their roots in intergenerational trauma; "what is overwhelming and unnamable is passed on to those we are closest to. Our loved ones carry what we cannot. And we do the same" (Castello, 2012). For Latinxs, the trauma may have its roots in the genocide of colonization, in the sequelae of the colonial period, in the Mexican-American war, or the multiple wars and occupations of Latin America in the 19th and 20th centuries, or in the segregation of Mexicans and other Latinxs in the United States prior to the Civil Rights movements, and the current urban social violence resulting from decades of oppression and marginalization (Flores, 2013). Such problems require a thorough evaluation of the family's structure, history, and resources and treatment approaches that are trauma informed, justice based, and culturally relevant.[1]

Injustice in the Family

The major forms of family dysfunction among Latinxs include substance misuse and abuse; family violence, including intimate partner violence (IPV); child abuse; marital rape; incest; and social violence (rape, stalking, homicide, and suicide).

Substance Abuse

According to a Substance Abuse and Mental Health Services Administration (SAMHSA, 2019) 2018 National Survey on Drug Use and Health (NSDUH) report, 1.1 million Hispanic/Latinx youth used illicit drugs in the past year, including 208,000 who misused opioids in the past year. Such high rates of substance use among Latinx youth places them at a greater risk for engaging in unsafe sexual practices linked to human immunodeficiency viruses (HIV), Hepatitis C virus (HCV), and sexually transmitted infections (STI). In addition, the report indicates that 92% of Latinx youth with a substance use disorder did not receive treatment in a specialty facility. Moreover, an estimated 17% of Latinx adults suffered from mental illness, and 15% of Latinx youth experienced a major depressive episode. The cooccurrence of a substance use disorder and mental illness increases the vulnerability for poor health outcomes for Latinx. The extent to which the family system is impacted by substance misuse and abuse has been documented by scholars (see Bernal & Flores-Ortiz, 1991). Of particular concern is the increased substance misuse among Latina girls and the early onset of alcohol misuse among Latinx youth. An earlier report found that Latina girls were abusing alcohol and illicit drugs at rates comparable to boys and higher than female youth from other ethnic/racial groups (National Coalition of Hispanic Health and Human Service Organizations [**COSSMHO**], 1999). Moreover, acculturative stress and family problems constitute risk factors for adolescent substance abuse (Flores, 2015).

Significant health disparities have been found among Latinx subgroups (Flores, 2013). As noted elsewhere (Flores, 2013) despite need, few Latinxs receive substance abuse treatment. Latinx also have low rates of health and mental health service utilization. The SAMHSA report also noted that *the need for treatment* for alcohol and

---

1   For an excellent formulation of working with Latino families in therapy, see Falicov (2014).

illicit drug use, as well as the receipt of illicit drug use treatment among those needing it, were more likely among Latinx born in the United States than among immigrants to the United States.

Alcohol remains the substance most frequently used and abused by Latinxs. Among the illicit drugs, opiate and marijuana use remains high; in the past decade there has been a rise among methamphetamine use among Latinx, particularly U.S.-born individuals (SAMHSA, 2019). Substance misuse and abuse affects not only the user, but also every member of their family. Substance abuse is highly correlated with all forms of family violence, including homicides and suicides. Substance misuse and abuse when treated must be done so holistically and with interventions that are culturally responsive and appropriate (Carrillo & Tello, 2008; Duran, 2006).

Family Violence

About one in three Latinas (34.4%) will experience intimate partner violence (IPV) during her lifetime and one in twelve Latinas (8.6%) has experienced IPV in the previous 12 months (Smith et al., 2011). The rates of IPV are higher for U.S.-born Latinas than for immigrant women. A study of 2,000 Latinas found that 63.1% of women who identified being victimized in their lifetime reported violence that included stalking, physical assaults, weapon assaults, attempted sexual assaults, and victimization in childhood (including physical and sexual abuse) (Cuevas et al., 2010). Most of the women reported having experienced more than one victimization, with an average of 2.56 victimizations.

A national sample of Latinas examining the forms of victimization, including physical assault, sexual violence, stalking, threat victimization, and witnessing violence, found that more than half of the women surveyed (53.6%) reported at least one victimization over a lifetime, and about two thirds (66.2%) of those women had more than one victimization. Among 362 Latinas seeking family planning services about half (51%) had experienced IPV and 34% reported reproductive coercion. Other studies have also reported a link between IPV, reproductive coercion, and unintended pregnancies for Latina survivors. In fact, one study found that 21% of pregnant Latinas experienced both reproductive coercion and IPV, increasing their risk for an unplanned pregnancy (Cuevas et al., 2012).

In author Flores's investigations of IPV in both Mexico and the United States, we found similar rates of domestic violence (Flores-Ortiz et al., 2002). Although some studies suggest that Latinas experience more violence than European American women, differences in rates of intimate partner violence between Latinx and non-Latinx have a tendency to disappear when factors such as age, urbanicity, and alcohol consumption are considered; in fact socioeconomic status was found to be the most predictive of IPV among African American, European American, and Latinx couples (Cunradi et al., 2002b). Cunradi et al. (2001a) also found that IPV patterns do not change over time; couples who experienced violence early in their relationship continue to face multiple forms of abuse well into their midlife. The victims of this violence include not only the spouse, but the children as well. In our binational studies (Flores-Ortiz et al., 2002), older women reported that they had hoped that with time the men "would calm down and stop being abusive"; however, the violence had persisted for most of their married life. Most of our respondents had spent their married life with depression and trauma but had remained hopeful that the man would change. Most did not and they regretted that their children had been affected by the violence they witnessed.

With regard to child neglect and maltreatment, during the fiscal year 2012 a nationally estimated 3.2 million children received either an investigation or alternative response at a national disposition rate of 42.7 children per 1,000 in the population. This is a 3.5% increase from 2008 when an estimated 3.1 million children received a Child Protective Services response at a rate of 40.8 per 1,000 children in the population (Children's Bureau, 2013). The majority of perpetrators were parents. More than three quarters (78.3%) of child victims were neglected, 18.3% were physically abused, and 9.3% were sexually abused. In addition, 10.6% of victims experienced "other" types of maltreatment such as threatened abuse, parent's drug/alcohol abuse, or safe relinquishment of a newborn (Children's Bureau, 2013). The same report indicates that children younger than 3 years were the most vulnerable and Hispanic or Latinx children represented 21.8% of cases (compared to 44% White and 21% African American). Among those who were sexually abused, 26.3% were between 12–14 years of age and one third (33.8%) were younger than 9 years. The same report identifies adults with domestic violence and substance abuse as high risk factors for child maltreatment.

From a family systems perspective, family violence, child maltreatment, and substance abuse are interrelated problems often with the same risk factors and underlying causes; therefore, they should be treated holistically. However, these family problems are rarely treated in a coherent manner. It is the nature of health care delivery systems to treat mental health, substance abuse, and child maltreatment separately; oftentimes families and individuals have two to three different systems or providers involved in their care provision. Less frequently is there communication among systems or providers (Flores-Ortiz & Bernal, 1989).

Causative Factors

From a family systems perspective, problems of injustice in the family must be understood and treated systemically. Families who present with such problems often face multiple stressful life events and lack more appropriate responses to deal with stressors. Likewise, it is critical to evaluate and consider the ecological factors that contribute to abuse, including poverty, social stratification, and the complex ecological niche that socioeconomically disadvantaged families occupy (Falicov, 1989, 2014).

In working with Latinx, as with other marginalized groups, historical legacies of injustice also must be considered, including the sequelae of colonization, which at the macro level [or the dimension of historical realities of facts, as articulated by Boszormenyi-Nagy (1987)], include the dependence of Latin American countries on more powerful nations and institutions (EU, United States, China; World Bank). This economic dependence often leads to pervasive conditions of poverty and corruption that adversely impact families and are a major reason for Latinx migration to the United States. In addition, institutionalized racism, classism, homophobia, and sexism affect the psychology of individuals and the family as a whole in both Latin America and the United States. **Historical trauma** also is associated with increased risk for substance misuse and abuse in both men and women

(Duran & Duran, 1995; Williams & Collins, 1995; Williams & Mohammed, 2009) as well as family injustice in all of its forms (Carrillo & Tello, 2008).

The legacies of migration also need to be understood. Cultural legacies and loyalties may remain invisible yet impact how individuals feel about themselves and their place in the world. At the level of individual psychology persistent experiences of micro- and macroaggression can result in despair, rage, and violence (Hardy & Laslofly, 2005). The changes in meaning systems that accompany migration (Falicov, 1998, 2014) can evolve into family problems ranging from mild to serious in severity. Acculturative stress, especially among adolescents and young adults, can tax their coping mechanisms and result in family problems that can be viewed as disrespect (see Chapter 2) or in more serious externalizing behaviors in young people as they try to fit in or find their place in the world (Aguirre-Molina & Betancourt, 2010).

Utilizing a contextual model, we can see problems of injustice as rooted in intergenerational patterns of injustice that can manifest at the level of individual psychology as the following:

- Destructive entitlement
- Feelings of powerlessness
- Dependency
- Depression
- Rage (which leads to outrage)
- Trauma

Neuroscience suggests that historical trauma compromises the neurobiology, leading to problems with self-regulation. In turn, this may result in the use of substances to quiet down the internal fury (Carrillo & Tello, 2008). A compromised limbic system results in poor impulse control, and hyperarousal, all of which may contribute to self and other injurious behaviors (Flores, 2013; van der Kolk, 2005).

Recent investigations of **minority stress,** which is defined by Brooks (1981) as the stress to which individuals from stigmatized social categories are exposed to as a result of inferior social status, find that the pressure to negotiate multiple identities (cultural, gender, sexual) increases the risk for LGBTQI youth to engage in high-risk behaviors, including substance abuse (Lehavot & Simoni, 2011). Although less research has focused on youth or adults of color, there is clinical evidence to suggest that questioning or queer Latinx youth would be at equal or increased risk as their European American counterparts. Wong et al.'s (2014) investigation of minority status and psychological well-being among African American and Latino men who have sex with men also found high-risk behaviors and reduced psychological well-being among this population as a result of minority stress. Their distress, however, was ameliorated by strong social support.

The impact of adverse circumstances on the family system include the following:

- Ungrieved losses related to migration or multigenerational trauma or of family members due to death, incarceration, deportation, addiction
- Difficulty making commitments
- Problems with communication
- Boundary problems
- Triangulated relationships

- Substance misuse and abuse
- Intimate partner violence
- Child maltreatment

Legacies of oppression intersect with the sequelae of more recent migrations, increasing the risk for dysfunction at the individual and family level among immigrants and children of immigrants (Flores, 2013). Falicov (2014) proposes that a family's MECA map is useful in understanding why and how things can go wrong with families. Specifically, from a social justice perspective we need to understand each family's ecological context, which is constituted by work, school religion, and community, as well as challenges related to migration and acculturation. These issues will include the losses associated with the migration (separations and reunions), trauma associated with migration, disorienting anxieties, and cultural identity conflicts or challenges related to migration and acculturation. From a cultural diversity perspective, which refers to values and beliefs, we also need to understand the family's life cycle (constituted by ideals, meanings, timings, transitions), the family organization (whether nuclear, extended, blended), patterns of communication, hierarchies, and degree of connectedness. Such maps will address the uniqueness of each family and help us understand that which is also universal—the life cycle processes and transitions—and how these can be disrupted by migration and injustice.

Latinx Families With a Problem of Substance Abuse

Contextual family therapy views substance abuse "as rooted in social and community dynamics that impact upon the family and the person" (Bernal & Flores-Ortiz, 1991, p. 80). These dynamics include legacies of abuse, wherein substance misuse is often a multigenerational pattern. For example, grandparents may have drank as a "cultural pattern," or to reduce stress, or for celebrations. The adult son may have increased his alcohol consumption after migration to deal with acculturative stress, work pressures, or feelings of anxiety or depression. The U.S.-born grandson may have begun to experiment with marijuana and alcohol and ultimately abuse heroin or methamphetamine to cope with marginalization, cultural identity conflicts, and a pervasive lack of belonging (Flores, 2013). The grandson's addiction must be understood contextually to develop treatment strategies that are more effective (Bernal & Flores-Ortiz, 1991).

Latinxs show a higher incidence of substance abuse when there are ungrieved losses; these losses could be related to migration, or to the substance abuse of earlier generations, or to the ecological context of the family, including the erosion of community that occurs in densely populated urban environments (Hardy & Laszloffy, 2005). Substance misuse is also associated with mood and anxiety disorders, particularly among men who use substances to contain their grief or sadness (Flores, 2013). In addition, contextual family therapists are concerned with the possibility that substance abuse itself may be a way of showing loyalty and concern for the family. In their early writings Bernal and Flores-Ortiz (1991) suggested that drug abuse was a self-sacrificing behavior, which might be a family member's last ditch attempt to make family members accountable, particularly when "integrity and trustable parenting are either not available or have eroded" (p. 81). Clearly an alcohol-abusing father is not sufficiently available to root, enculturate, or support his children, who may in turn seek emotional sustenance in alcohol or other drugs, particularly if the social ecology of their community makes substances readily available and the youth have internalized stereotypes of Latinxs as drinkers.

The substance abusing family member often is the child who was maltreated, abused, or parentified. From an individual psychology perspective, they are seeking to soothe the fire/pain within (Carrillo & Tello, 2008). The substance-abusing individual also may be the mourner or underaculturator (Sluzki, 1979) in a family with a history of migration.

Many Latinx families with substance abuse problems engage in a code of secrecy that helps maintain the problem. Often this is related to concerns about social appraisal (*el qué dirán*) or to hide other problems related to substance abuse, such as family violence. In these families dysfunction may be masked as a "cultural" pattern or expectation: All men drink; drinking is central to having fun . These families may also manifest diffuse boundaries wherein it is not clear who is in charge. Indirect communication is also common and facilitates lack of accountability. U.S.-born or -raised children who may be more accustomed to direct communication may disregard messages that are not directed at them specifically. For example, parents may say *Los jóvenes no deben tomar alcohol* (Young people should not drink); to the children this may sound like an opinion and not a direct message about parental expectations. A direct statement, "I do not want you to drink alcohol until you are an adult," would convey a more direct rule from the parents, but it may feel culturally incongruent to immigrants who are more comfortable with indirect messages.

As stated, Latino families who present with substance abuse often manifest both intergenerational and contemporary patterns of loss, despair, migration-related traumas, multiple economic and health disparities, and/or minority stress. Bernal and Flores-Ortiz (1991) discussed the case of the Soto family. The mother, Mrs. Soto, was an immigrant from El Salvador, who lost custody of her daughter Rita after she broke a jar of peppers on Rita's head when she discovered that her daughter was sexually active. The hospital blood tests revealed that Rita, who was 14 years old, had high levels of methamphetamine and cocaine in her system. Rita admitted the drug use to her mother's growing consternation. Mrs. Soto could not understand why her child had become a drug user.

An evaluation of the family revealed that Mrs. Soto had been a teen mother who left her two children (from different fathers) in El Salvador with her own mother when she migrated to the United States to seek better economic opportunities. Rita was only 18 months when her mother left her. In the United States, Mrs. Soto partnered with a new man and had four more children. Her attempts to reunify with her children left behind were delayed for several years. Once she was able to bring her children to the United States, family reunification was fraught with difficulties, as Rita and her brother considered their maternal grandmother their mother. Mrs. Soto had not visited El Salvador since she left, though she sent money for the children's care; however, they felt abandoned by her and were depressed and angry. When Rita and her brother arrived in the United States, their mother was expecting twins and had a 5-year-old son. Rita resented her baby brother, disliked her stepfather, and was angry with her mother. Rita was 9 years old. Shortly after her arrival, a family friend molested her. Her mother blamed her for the abuse and beat her. According to the children, their mother was abusive and showed them no love. Mrs. Soto argued that her older son and daughter were ungrateful and disrespectful. She denied being abusive; she explained that she had learned *a punta de palo* (due to corporal punishment) and that is why she had mended her ways and now had a relationship with a good man.

Rita's sexual behavior and drug use coincided with her mother's last pregnancy and her grandmother's arrival from El Salvador. Bernal and Flores-Ortiz's contextual analysis of the case highlighted a number of multigenerational patterns: daughters having children out of wedlock and leaving them with their own mothers for care, alcohol abuse, abandonment and illegitimacy among the men, and parentification of children and extreme disciplinary practices. All the women in the family also were molested and blamed by family members for their own victimization. In this case, multigenerational patterns, as well as the migration process, separation from family members, and involvement in the social welfare systems all compounded the family dysfunction. Rita used drugs to self-soothe and to fit in with her peer system. The therapists working with the family identified multigenerational patterns of incest, desperation, substance abuse, and abandonment that needed to be recognized in order to make change in the present and prevent repetition in future generations.

From a contextual family therapy perspective, the multigenerational patterns of molestation, substance abuse, and family violence created invisible loyalties to previous generations that manifested as dysfunction. The therapists reframed Rita's "misbehavior" as an effort to make visible the hidden suffering of the women in the family. Her mother's violence toward her reflected her own dehumanization caused by incest and abandonment. The grandmother, mother, and Rita were connected across time by legacies of suffering and violence. To break the cycle and prevent Rita from continuing to use drugs, have unplanned pregnancies, and become an abusive mother, the women needed to begin a process of healing. To become accountable to Rita and the other children, mother and grandmother needed to understand, and change, the meaning of their own victimization. To prevent the boys in the family becoming abusive, the male legacies of dysfunction and abandonment also needed to be understood and changed (Bernal & Flores-Ortiz, 1991).

From a narrative perspective, we can analyze this case in terms of the saturated story and the dominant narratives that impacted the family negatively. Rita's saturated story was one of being unwanted. Her father did not parent her; she never knew him. Her mother left her in the care of a grandmother, who was kind but not loving given her own history of victimization. Her mother and stepfather minimized Rita's sexual abuse; instead of being supported and taken care of, she was beaten and called a whore by her mother. Mrs. Soto was influenced by a similar dominant story. Her own father sexually abused her; then he left the family. Tacitly her mother blamed her for her father's abuse and disappearance from the family. Mrs. Soto became a teen mother and felt unwanted, unloved, and unworthy. While she did not abuse alcohol or drugs, she could not parent her first two children. She left her children as a gift to her mother and fled to the United States to start a new life. A grand narrative that women should sacrifice for the family also influenced Mrs. Soto's mother; she protected the men (even if they did not deserve protection), guarded secrets for the sake of *el que dirán*, and raised her grandchildren the best she could. These grand narratives had to be deconstructed; the influence of family history, cultural norms, and adverse circumstances had to be understood in order to reconstruct and cocreate with the therapists more fulfilling and healthy alternatives for all.

Ultimately the goal of working with families where substance abuse is a problem is to focus on recovery from the addiction and from the sociocultural, political, and ecological factors that led to the onset. For Latinxs, as stated, the treatment must be attuned to the level of acculturation of the individuals who form the family, their ecological niche, their individual psychology and family system, as well as the cultural resources they have. Treating the substance abuse without consideration of the factors that led to it is not likely to produce long-term health or prevent repetition of the patterns in future generations (Bernal & Flores-Ortiz, 1991; Duran, 2006).

Moreover, when girls abuse substances it is very likely that they experienced previously some form of sexual violence; therefore, the treatment also must be trauma informed (Flores, 2013). When teen boys abuse substances it is likely they also have experienced some form of violence or denigration, either in the family or society (Hardy & Laszloffy, 2005). Substance abuse and the correlates of suicidality and violence are often expressions of the rage caused by marginalization, dehumanization of the losses they have experienced, and the erosion of their communities.

Latinx Families With a Problem of Violence

Similar to families with substance abuse problems, Latinx families who maltreat often show legacies of abuse, that is multigenerational patterns of domestic violence, child maltreatment, and sexual abuse, as evident in the Soto family described earlier. Likewise these families often have a higher incidence of substance misuse when compared to families where abuse is not present. At times the dysfunction is masked as a "cultural" pattern or saturated stories (i.e., internalized stereotypes that all Latinx men control their women with violence); diffuse boundaries and indirect communication also are common. In cases of child maltreatment, the abused child often is the identified patient (as was Rita) or a parentified child.

Almeida et al. (1994) propose that the roots of interpersonal injustice within families and in society are located in the historical legacy of oppression and colonization, as well as the stratified caste system based on race, ethnicity, religion, sexuality, and ability instituted when the First World (Europeans) collided with the American, African, and Asian continents. As a result of colonization, injustice was institutionalized through education, employment, and limited access to power. This institutionalization in turn resulted in a pyramid of oppression where belonging and dispossession or psychological homelessness is predicated on the degree of acceptance by those in power (Flores-Ortiz, 1999b). Thus, it is important to understand the role of power in human relationships and in particular the distinction between having power and using power *over* others.

Injustice results in a hierarchy of oppression in which those with more power use it over those who are perceived to have less. At an interpersonal and intrafamilial level, power over relationships (man over woman, adults over children, employer over worker) result in a culture of terror and disrespect where abuse of power and violence can easily occur (Flores-Ortiz, 1999b). At an individual psychological level, oppression, particularly injustice that is racially, ethnically, gender, or class based, results in psychological homelessness (Hardy & Laszloffy, 2005). As Carrillo and Tello (2008) also have noted, racism inflicts pain; discrimination creates soul wounds. Disempowerment causes pain; that pain, when compounded by loss of community and place or sense of belonging, can lead to outrage, and in time to rage and explosive anger. Thus, the violence engendered by racism cannot be isolated from intimate partner violence, child maltreatment, and acts of violence toward the self and others.

To understand male violence toward women of color, we also need to understand men's own victimization and the gender oppression and disempowerment that is a legacy of colonization. As we have noted elsewhere (Carrillo & Tello, 2008; Flores, 2013) oftentimes Latino men hurt the women and children they love because their rage cannot be directed at the perpetrators of the violence they endure. The daily indignities they face as men of color accumulate and sometimes detonate when their coping mechanisms falter, their neurobiology is compromised, or they abuse substances.

At the very least social injustice leads to unfairness and imbalance in relationships; inauthentic connections may exist because individuals are afraid to show their true self. Others may disconnect from feelings and develop a veneer of stoicism and invulnerability. When oppression occurs, it can lead to isolation, the break-up of families, or the development of unfair patterns of relationships where some members are overburdened. Injustice also can lead to the erosion of culture, particularly if dysfunctional patterns are associated with a particular group. At times Latinas who have experienced the dark side of *machismo* will not date Latino men because they believe that they will be oppressive or abusive, as were their fathers. The pain of injustice can transform into explosive anger or rage. Intimate partner violence, child maltreatment, social violence, and self-abuse (including alcohol and other drug abuse and suicidality) are some of the expressions of injustice and despair (De La Rosa et al., 1990).

Moreover, the social context of gender violence has to be considered. As Straus and Gelles (1989) have noted, in most societies men hit women because they *can*. However, when Latino and other men of color abuse those they purport to love, they do so because they can *and* because they too are victims of violence. Therefore, they need treatment as well as social accountability, not merely punishment (Carrillo & Tello, 2008). Everyone in the family suffers when intrafamily injustice occurs. Therefore, treatment of family violence must be justice based and multimodal, often including individual, group, marital, family, and social network therapies, as well as be interdisciplinary and culturally attuned (see Flores-Ortiz, 1993, 1998, 1999a, c; Flores-Ortiz et al., 1994).

Families where incest occurs are characterized by rigid and hierarchal gender roles that ensure male supremacy and over-privileging of male children. These families typically have diffuse boundaries and unclear and indirect patterns of communication. Such families create a climate of fear where women and children have no voice. Moreover, much of what occurs in the family is normalized and hidden under a mask of culture (Montalvo & Gutierrez, 1983). Secrecy is labeled good behavior and family loyalty; behavioral compliance motivated by fear and terror is considered respect, and silent suffering of the abuse is reframed as loyalty (Flores-Ortiz, 1993, 1995, 1997b). In these families when the perpetrator is a father or brother, and the mother does not "see" the abuse, it is likely that she also was sexually abused in her own family. Her own trauma prevents her from protecting her children or seeing the abuse when it is occurring (Flores-Ortiz, 1997b).

Injustice in all of its forms causes trauma. In psychiatric nomenclature it is understood as post-traumatic stress disorder (PTSD). In the explanatory model of traditional Latinx it may be viewed as *susto* or *espanto*, the manifestations of soul loss after a particularly difficult or traumatic incident (Flores, 2013). Such trauma then is a causative factor for subsequent substance abuse and violence against the self and others, as well as mood and anxiety disorders at the individual level. In addition to the formulations offered by MECA, contextual, and narrative family therapy approaches, it is critical to understand the nature of trauma from a feminist social justice perspective.

In addressing gender violence, Flores-Ortiz (2001b) noted that

> the body speaks in languages left unread. The body encodes the *agravios*, the assaults that sometimes lead to numbness and alienation, to depression and despair, to a desire for an endless night of sleep. ... Women's bodies are dismembered by the ravages of institutionalized racism, by the patriarchal structures that accord privilege on the basis of gender and class, by the sexism and heterosexism that forbids love and silences desire. (p. 263)

A basic premise of feminist theory is that gender violence will not end while patriarchy prevails and until there is gender equity; likewise the proprietary perception of women and children contributes to violence against women and children. At the root of intrafamily violence is gender oppression, distorted notions of masculinity, imbalances of power, and social injustice. Dominant ideas about gender contribute to the abuse of women, as some men (and women) believe that women must be disciplined to be protected. Likewise, among Latinx and other patriarchal cultures the cult of virginity leads to repression of female sexuality, objectification of women, and the virgin-whore dichotomy. Women often are viewed as weak, seductresses, unable to control their sexuality, thus in need of "protection" from men (Flores, 2013).

Across different cultures, childrearing patterns promote dependence of females and privilege male power. The boys and men are positioned as protectors (and controllers) of women. Women who contest these practices are viewed as bad women (Souza, 2001). In some cultures, men are viewed as morally weaker, thus women are made to feel responsible for controlling male sexuality. Family loyalty as a cultural dictum also silences women and prevents disclosure, as does the shock of being betrayed by one's own family. How to name the unnamable? How can those who love me hurt me? (see Flores-Ortiz, 2001, 2004, 2005.

In our research with college students in the late 1990s (Flores-Ortiz, 2003), 85% of the women disclosed personal experiences of physical violence in their childhood home, where the father or mother was the perpetrator. One hundred women (out of a sample of 168) reported witnessing at least one incident of domestic violence between their parents. Fifty women reported being abused by a family member. Of these, 20 were sexual violations. Among the sexually abused women, the age when the abuse began ranged from 4 to 18 years. Twenty-nine of the women reported verbal or physical attacks because of their race and witnessing violence among peers and neighbors, as well as police violence. The women manifested both psychological and academic problems, which likely were connected to their experiences of victimization. Traumatic memories can manifest in the body, in the thoughts or cognitions of the victim, as well as in their emotions and interpersonal relationships.

Encoding Violence in the Body

Women's narratives often show the location of the trauma:

> I know I am depressed because I can't stop crying. I feel tightness in my chest; I can't breathe. It's like my body remembers certain things, even though I don't want to remember, and then I try to give a name to it. Oh yes, I say to myself, this is depression. What is my body remembering? All the times he came to my room late at night, sat on the side of the bed, then climbed on top of me. At first I was scared, then I would just close my eyes and fly away. I don't consciously want to remember anything. But my body does (Flores-Ortiz, 2003).

Violence in all its forms attacks the self; sexual violence leads to a mind/body split. Racial violence affects self-image; repudiation and multiple erasures also foster disconnection between mind/body and spirit (Flores, 2013; van der Kolk, 1994, 1997, 2005). Given the gender socialization of women, all forms of violence often lead to self-blame. Women victimized by violence often internalize blame for the abuse and "punish" themselves for their own victimization, culminating frequently in multiple forms of self-denigration, eating disorders, substance abuse, self-mutilation, myriad physical maladies, depression, high-risk behaviors (including sexual acting out), and suicide. At times women "punish" their bodies for the assaults they have suffered; they may attack what they perceive to be the culprit—the physical attribute that calls attention to themselves.

> Here in the U.S., I used to think women had more rights, but I've learned that if you are a Latina, you can't stop this stuff from happening. My boss was coming at me with compliments, or so he claimed, when I confronted him. He used to call me "chiquita" and tell me how beautiful my long hair was. I told him he made me feel uncomfortable. So he said I must be a feminist. Yes, I was angry, but what could I do? I needed the job. I just tried to ignore him, but the one thing I did was cut off my long hair. *Daniela, age 22*

As stated, violent experiences affect the entire self and can be manifested somatically and psychologically. The long-term sequelae may compromise not only the physical and emotional health of those affected by injustice, but the spirit as well:

> Who are we if not the sum total of our victimization? *Luisa, age 35*

> I feel at times that I am the walking dead. I don't believe in God, how could a God, whether Christian or something else, allow little children to be hurt by those who are supposed to care for them? My body will walk the earth until I die, but my spirit left a long time ago. *Tina, age 35*

> The spark of life grows ever dimmer. I was once a vibrant child, a happy little girl. Then her assaults began. I could feel myself shrinking. I may be over 50 years of age, but a

hurt little girl lives inside of me. She is the only part of me that is alive. *Se me fue el espíritu desde hace tiempo. Olga, age 55*

As noted elsewhere (Flores-Ortiz, 1997a), battered women and sexually abused children are similar to survivors of state terror and prisoners of war. The process of victimization attempts to rob the individual of her will, her sense of self, and her ability to control even basic physical functions. The victim's thoughts and behaviors are subject to the control of the more powerful perpetrator (Herman, 1992). The perpetrator isolates the family through rigid control, often forbidding the women and girls from going anywhere without him, even visiting their own families. Michael Johnson (2008) labels such perpetrators *intimate terrorists* because they use tactics similar to those utilized in warfare to instill terror and gain control of the enemy.

In these families, boys often are enlisted or coerced to function as enforcers of discipline and controllers of sisters. The wife/mother in such families may be unable to protect the children due to her own victimization as a battered woman or victim of sexual abuse herself. In the climate of fear created by the perpetrator and often supported by social institutions, women and children suffer violations silently, or turn against one another. Women may blame the girls for "the seduction of the husband." Nuclear and extended family members may collude in the maintenance of the abuse "as love is confused with sex, loyalty with obligation, and respect with silent endurance of violations" (Flores-Ortiz, 1997a, p. 57).

Treatment Considerations

In the treatment of IPV the focus should be on why men abuse, not why women stay in unjust relationships. Such a question blames the woman and de-contextualizes the experience of abuse. In cases of IPV and sexual violence, community accountability is essential. Services are needed for women and men who are victims and/or perpetrators. Ancillary services for men who batter and sexually abuse are essential to help the perpetrator become accountable. Once the perpetrator of violence becomes accountable the family can be treated together (Flores-Ortiz et al., 1994 [For a different modality of treatment see Madanes (1990)]. From a contextual family therapy perspective the treatment includes reconstructive dialogues (Flores-Ortiz, 1998) to foster accountability among those who have hurt, breaking the silence for those who have been injured, and rebalancing the relational scales to prevent the repetition of these patterns in future generations.

From a narrative perspective that is rooted in social justice, the path to healing entails finding meaning among those who have been hurt. An important step is externalizing the blame, giving testimony to break the silence and thereby contesting, challenging, and holding accountable both the perpetrators and those who did not protect the family member who was victimized. Cultural narratives of victimization and dominant stories of suffering and victimhood must be rescripted. By building a community of support, the larger society collaborates in the healing. As stated earlier, the Dulwich Center advocates for the use of humor, storytelling, and (re)connecting to ancestral culture in order to heal. Remembering the body is often the first step to integrating body-mind-spirit, which is crucial to heal from trauma.

Our work with survivors of incest and marital rape focuses on healing the trauma through an integrative therapy of bodywork, art, and feminist relational therapy (Flores-Ortiz, 1997a). Whether in individual or family therapy, the woman is helped to heal the body, mind, and soul, rebalance relationships with family members, and externalize the blame. Incest in particular creates soul wounds that interfere with a woman's enjoyment of her body and overtime may contribute to physical illness (Flores-Ortiz, 1997a; Flores, 2013; van der Kolk, 1994).

In author Flores's work with incest survivor "Becky" we focused on releasing the shame associated with sexual abuse. In addition, through ritual and artwork she was able to express her grief, shame, horror, and guilt. Over time she was able to contextualize those who abused her and rescript her story of victimization into one of survival (Flores-Ortiz, 1997a).

> I am far more than the paintings I give birth to out of my pain. I don't want to be remembered as an incested woman, a survivor of family violence. I want to be remembered for the totality of my being, for everything I have done, not for what was done to me.

> I finally inhabit my body. I feel the beating of my heart, I know what I am thinking in the moment, I can translate my emotions, and I have conquered fear. I can say I am no longer afraid to love, to make love, to be touched. But more importantly, while I cannot recover the innocence he robbed, I got back my soul.

> Joyfulness, playfulness, aliveness have replaced depression, dissociation and despair; pretty cool huh? *Becky, age 29*

Male incest survivors also struggle with questions about their masculinity if the perpetrator was male and with the minimization of his suffering by others if the perpetrator was female. Latino boys and young men who were victims of sexual abuse by women and told their fathers often encountered congratulatory responses, as if the boy or young man had been a willing sexual partner of the perpetrator. Consequently, they often are filled with shame and are silenced. Given the likelihood of homophobic responses to sex with men, males often are silenced if the perpetrator was male for fear that he will be considered gay. In many families, unless the boy was very young and the perpetrator was not a family member, sexual victimization is rarely reported and the child is not given enough support. Many Latinx families hide such victimization for fear of *el que dirán,* under the guise of protecting the child from shame and humiliation. The implicit message the victim receives is that he is somehow complicit or to blame for the victimization.

However, recovery from incest and IPV is a lifelong struggle; the survivor must learn to identify and avoid the triggers to PTSD symptomatology. They must learn to live with their story and transform it. Reconnecting to the body, healing the spirit and emotions, advocacy, and breaking the silence are important paths to healing. Family accountability and social support are essential for long-term recovery.

Summary

Injustice in Latinx families is multidetermined and must be understood in terms of the individual's intersectional identities and the family's ecological realities. In order to heal from family or intimate partner violence or substance abuse or misuse, the following must be evaluated: family's contextual history, current stressors related to educational and health disparities, exposure to micro- and macroaggressions, and minority stress. While a variety of treatment approaches exist, along with healing strategies, the individuals and family's coping mechanisms, cultural wealth, and social resources must be mobilized to promote healing and recovery.

HOMEWORK ASSIGNMENT

- Develop a MECA family map.
  - What is the ecological context of your family?
  - What are salient migration and acculturation issues?
  - What do you see as the most pronounced patterns of injustice affecting your family?
  - What is the life cycle of your family of origin? (Note that your family may be in several stages simultaneously, e.g., both school-aged children and launched offspring.)
  - What are the most important values and beliefs evident in your family?
  - What is your current family organization? What was it while you were growing up?
  - How would you describe your family's patterns of communication?
- Identify injustice or dysfunctional patterns in your family of origin.
- Once you have completed your genealogy, identify patterns of injustice that repeat over generations (e.g., substance misuse or abuse, IPV, divorce, abandonment)
- Reflecting on your family's history, what hypotheses do you have regarding these patterns of injustice? What may be some causative or contributing factors?
- Given your family history, what is your dominant story?
- What cultural, gender, or social scripts currently influence you and your family?
- What cultural grand narratives might affect you in terms of your gender, sexuality, or class position?
- Reflecting on your family history, what are the sources of resiliency and strength?

KEY TERMS

Acculturative stress: The stressors associated with being an immigrant or ethnic minority and going through the acculturation process. Acculturative stress can have a negative impact on children's psychological health.

Dissociated: The result of suffering from dissociation. The person may feel disconnected from thoughts, feelings, memories, and surroundings. It can affect sense of identity and perception of time. The symptoms often go away on their own. It may take hours, days, or weeks.

Ecological factors: External conditions that impact individuals and are framed within ecological systems theory (also called development in context or human ecology theory, developed by Urie Bronfenbrenner). It offers a framework through which community psychologists examine individuals' relationships within communities and the wider society.

Erosion of community: How a community may suffer the consequences of losing cultural aspects and being deprived from access to resources.

Externalizing behaviors: Maladaptive behaviors directed toward an individual's environment, which cause impairment or interference in life functioning, for instance misbehaving at school.

Family's ecological context: External characteristics impacting and shaping families' experiences. For instance, the ecological contexts of parenting success of children with disabilities is particularly important by having support at school.

Historical trauma: Used by social workers, historians, and psychologists to refer to the cumulative emotional harm of an individual or generation caused by a traumatic experience or event. Historical trauma response refers to the manifestation of emotions and actions that stem from this perceived trauma.

Hyperarousal: Primary symptom of post-traumatic stress disorder (PTSD). It occurs when a person's body suddenly kicks into high alert as a result of thinking about their trauma. Even though real danger may not be present, their body acts as if it is, causing lasting stress after a traumatic event.

Intimate terrorist: In domestic violence situations a partner uses physical abuse plus a broad range of tactics designed to get and keep control over the other person in the relationship.

Limbic system: A set of structures in the brain that deal with emotions and memory. It regulates autonomic or endocrine function in response to emotional stimuli and also is involved in reinforcing behavior.

Mara Salvatrucha: Commonly known as MS-13, this is an international criminal gang that originated in Los Angeles, California, in the 1970s and 1980s. Originally, the gang was set up to protect Salvadoran immigrants from other gangs in the Los Angeles area.

Mask of culture: Refers to the justification of certain behaviors as part of cultural practices.

Minority stress: Describes chronically high levels of stress faced by members of stigmatized minority groups. It may be caused by a number of factors, including poor social support and low socioeconomic status; well understood causes of minority stress are interpersonal prejudice and discrimination.

MS 18: 18th Street, also known as Calle 18, Barrio 18, Mara 18, or simply La 18 in Central America, is a multiethnic transnational criminal organization that started as a street gang in Los Angeles.

Parental child or parentified child: Those children who become the "parents" to their parents and younger siblings by providing emotional and or instrumental support. These children perform responsibilities of adults, which can have a psychological cost for them depending on the circumstances of this role reversal.

Reconstructive dialogues: In the context of family therapy it helps families to understand, heal, and move forward.

Susto or *espanto*: Scare. It refers to a culturally embedded expression of illness, primarily among Latin American cultures. The condition implies a chronic somatic suffering caused from emotional trauma or from witnessing traumatic experiences lived by others.

Trauma-informed care: An approach in the human service field that assumes an individual is more likely than not to have a history of trauma; recognizes the presence of trauma symptoms and acknowledges the role trauma may play in an individual's life.

5

Politics, Policies, and the Formation of Transnational Families

---

Scholars have described the process of transnational migration as one entailing "ambiguous losses and gains"[1] (Falicov, 2014). Leaving the homeland, regardless of the type of migration, results in losses, grief, and mourning for migrants, as they leave behind loved ones, networks of support, and their familiar context and ecological niche. As stated in earlier chapters, post-migration adjustment is facilitated or hindered by the degree of reception of the receiving country. Every immigrant to the United States has encountered particular circumstances and varying degrees of acceptance that determined in part their structural integration to the United States.

Latinxs have had a particular history with regard to migration. In the 1840s the Treaty of Guadalupe Hidalgo incorporated Mexicans into the United States (Rosales, 1991); they did not migrate. As Antonio Burciaga (1993) stated, "We did not cross the border; the border crossed us." This border became an open wound that many would later traverse by foot, water, and air to rejoin family members, flee political oppression, escape wars and revolutions, and seek better economic opportunities. At various points in U.S. history policies have welcomed Mexican migrant labor (i.e., the Bracero program between 1942–1964)[2] but disinvited them to stay after their *brazos* (arms and labor) were no longer needed. Some remained and adjusted their status; others left and returned to Mexico, creating a legacy of transnational migration. *El Sueño Americano* (the American dream) of greater economic prosperity offered a path out of poverty for rural Mexicans who

---

1 These losses and gains are ambiguous because there are typically no rituals to denote the departure; the losses entail leaving behind intangibles as well as loved ones with the expectation and hope of attaining gains at some future time—the American dream—which may or may not occur. There are at times feelings of shame about leaving in the midst of the excitement and anxieties about the journey. As Sluzki has noted and was described in earlier chapters, what occurs in the journey and how prepared for the migration the immigrant is will mitigate the challenges of arrival and settlement.

2 For a historical review of this program read about the Bracero History Project: http://braceroarchive.org/.

imagined a better life for their families if they sought work in the North. *El Norte* became the promised land. Thus, since the 1960s millions of Mexicans have continued the journey north, many to reunite with relatives who had obtained legal status for them, while others crossed the border without documentation and became unauthorized migrants (see Flores et al., 2019).

In the 1990s Mexican migration to the United States increased; some attribute this increase to the Free Trade Agreement (NAFTA), which resulted in increases in unemployment and reduced agricultural production in Mexico (see Massey, 2001). As a result, official Mexican government data indicates over 12 million of its citizens live abroad, mostly in the United States. Of these, 45% are women and 55% are men (Rivera Heredia et al., 2014).

Central Americans, particularly from El Salvador, Nicaragua, and Honduras, migrated in large numbers to the United States in the mid and late 20th century as a result of civil wars, natural disasters, and the legacies of U.S. intervention in the region that destabilized economies, pushing hundreds of thousands into poverty and despair (Mahler & Ugrina, 2006). Most recently, the proliferation of drug cartels and the violence attributed to gangs such as the *Mara Salvatrucha* (MS-13) and their rival M-18 have led to mass migrations of Hondurans, Salvadorans, and Guatemalans, many of them children (Savenije, 2007; Wolf, 2012). These unaccompanied minors recently have been the focus of significant media attention and have challenged existing U.S. immigration policies under the Obama Administration (Restrepo & Garcia, 2014).

Since the 2016 election of Donald Trump, immigration policies have toughened along with an increase in xenophobic and anti-immigrant rhetoric, particularly for immigrants of color, and Mexicans specifically. In 2019, these policies translated into massive family separation, caging of children in the U.S.-Mexico border, detention of asylum seekers, and forcing Central American refugees to linger in shelters along the border, remaining in Mexico indefinitely. The COVID-19 pandemic most recently has been used as an excuse by the current administration to refuse asylum seekers a chance for a hearing, and most recently, the president signed an executive order denying legal migration to the United States and deportation of children back to their countries of origin (Hackman et al., 2020). Such draconian policies have torn families apart and increased anxiety among undocumented, mixed-status families, as well as legal U.S. immigrants and residents as well. These policies have fueled racism across the country and open discrimination of Latinx individuals and families (Kriel, 2020).

As a result of the continuing influx of Latinx immigrants to the United States, families may be formed by transnational migrants from different countries and by U.S.-born Latinxs and migrants who are authorized or unauthorized; Latinxs of different generations may partner and have children who may hold varying degrees of identification with their Latino ethnocultural roots. Other families have mixed status, as some members are U.S. citizens or authorized residents while others are undocumented. Others are of mixed race as Latinxs partner with African Americans, Middle Easterners, Asian Americans, South Asian Indians, and European Americans.

This chapter focuses on the impact of immigration policies on Latinxs from various national origins. First, we examine the pursuit of the American dream and the push-and-pull factors that result in the migration of men and women from Latin America. Second, we examine the sequelae of deportations and exclusions on Latinx families and the forced formation of divided families due to mixed status. This section is followed by a discussion of the impact of microaggressions and macroaggressions on children and youth in mixed-status families. The last section offers an analysis of rooting and belonging in the context of being positioned as an "other."

Migration and Family Life: Why Migrants Leave and Why They Do (Not) Return

Today around 214 million people, approximately 3% of the world's population, live outside of their country of birth. Stiglitz et al. (2013) document that women and girls account for half of international migrants, and 16% are under the age of 20. Significant female migration in the 21st century is motivated by poverty but also by efforts to escape social and family violence, or due to being victimized by labor and sex traffickers (see Sidun & Flores, 2020). Moreover,

> South-South migration is now as frequent as south-north migration has been in the past, and while 97 percent of the world's population does not move, migration is a global phenomenon that touches millions of lives, including many of those who haven't themselves migrated. (Stiglitz et al., 2013, p. xv)

As stated earlier, many factors motivate a migration away from one's homeland.[3] There are push factors, such as unemployment and poverty, war, social unrest, and political or religious persecutions that push people out of their countries. There are also pull factors that "invite" people to migrate to particular countries, such as the United States. Typically, the pull factors are the expectation of work and improved economic opportunities. Family reunification is also a motivator for transnational migration. Likewise, migrants often have "official stories" and more covert or secret reasons for leaving. Author Flores narrates,

> My father left his homeland at age 19 after his mother died in order to seek better economic opportunities, and thereby help support his younger siblings. This was the official story. However, the unofficial story was that his father's philandering and his bringing a young mistress to raise his orphaned children outraged my father. Thus, my father left Costa Rica for Panama to seek work and escape an untenable situation. He was also following the legacy of his paternal and maternal grandfathers who had migrated from Spain and China respectively and partnered with Indigenous women, thereby contributing to the racial tapestry that became my family of origin. Although he migrated to work and support his sisters, in Panama my father met my mother. He became her protector and provider for her two young sons, products of her failed first marriage, thus adding a layer of responsibility to his life that he had not anticipated upon migration. Although he now had a woman and children to support, he continued to help his sisters financially and emotionally.

---

3   Migration is a phenomenon that has occurred since the beginning of time; the focus in this chapter is contemporary migrations in the 20th and 21st century. Clearly European migration to the Americas left a legacy of migration for future generations, as well as the sequelae of colonization, genocide, and trauma (see Flores, 2013).

In the migratory experience of author Torreiro-Casals's family from the countryside of the northern part of Spain, Galicia was characterized by relatives seeking better economic opportunities. She states

> My family's previous generations migrated to Cuba, Argentina, and Uruguay. Some family members returned after years of hard work with some savings, and others never came back. I remember my grandmother's comments on why some of her siblings left without a real necessity for migrating. According to my *abuelita*, grandmother, her family of 14 siblings who lost their mother at an early age had enough to live with dignity after the Civil War in Spain. As previously mentioned, families have "official" reasons to leave and others' reasons may be unclear. Our families grew apart and divided; their losses in times of minimal opportunities for communication were accepted with resignation and always with some romanticization of the migratory experience and the new opportunities. During the dictatorship my father also left Spain and moved to France at the age of 18 as a single man. He easily found a job in a car factory; from age 14 he worked as a mechanic. My dad always shared that this temporal migration was a transformative experience in a more liberal country than Spain at that time. This migratory experience motivated him once back in Spain to continue studying and improving his life. I grew up under very different sociopolitical realities and I left Spain when I finished college. I moved first to the Netherlands and later the United States. Indeed, it was part of my family legacy to follow the tradition on migrating.

This legacy of migration is often the experience of young men who migrate alone seeking better economic opportunities to help their parents. Eventually, they form their own families, adding to the financial responsibilities that propelled their migration. The departure of sons and brothers affects the entire family left behind. Thus, drawing on the experiences of high sender communities of Mexico, Rivera-Heredia et al. (2014) argue that migration cannot be considered an individual process, as it affects all aspects of the private and public lives of relatives, neighbors, and friends. Due to the reliance on remittances sent from the United States, many Mexican communities depend on the migration of the young and able-bodied to subsist since not only do remittances support people, they may also contribute to the infrastructure of the town.[4]

Why Men Migrate

The majority of Mexican men who come to the United States from rural communities do so to improve the financial situation of their families left behind (Flores et al., 2014, 2019; Rivera-Heredia et al., 2014). Author Flores et al. (2019) further document this pattern in their study of agricultural Mexican workers in Central California; all the men had migrated for economic reasons: to support their parents, help out their siblings, and to build capital with the hopes of eventually returning home. Most had migrated in their late teens and had male relatives who had migrated before them—most notably cousins and uncles. Most of the men had been unable to return to visit their families and had endured losses due to death, long-term separation, and failure to attain the American dream. The majority

---

4 Civic groups may form in the United States to raise funds for maintenance of churches, building clinics, or childcare centers "back home."

were unauthorized migrants who had risked border crossings multiple times in order to visit their parents in the first few years after their migration. They worked to send back remittances. A few had met and married women from their *ranchos* and left them behind when they returned, thereby creating transnational families. Some returned annually for visits; the women became pregnant during these visits, thereby increasing the economic demands on the migrant man. The men also worked to send money back so that their wives could save to build a home for him and the family for his return.

However, after the attacks of 2001 and the increased militarization of the U.S.-Mexico border, many of these men were unable to return to Mexico for fear of the more treacherous journey across the desert and increased risk of detention and deportation. In some cases, the women made the journey north to join their husbands, leaving their children in their parents' care. In the United States, both worked to support themselves and the children were left behind. For the men, having new family responsibilities created a burden of guilt, as they were less able to help their parents, the original purpose for their migration. These couples often had children in the United States, thereby creating mixed-status families. The younger children were U.S. citizens, the parents unauthorized immigrants who lived in fear of detection and deportation. The older children were in Mexico separated from their families and siblings. All dreamed of an eventual family reunification, which if it came to pass was fraught with conflict and anxiety, as will be discussed later in this chapter.

In some cases, the wife and children migrated together to join the male migrant. As the children grew up, they faced the challenges of being unauthorized as well. These young people lived in the shadows, unable to obtain driver's licenses (a rite of passage for many adolescents), work, or obtain financial aid to attend college. Thus, immigrant parents often saw their dreams of affording their children a better life through education thwarted by immigration policies and their decision to bring the children to the United States without proper documentation. It was until the Development, Relief, and Education of Alien Minors Act (DREAM Act) was created as an opportunity to enlist in the military or go to college and have a path to citizenship for unauthorized child immigrants to the United States that some of their situations got better. This Obama-era policy is under attack by the Trump Administration and is currently being considered by the U.S. Supreme Court, which due to new appointees by the Republican-controlled Senate has swung dangerously to the right. At the time of this writing, Dreamers await their fate with great trepidation.

Don Alberto

For Don Alberto, a 45-year-old Mexican immigrant who had spent 28 years of his life in the United States, the primary reason for migrating was to help his family. He was the eldest of 11 siblings. For the first few years post-migration he lived in central California; he worked in the fields and returned to Mexico during the off-season. He did not seek a wife or partner because "his mission was to work to help out" his parents. He did not want to be "sidetracked" or add other responsibilities that would deter him from his original goal of building his parents a more livable home. Each time he visited Mexico, he brought money and some materials to expand his parents' modest home. Eventually, he built a house with four rooms so that his parents could have their own room and his seven brothers could share two rooms and his three sisters the remaining room. Overtime, his siblings married and formed families of their own. Don Alberto indicated that he discouraged his brothers from migrating; he sent extra money when he could to make sure they remained in Mexico to avoid the suffering he endured—the loneliness away from family, the lack of well-paid work opportunities, the temptations to escape into alcohol and drug use.

In one of the visits to his *rancho* in rural Michoacán, Don Alberto met Alicia, a woman 15 years his junior. They fell in love and married. Don Alberto continued the migration to California annually, now also to support his wife. Two years after they married, Marisol was born. As their daughter grew older and his visits became less frequent, his wife insisted on joining him. Alicia and Marisol crossed the border without inspection and the family reunified. Don Alberto commented that since their arrival his life had become more stressful. His wife had to go to work, as he could not afford a house for them solely on his income. He had rented a room with a number of other migrant men prior to his wife's arrival. However, he could not bring her and their 13-year-old daughter Marisol to live with a group of men. As a result of both partners having to work, Don Alberto felt the quality of his family life had diminished. They had little time to spend together. Now his worries also included concerns about his daughter's education, as she struggled to learn English and perform at grade level in a different educational system. Doña Alicia worried about her daughter's future and was committed to finding a way to support her academically so that she could succeed. Both she and her husband were aware that Marisol would face significant challenges as an unauthorized person in the United States but felt the sacrifice was worth the hardship. They wanted the best for Marisol. Don Alberto, however, was distressed about the added responsibility and felt guilty that he now had to focus on his own family and less on his parents, who still depended on him for support.

At the time of this writing, Don Alberto continues to work in the agricultural fields, despite the pandemic. His wife, who worked at a local restaurant, is unemployed. The restaurant had to close. Therefore, Don Alberto works longer hours with insufficient protection. His crew did not receive masks or any other personal protective equipment from his employer. Community volunteers made masks and brought them to the men when it became evident the government would not protect these essential workers.

Given the limited work opportunities available to unauthorized male immigrants, the American dream becomes elusive. For those men who migrate alone and are young, sadness and loneliness can lead them to substance abuse. For older men, alcohol may also be an outlet to manage the grief and losses that accompany migration. One of our male research participants noted that sometimes they drink too much and do not have enough money to send their wives; they then make up stories that work was slow or they were not paid to explain why they could not send money back that particular time (Flores et al., 2014, 2019).

Most of the men we have interviewed dreamt about eventually going back to their home and their families. Few realize that dream voluntarily. Many are deported only to try to return promptly to continue the pursuit of a better life. With each migration, debt is incurred both in the United States and in their country of origin, as few men have the resources to pay for the passage. Often they borrow from relatives in the United States, who have to pay *the coyote*, the smuggler, for the transport of the migrant. Thus, in the first few months in the United States men work to generate the income needed to pay back the debt. Many men and their families in the country of origin spend years in debt because of the increased costs of migration.

As noted elsewhere, male migration to the United States creates risk factors for substance abuse, mood and anxiety disorders, and disruptions in family life on both sides of the border (Falicov, 2014; Flores, 2014). Men we have interviewed refer to the risk factors as the "emotional costs of migration" (Flores et al., 2014). As noted in Don Alberto's story, some of the stress men experience post-migration is related to their wives' entry into the labor force.

In our study of rural Mexican men in Central California, we interviewed two men whose wives had "changed dramatically" after they began to work (Flores et al., 2020). One recounted how his wife began to socialize with coworkers after work; she began to go out dancing to a nearby town while he stayed home with their two children; she eventually began an extramarital affair that resulted in their separation. This man blamed the end of his marriage on his wife's encounter with temptation. He blamed himself in part for not being able to afford a lifestyle that precluded her having to go to work. The dissolution of the marriage led him to become suicidal, as his American dream had become a nightmare.

However, not all couples find family reunification or transnational relationships fraught with conflict and challenges. Hirsh's (2003) study of transnational couples in Atlanta, Georgia, addresses the ways "gender structures [are] in turn structured by transnational social ties" (p. 17). Hirsh noted how both men and women understand the gender differences in the United States and Mexico and how gender roles are negotiated to deal with those differences. She introduces the term "companionate marriages" to describe the type of bond created by transnational couples to maintain both emotional and sexual intimacy, despite the distance that separates them. These bonds are based on mutual respect and trust. Women who are left behind focus on raising the children and maintaining the dream of *familia* alive for the benefit of the husband and their children. While the man is away, they are de facto authority and decision makers. Women in our studies often refer to this as "borrowed power," which they surrender when the husband arrives for a visit (FloresOrtiz, Valdez Curiel, & Andrade Palos, 2002).

In the U.S. context, once reunified some couples work to address gender inequalities that may have been more culturally appropriate in their town of origin but are not functional in their new social context. In author Flores's research (Flores-Ortiz, 1993), her Mexican immigrant women respondents indicated that they found life in the United Statets to be more amenable to shared decision making and to have a greater voice in their marriages. Husbands adjusted to relationship changes; although men expressed some regret at their loss of power within the home, some welcomed their wives' increasing independence. A few men feared that the increased independence afforded by having their own earned income would result in the wives leaving them. A man, whose wife began to jog, feared that one day she would start running away from him and never turn back (Flores-Ortiz, 1993).

Why Women Migrate

The increase in female migration to the United States is associated primarily with escape from poverty, situations of family or social violence, or to reunify with family members already in the United States (Flores & Valdez Curiel, 2009). Central American female migration increased during the civil wars of El Salvador and Nicaragua as well as the repression against Indigenous groups in Guatemala and Mexico. In some of her earlier writings (Flores-Ortiz, 2002, 2003; Flores, 2012), author Flores examined the push-and-pull factors that bring women to the United States. The increased migration of Mayan women from the Yucatan Peninsula of Mexico, for example, has been labeled "the new Mayan route." Many of these women escape persecution by government officials and the military and seek political asylum in the United States. Many left children behind in hopes of reunifying with them in the future. Many experience rape and physical abuse during the journey, arriving in the United States with extreme trauma (see Sidun & Flores, 2020). Others both flee persecution as well as travel to join their husbands in the United States, who fled before them.

Although female migration often is the result of violence, the harrowing accounts of female asylum seekers shed light on the pervasiveness of gender violence in Latin America. Femicide is the leading cause of death for women in Mexico and many Central American countries (UN Human Rights Council, 2015). In El Salvador, the rise of **Mara Salvatrucha** and **MS 18**, among other gangs, has led to increased extortion, kidnapping, torture, and violent assaults on women. Many of these assaults are in retaliation to opposing gang members' violence or in turf wars to intimidate family members into submission and payment of "taxes" for running small businesses, or simply to promote terror in the neighborhood. Young women are targeted as well to become sexual slaves of gang members. Those who refuse are tortured and dismembered to send a message to the community (De Jesus & Hernandes, 2019). The majority of female asylum seekers from Central America report fleeing family and social violence, in particular gang persecution. These are asylum categories Jeff Sessions precluded from consideration while he was in the Trump Administration. Although challenged in the courts, immigration judges cannot grant asylum on the basis of these forms of persecution.

For Guatemalans and other Central American female migrants the journey entails negotiating multiple borders and facing detection, detention, deportation back to their countries, and being robbed, beaten, and raped by Mexican police, gang members, and even other migrants (see Brown & Oden, 2011). Many women migrate to escape family violence only to encounter equally adverse conditions in the United States.

Maritza's Story

Maritza is the third of seven children born to a *mestizo* family in Chiapas, Mexico. She described a childhood filled with violence and despair. Her parents were very poor; an older brother left for Mexico City to work when he was still a child. An older sister also had left the family to seek work; consequently, her mother relegated house chores to Maritza from a very early age, as she was the oldest girl at home. She felt that her mother mistreated her for being female. She beat her when the chores were not done to her satisfaction. Maritza had to prepare meals, take care of her younger siblings, and remain in the home. She was not allowed to go outside to play or to attend school. Her younger brothers worked in the fields, and she had to cook for them and wash their clothes. Her parents reportedly told her that her place was at home because she was a girl.

When Maritza was 7 or 8, she does not recall exactly, her 17-year-old brother who lived in Mexico City began to sexually abuse her when he came home on vacation. He also beat her whenever he felt like it. When she complained to her parents about the physical violence, she was told that because he was older he had the right "to discipline" her. She did not tell her parents about the sexual abuse. She feared they would not believe her and beat her "for lying." Her parents favored their sons over their daughters.

The first time her brother sexually abused her he had come for a visit and began to rub himself against her back. Because she told him to stop, he hit her on the head with the belt buckle. He gave her a choice: to beat her or rape her. She began to cry and he raped her and then beat her. Thereafter, whenever he came home from the city, he brought her pretty dresses and had her put them on. He would then remove the dresses and rape her. He sodomized her, made her perform oral sex, and vaginally penetrated her on multiple occasions. Maritza stated that her spirit left her body when he did these things. She dissociated. Overtime, she became increasingly despondent. She considered suicide many times. As she grew older, she began to experience night terrors, episodes of severe anxiety, which she did not know were symptoms of trauma. She migrated to the United States at age 19 to escape her abusive family. She began to work and tried to put the past behind her. However, eventually she became involved with a man who drank to intoxication and physically and verbally abused her. She had a daughter, Kristina, with him, but eventually left him due to his abuse and infidelity. He flaunted his affairs and brought his lovers to the house for her to feed them. After being alone for a few years, Maritza then became involved with another man who also drank and verbally abused her. She had her daughter Celeste with him. Neither man provided financially for the girls.

Maritza worked long hours to provide for her daughters; thus, she relied on Kristina to take care of the home and help with Celeste. Economic circumstances and her position as an unauthorized migrant forced her to repeat childrearing patterns that she had endured and abhorred. Kristina felt it was unfair to have to be a mother to her younger sister and began to rebel. She cut school and spent time with gang-involved youth. Maritza indicated that she did not know what to do. Kristina was becoming increasingly rebellious. One day she saw that her daughter was sending nearly nude photos to her boyfriend. Maritza stated that she lost control; she began to hit her daughter and screamed and cried without being able to stop. She saw her mother in herself and wanted to die.

Because of hitting her daughter, Maritza was arrested and lost custody of her daughters. When she was jailed, she was evicted, lost her two jobs, and became homeless. Child Protective Services (CPS) became involved and her daughters were placed in foster care until Maritza completed a treatment program and found suitable housing. Maritza stated that CPS referred her to individual and family therapy. In the course of therapy, she disclosed her childhood physical and sexual abuse. This began a slow, gradual healing process. She spent a year in therapy and reported being grateful that due to CPS "and God" her daughter Kristina had begun to recover. She finished high school and began to attend a local junior college.

After her arrest, Maritza lost custody of Kristina for 18 months and of Celeste for 10 months. These were her darkest days, she indicated. Celeste was only 1 year old and developed attachment problems. Although improving with therapy, she feels that Celeste continues to have problems. Maritza is devastated that her loss of control affected her daughters and caused a long separation. She wept as she confided that she had come to the United States to escape violence only to encounter more and to become violent herself.

She had wanted instead to end the generational cycle of violence in which she grew up. She fled her family to escape their violence and found herself hurting her daughters. With the aid of therapy, she came to understand that the verbal abuse, the physical violence, and the sexual abuse she endured affected her emotionally and behaviorally. She carries within her, her own mother's words that she is useless, worthless, good for nothing. She understands that her involvement with abusive men is a result of her childhood victimization and lack of self-esteem. She wants to make sure her daughters do not have her same fate. Yet, she continued to become involved with men who did not treat her well.

However, because of her arrest on child abuse charges, Maritza is on deportation proceedings. She fears that if she is deported she will lose her daughters forever. She doesn't want her daughters to experience the poverty in which she grew up. She cannot return to her family, as the abuse from them will continue. She has no one else in Mexico who can help her. She would have to leave her daughters. Kristina is attending college and she does not know where Celeste's father is; therefore, she could not obtain his consent to take Celeste with her. If she is forced to return to Mexico, Kristina will need to take care of Celeste or her youngest child will once again enter the foster care system.

Many immigrant women experience the same circumstances as Maritza; others are able to thrive and form functional families. However, living in the shadows due to unauthorized status increases the risk of family separation and creates a climate of anxiety and fear for many immigrants and a pervasive sense of lack of belonging and rootedness for their children, which can manifest as adolescent acting out, as in Kristina's case.

Returning "Home"

When we asked migrants to identify the barriers to returning home, most stated that they could not leave until they were financially solvent, have enough savings to live better in their country of origin, or when the political situation in their country had improved (Flores et al., 2014). For most, returning home becomes complicated when they have children in the United States, they become ill, or they cannot go back due to increased violence in their homelands. Most immigrants who migrated as adults experience the nostalgia of home, as discussed in earlier chapters (see Flores et al., 2019). They may experience psychological homelessness (Hardy & Laszloffy, 2005) and feel they are neither "from here nor there," a situation also experienced by their U.S.-born or -raised children, as will be discussed later in this chapter.

In her study of Mexican returnees to rural Michoacán, Cervantes-Pacheco (2014) found that most men hope to return to the United States. Many of the men were deported; sometimes they were stopped for minor traffic violations or driving without a license, or after a car accident. Unable to pay for an immigration attorney, they were deported after days, weeks, and sometimes months of detention and frequent maltreatment. They returned to a Mexico that was unfamiliar, to a social context that resented, devalued, and at times envied them. They relived the stages of migration discussed in earlier chapters, but this time without hope of improving their life circumstances. Some were able to establish businesses, but most returned to their country to struggle economically to support their families. This situation often resulted in depression. In instances when the family remained in the United States, the women had to work to support themselves and send remittances to the husband until he could "get back on his feet."

For Central Americans who fled their homelands due to social violence, in particular persecution from *maras* (gangs), deportation increases the risk that upon return to their country they will be killed. Recent news reports document the rise of deportee homicide in El Salvador, for example (Parker, 2020).

The formation of transnational families as a result of migration and deportation back to the country of origin complicates the family's ability to negotiate life cycle stages and support the children emotionally and perpetuates the legacy of migration (Cervantes et al., 2010; Falicov, 2014).

Impact of Immigration Policies on Latinx Families

The Illegal Immigration Reform and Illegal Immigrant Responsibility Act of 1996 (Cervantes et al., 2010; Hing, 2004) adversely affected mixed-status families. These are families where one or more children or a spouse are either citizens or legal residents, and others are unauthorized. Individuals who entered the United States without inspection were criminalized. In various states, drivers' licenses were no longer available without proof of legal residency or citizenship. After 2001, the USA PATRIOT Act allowed for the mandatory detention of "certified aliens," that is, individuals who could not produce documentation verifying legal residency or citizenship (Sinnar, 2003). Immigrants who might have lived for decades in the United States were subject to detection and detention. Workers became more vulnerable to exploitation as fines were issued to employers if they hired undocumented workers, so the immigrants were paid "under the table" without any benefits or fair compensation. Many immigrants lost well-paying jobs in construction and other industries if they lacked legal status or a work permit. With the loss of these jobs came loss of health insurance benefits. Many Latinxs also lost their homes, as they could no longer afford mortgages.

As noted in the American Psychological Association's (APA, 2012) report on immigration, 79% of the children of undocumented immigrant adults are citizens, as the 14th Amendment grants them automatic citizenship. Moreover, more than 4 million citizen children live in homes with undocumented parents, and another 1.1 million children are undocumented themselves. According to Passel and Taylor (2010), most immigrant children live in mixed-citizen-status families whereby some members are citizens and others are not. This situation creates complicated dynamics and ambivalent relationships within the family according to Carola Suárez-Orozco et al. (2010). Celia Falicov describes how the varying levels of access family members may have depending on their immigration status contribute to family conflict. Moreover, Yoshikawa (2011) has noted that although children who grow up in homes with undocumented parents are more likely to live in two-parent families, they are also more likely to live in poverty because their parents work in poorly remunerated and precarious jobs. As a result, many of these citizen children are less likely to be enrolled in programs that could help foster their early learning (e.g., preschool, Head Start) or to have access to health care (Yoshikawa, 2011). Thus, mixed status contributes to maintaining health disparities among Latinx groups. These disparities have become evident during the current COVID-19 pandemic, as Latinx are testing positive and dying in disproportionate numbers in major U.S. cities, including Chicago, New York, and Los Angeles (Hayes-Bautista & Hsu, 2020).

With the passing of the USA PATRIOT Act and subsequent U.S. Department of Homeland Security measures, life for mixed-status families became more stressful due to economic uncertainty and fear of apprehension. U.S.-born or -raised children lived in fear of their parents being detained and deported, particularly as Immigration and Custom Enforcement (ICE) raids became commonplace in Latinx neighborhoods. Chiu et al. (2009), in a report of the Cardozo Immigration Law clinic titled "Constitution on ICE," document that during the last 2 years of the Bush Administration "[ICE] vastly expanded its use of home raid operations as a method to locate and apprehend individuals suspected of civil immigration law violations" (p. 1). ICE officials indicated that these raids could be done without a warrant, but any entries into homes required the informed consent of residents.

> However, frequent accounts in the media and in legal filings have told a similar story of constitutional violations occurring during ICE home raids—a story that includes ICE agents breaking into homes and seizing all occupants without legal basis. (Chiu et al., 2009, p. 1)

Other raids consisted of entering job sites in factories, construction, and agricultural fields to demand proof of legal residency. At times, ICE agents waited outside people's homes to detain them, as happened to the Arias family of Sacramento, California. Through a public records request of ICE, Ryo (2019) obtained data on 1,199,026 ICE encounters, 381,370 arrests, and 650,944 removals that occurred between January 2016 and September 2018. These encounters demonstrated the Trump Administration's focus on deportation of all unauthorized immigrants, particularly from Mexico and Central America, regardless of whether they were long-term residents, lawful citizens, or had U.S. citizen spouses or children.

The Arias Family

Luis and Angela Arias met in the United States; they both had migrated in their youth to join their parents, unauthorized immigrants, who sent for their children once they established themselves in northern California. Luis and Angela met at the restaurant where she worked. They married and had three children. Luis worked in construction and with both of their salaries they were able to buy a home. Their son Gabriel was a sophomore in high school when ICE knocked at their door one morning. Lolita, an eighth-grader had been braiding her 7-year-old sister Elena's hair when she heard a commotion and her mother scream. She ran to the door and saw three men had thrown her father on the floor; their mother was begging for an explanation. Gabriel was terrified. An ICE agent reportedly told the parents, "I'm gonna be nice, so one of you has to come with me right now; the other can stay until you find someone to take care of your kids, but must turn yourself in within a month. You are illegal and gotta go back." This is how Gabriel and his siblings learned that their parents were not U.S. citizens. Luis told the agents he would go with them. He was handcuffed and arrested. Within 72 hours, he was back in Mexico, a country he had left at age 15.

In the following month, Angela struggled to control her feelings of devastation and began to sell everything the couple owned; with the help of her legal resident sister and parents, she rented out her home, as she hoped she and her family could be back in a short time. Angela arranged for her two older children to go live with her sister until the end of the school year. Prior to the end of the month she was given, she signed a voluntary departure and returned to Guanajuato, Mexico, with Elena. Her husband had been unable to find work in Jalisco, where he was from, and joined her in Guanajuato, where her maternal grandparents lived. As soon as school was out for the year, Gabriel and Lolita left for Mexico. Gabriel had been an A student and basketball player. In Mexico, school officials told him that he would have to enter the sixth grade because he was not fully literate in Spanish. He stopped going to school and became suicidal. The couple's relatives in the United States sent them money to pay for psychiatric treatment for Gabriel.

Prior to her departure, Angela had contacted an immigration lawyer who began the process of petitioning for their return. Angela's mother was a legal resident with a chronic and debilitating illness. Therefore, the attorney argued, she needed her daughter's help in the United States As Hing (2004) and de la Torre et al. (2010) have noted, criteria for adjusting status after unauthorized entry into the United States has become increasingly stringent and require demonstration of extreme or unusual hardship or beyond that which would be expected as a result of separation from a loved one. The family's situation was complicated by Luis's deportation and Angela's "voluntary departure." However, the attorney could demonstrate, with the help of medical and mental health experts, that Angela's mother and Gabriel in Mexico were experiencing extreme hardship. Angela and the children were able to return to the United States 2 years after their departure. Gabriel could not graduate with his class because he lacked the credits. He had to obtain a GED before he could apply to college. He continued to be depressed and unmotivated, so he took a job at a gas station, vowing to return to school when his father rejoined the family. Lolita began high school, but "life never was the same"; her friends had moved on to other relationships. She had to rely on her cousins and brother to make sense of what had happened.

Although back in the United States, the children remained separated from their father for 3 more years. Angela struggled with depression and a pervasive shame that they had been treated like criminals; Luis had been chained and handcuffed prior to his deportation. Her parents, as well as Luis, lived with the guilt that they had brought their children as teens to give them a better life, but in so doing had broken laws that ended up criminalizing their children and separating the family. In Mexico, Luis also struggled with depression, as he could not find work. He migrated to the border and sought work in Tijuana, so that when finances allowed it, the grandparents could bring his U.S. citizen children for a visit. Five years after his arrest and deportation, Luis returned to the United States "a broken man"; although the children were happy to have both parents with them, the disruption in family life they had endured left an indelible mark on all of their lives.

Mixed-status families also can face the precarious process of the documented spouse attempting to adjust the status of their unauthorized partner. This legal process also entails documenting unusual hardship. For many Latinxs, the waiver process, that is, the unauthorized immigrant's petition for a pardon and a waiver of inadmissibility, can open childhood wounds if they themselves were children of transnational immigrants who often were away from the family. This is particularly the case when children were left behind and experienced adverse circumstances, as did Veronica.

Veronica's Story

The youngest of five children, Veronica was left by her parents in El Salvador when she was 4 years of age. She and her older sisters and brother were left in the care of their maternal grandmother. Veronica described a painful childhood; her grandmother was a stern, negative woman who mistreated them physically, verbally, and emotionally. An uncle who lived with them brought home male friends who sexually abused her. At age 8, she, her older sister, and a brother left El Salvador hoping to reunite with their parents. She and her sister were caught at the border while trying to enter the United States without inspection. They were sent back to El Salvador. Her brother was separated from them and kept by a Mexican family who saw what had occurred. Veronica's mother thought her son had been lost forever. This was a stressful and painful period; Veronica was frightened and confused, as she did not quite understand why they had left El Salvador and traveled so far to see parents she did not even remember.

After a successful entry into the United States a few months later, Veronica was reunited with her parents. However, she did not remember them and had difficulty adjusting to family life, particularly since her father was physically abusive toward her mother. Her mother, still distraught about her son's disappearance, did not ease Veronica's emotional distress. As a result, Veronica had to become self-reliant and grew into an adult who tried not to feel her emotions and attempted to block painful memories of her childhood.

Veronica became a single parent at age 20. She had a daughter, Jazmin. Veronica later married, "but the marriage did not work out" largely due to her distrust of men and her fear of intimacy, which is the result of her childhood sexual abuse. She separated in 2005 and divorced in 2006. From her early 20s she worked as a janitor at a college campus. In 2010, she met her second husband when he came to the campus to work as a painter. Antonio, originally from Leon, Nicaragua, came to the United States in 2008. They married in 2011 and had a daughter, Julia, a year later. Given the precarious work situation he experienced as an unauthorized migrant, Veronica decided to adjust his status. She became a citizen and petitioned for her husband.

The I-601 process[5] and the potential separation from her husband reopened childhood emotional wounds, leading to feelings of loneliness, isolation, and intimacy problems.

5　The I-601 waives the "unlawful presence" and "misrepresentation" grounds of inadmissibility for foreign nationals if they can demonstrate that their U.S. citizen or lawful permanent resident spouse or parent would suffer "extreme hardship" if the foreign national is not allowed to remain in (or return to) the United States. A U.S. citizen fiancé(e) may also be a qualifying relative for purposes of the waiver. Unlawful presence is defined as any period in which a foreign national is present in the United States after expiration of their period of authorized stay (e.g., after the expiration date found on their I-94 entry/departure card) or after entering the United States without being admitted or paroled (e.g., after entering the United States illegally without inspection). The "unlawful presence" ground of inadmissibility typically poses a problem for spouses of U.S. citizens who entered the United States illegally without inspection (e.g. through the U.S-Mexican border) (U.S. Citizens and Immigration Services (n.d.).

Veronica complained that since her daughter Julia was born she "pushed her husband away due to flashbacks of childhood victimization and fear that he would have to leave" and she would be alone again. Veronica indicated that she did not know what she would do if her husband was not granted a waiver. Of late, she had become increasingly anxious. She felt that a separation from her husband would constitute another trauma; she did not know if she could cope with it.

Veronica also stated that she could not go to Nicaragua with her husband. She had never been there. Her daughter was doing well in school and her baby had good health care available through her job in the United States. She did not want her daughters to experience the poverty and violence she did during her early childhood. Therefore, she and her daughters would remain in the United States. However, she would be alone and bereft again. She already had experienced the hardship of being a single parent. Veronica could not bear the thought of being a single mother again. The mere thought of a separation from her husband was profoundly devastating.

As a result of her victimization in childhood and the dysfunction in her family of origin, Veronica had learned to block her emotions and detach from strong negative feelings; moreover, she believed that if she sought mental health services it would signify that she was weak (see Flores, 2013). However, Veronica agreed to enter therapy since acknowledging her distress and seeking mental health services could be an avenue to document the extreme hardship that a separation from her husband would cause. In therapy, her history and the sequelae of her victimization in childhood could be documented; a psychological evaluation also could explain how those experiences could result in extreme hardship if her husband was not granted a waiver. In this case, the difficulties inherent in being in a mixed-status family and initiating the waiver process opened the door for healing to begin. Regardless of the outcome of the immigration case, psychotherapy could be beneficial and a pathway for her to learn more effective coping mechanisms that could break the parenting and partnering patterns she had learned in her family of origin.

Deportations, Exclusions, and Divided Families

Several of the cases described illustrate the suffering of adults and children that result from deportations or exclusions based on unlawful entry. When families are divided, a pervasive sadness occurs among adults and children (Miranda et al., 2005). Children who are left when young typically feel that they were abandoned, since they may not understand the notion of "legal immigration status" or why their parents had to leave. Older children may experience anger/rage and sadness (Diaz & Lieberman, 2010). Typically, these feelings are manifested at home and at school. Academic underachievement is common as childhood depression interferes with learning (Suarez-Orozco et al., 2010). These children also may misbehave. Parents or guardians at times do not inform school officials that a parent has been deported due to feelings of shame or fear that they too may be deported if someone discloses this information. Therefore, children may not receive the help needed to deal with the family disruption.

Technological advances have made it possible for some families to remain connected despite geographic separation. For example, some fathers and mothers who remain in the United States use Skype to speak to their children who are in Mexico with the other parent. In this way, they can see the developmental progress of their children who in turn can see the absent parent. Nevertheless, parents who are separated from their children often tell heartbreaking stories of their children begging for them to bring them "home" or join them wherever they are. Some children begin to express their anger at the absent parent and refuse to speak to them. The parent who remains in the United States needs to work to support two households, often finding it difficult to travel to visit their family due to economic difficulties. Thus, the children see their parents' absence as lack of caring or abandonment as well. In cases of prolonged separation, sometimes the older children want to return and join their parents who are in the United States. However, they miss their younger siblings and parents left behind. Such return migrations to the United States by citizen children invariably result in academic difficulties, anger, and depression.

Javier's Story

Javier was 15 years old when his 50-year-old mother, Leticia Lopez, was caught in a work-placed raid and arrested. Mr. Lopez and his wife have four sons. The eldest, Joaquin, was born in Mexico and was without status. He came as a baby when Mrs. Lopez crossed the border without inspection to join her husband, who had been a transnational migrant since his teens. After his wife's arrest, Mr. Lopez scrambled to hire an attorney to obtain his wife's release but lacked enough funds to pay the bond. Mrs. Lopez was transported from a jail in Sacramento to a jail in San Francisco. By the time the family arrived in San Francisco to see her, she had been sent to a detention facility in Arizona. Two days later, she was back in Michoacán, México, a country she had left 30 years before. She went to live in a *rancho* with her aging parents.

Javier was devastated. He wanted to be with his mother. Mr. Lopez worked long hours and worried that without his wife's supervision Javier and his older brother Danny would get into trouble. The fears were warranted, as Danny had been cutting classes before his mother left. The couple's second son, Enrique, born in the United States quickly petitioned for his mother. Shortly after her departure, Joaquin was arrested for a DUI. He had been despondent since his mother left and had relapsed into alcohol abuse. As the DUI was his second offense, the arresting officers called ICE. Within a week, Joaquin was deported to Mexico, a country in which he had not lived since 9 months of age.

When school let out for the summer, Javier told his father he wanted to be with his mother. He joined her in Mexico and stayed there 6 months. However, he could not attend school because the closest to his *rancho* was an hour away by bus. He also was not literate in Spanish and would be placed back in fourth or fifth grade. He returned to the United States and reentered high school but soon became clinically depressed. Author Flores evaluated him to document the hardship he was experiencing due to his mother's deportation. Javier was brilliant, a critical thinker, and a great writer. However, his depression about his mother's absence, his brother's deportation, and Danny's increasing acting out were interfering with his academic and psychological functioning. He felt worthless as a child of unauthorized immigrants; he felt powerless to change his family's situation. The family obtained an honest and ethical attorney after they learned that the one they had initially hired had been disbarred for failure to properly represent clients. The immigration process, however, took a long time; Javier continued to struggle with depression and suicidal ideation. Danny was arrested for fighting and carrying a concealed weapon—a small knife—and was incarcerated for several weeks. Mr. Lopez became increasingly depressed, and his diabetes became out of control. Enrique attempted to balance his obligations to his wife and sons and to his family of origin, which he felt ill equipped to do.

The Lopez family, as many others in similar circumstances, may well spend years attempting to recover from the crisis caused by the deportation of a family member. These experiences create feelings of regret, remorse for having come to the United States, failure because the migrants could not establish themselves with greater economic solvency to provide better for their children, and devastation at the family separation. Fear, anger, and depression are common among the children of such immigrants either because their unauthorized status limits their opportunities or because, despite their citizenship, they do not feel fully "American" given their loved ones' immigration status.

Impact of Micro- and Macroaggressions on Mixed-Status Children and Youth

It is well established that the discrimination, prejudice, and myriad micro- and macroaggressions[6] youth experience may contribute to a compromised mental health (see Falicov, 2014; Flores, 2013). The family first and then the school provide protective and risk factors for Latinx children. Underresourced schools and educational policies that ignore or disrespect the cultural capital that children bring from their home and home culture create great risk. Racist attitudes and biased assumptions about Mexicans and other Latinxs affect how teachers treat students, how students treat each other, and how police respond to Latinx youth. Parents who work all the time to provide economically for their children unwittingly may neglect their emotional well-being, exacerbating the stress created by a disenfranchising school climate and daily microaggressions. Parents may be unaware of the disparaging treatment their children receive. Others are fully aware that teachers devalue their children and do not consider their parental involvement in their children's life as important or valuable (Manzo, 2014). Moreover, differences in value orientation, because of the acculturation and biculturality of their children, also pose challenges to immigrant families and create tension between parents and children (Falicov, 2014).

Less attention has been paid to the impact of parental immigration status on the psychological well-being of Latinx children. The APA (2012) report reviews in detail the existing studies and documents the academic and social, as well as emotional, costs of immigration policies on immigrant children and youth and those who are children of immigrants (both authorized and unauthorized). Falicov (2014) as well addresses

---

6   Psychologist Derald Sue (2010) used the term *microaggressions* to refer to the brief and commonplace daily verbal, behavioral, or environmental indignities, whether intentional or unintentional, that communicate hostile, derogatory, or negative racial slights and insults toward people of color or those who are different on the basis of gender, ethnicity, sexuality or ability. Macroaggressions refer to institutional patterns of racism, classism, or sexism, such as unequal wages for men and women, substandard schooling in poor communities, police profiling of men and women of color, and the murder of Black men and women by police.

the long-term impact of parental separation on children left behind when mothers or fathers migrate. Younger children may manifest distress in their bodies, eating disorders (over- or undereating), depression, nightmares, and academic problems. Older children may show rebelliousness along with the other symptoms. Siblings left behind may hold mixed feelings toward those who presumably have a better life with the parents in the host country. Falicov (2014) also notes, "Separation of parent and child intensifies the attachment of the child with the new caretaker, and by extension, with the entire maternal or paternal line, but may weaken the attachment with the biological parent" (p. 115). Reunification, although often desired and anticipated for years, often is fraught with anxiety, conflict, and challenges once it occurs. Such was the case of Veronica, discussed earlier. Falicov (2014) encourages families to prepare for potential long-term separations and once reunited engage in "catching up narratives," wherein parents and children hear each other's stories of their lives prior to reunification. This is a useful family therapy technique to help families reconnect in mutually satisfying ways.

Often families are brought into the mental health care system after police or social services involvement, as in Maritza's case previously discussed. Although not separated from her daughters due to migration, Maritza became abusive and lost custody of her children. In addition, she was forced to enter individual and family therapy, which proved helpful to begin a healing process for all. Falicov (2014), among other mental health professionals, suggests a reframing of the adjustment problems that occur after reunification, away from "family dysfunctions" to problems in cultural transition and family reunification stress. By shifting the burden away from parental behavior to changes in family organization post-migration, parental guilt may be reduced, and children's resentment can be heard without being censored.

Migration and the less than hospitable social and educational climate young migrants encounter may exacerbate the psychological distress caused by parental separation and being "left behind" (see Suarez-Orozco et al., 2010). Adults who were left behind as children often recount the difficulties of feeling connected again to the absent parent. Long-term separation often creates a breach in the parent-child relationship that may not be fully mended.

When youth migrate to rejoin families, they often encounter the circumstances that Hardy and Laszloffy (2005) have identified as leading to anger and violence in children: devaluation for being "foreigners," whether documented or not; disruption of community due to leaving behind caregivers who were parent substitutes and friends and leaving behind the familiar environment; and devaluation of losses, as parents and teachers may not have the time or the awareness of the importance of the losses accompanying migration. Without support to experience, process, and contextualize their pre-migration, migration, and post-migration experiences, youth may be left adrift. In addition, older adolescent males often are expected to work after their migration in order to lessen the burden on their fathers. As a result, many do not attain sufficient education to prosper in adulthood; they do not master the English language or develop bicultural skills to help them obtain well-paying jobs. Some sacrifice their education so that younger siblings remain in school. Many of these men then experience the sorrow and frustration that their brothers or sisters "do not take advantage of these opportunities and instead drop out of school, become parents at a young age, or join gangs." The quote comes from a male's focus group conducted by author Flores (Fresno County, Ca. December 2018).

Older daughters may find themselves providing childcare for younger siblings they had not met prior to rejoining their mothers or fathers. Some describe feeling like "Cinderella." Few recognize the parental stress felt by their progenitors who work sometimes two jobs to keep the family afloat financially and therefore do not have the time to help their children adjust to their new life. Others meet stepfathers whose existence they did not know and may feel resentful toward them, even though they may have been the ones who sponsored them or paid for their travel. In such cases, clear communication and "catching up narratives" are essential to help integrate the newly arrived into the family.

In sum, it is critical that educators and health care providers understand the context of immigrant families affected by immigration policies as they may be in a position to promote family well-being by supporting the family's efforts to reunify the children's efforts to become members of the school and family community. Furthermore, school curricula that respectfully address Latinx diversity and the challenges faced by immigrant families and children can do much to prevent the marginalization and feelings of not belonging so often experienced by mixed-status and immigrant children.

Ni de aquí ni de allá: Rooting and Belonging in the Context of "Otherness"

Children of immigrants, whether born in the United States or not, often describe feelings of otherness; sometimes these are caused by microaggressions, when they are asked their national origin—the assumption being that due to phenotype or accent or skin color they could not be American (Flores, 2014). Young children may find the question confusing; teens may respond with irony or anger. For most of her adolescence, author Flores was posed that question time and time again. Sometimes it was a crude "What are you?" Other times it was "Where were you born or where are you from?" Initially, she would answer it without much commentary. As she grew older and more aware of racism in this country, she would answer more defensively or pose a question of her own "How much time do you have? Because to answer your question, I have to tell you a story of multiple migrations." Few people really cared to hear the story and would simply walk away.

Gloria Anzaldua (1987) offered that children of Mexicans (and we would add any Latinx) must construct their own identities and become the new Mestiza/os because we often feel, or are made to feel, that we are neither "from here nor there." In a world of binaries, despite globalization and transnational migrations, hegemonic notions of nativity prevail. In the popular imagination "American" citizenship is usually accorded to Whites whose ancestors came from Europe; everyone else is foreigner whether born on U.S. soil or not. Therefore, identity formation is complicated for youth of color (Hurtado & Gurin, 2004), especially those who are mixed race or who do not look "White" (Collins, 2009; Root, 1996).

For many immigrant Latinx parents the ethnic identification of their children may be a source of confusion, if not concern. In a particularly heated family therapy session, the exchange between Mr. Gonzalez and his son, Juan, a sophomore in college, was as follows:

Mr. Gonzalez: *Qué son esas chingaderas de decir que eres Chicano. Eres Mexicano.* (What the hell do you mean by saying you are Chicano. You are Mexican and that is that.)

Juan: Dad, I have never been to Mexico; I don't want to go to Mexico. I don't eat beans and I hate tacos. I was born in the United States and have to deal with all the assumptions people have about Mexicans. I am not from there, but I am made to feel that I am not from here either. That is what a Chicano is, dad, someone who has that consciousness; someone who is aware of the racism we experience because we are children of Mexicans. But you know what; if I went to Mexico they would not want me either. There they call us ***pochos***.

Mr. Gonzalez turned to the therapist and complained that his son never answered in Spanish, which he viewed as a sign of disrespect. Frustrated, Juan retorted that he went to English-only schools; his parents worked all the time and he did not have anyone to teach him Spanish. He had to learn English in order to do well in school and to be treated better. That had helped him get into college. What more did his father want?

Such exchanges are common between U.S.-born youth and their immigrant parents. Often neither fully understands the context and experiences of the other. Falicov's (2014) and the other therapy approaches outlined in earlier chapters facilitate the negotiation of differences within the family in order for all family members to feel respected, heard, and understood.

The intersectionalities of race, ethnicity, gender, sexuality, and nativity need to be understood by all family members in order to adjust to the increasing demands of a more globalized world, while at the same time preserving the cultural traditions and values that have helped the family survive as a system—all of this despite the adversities and challenges related to poverty, migration, and disruptions brought about by family separation.

Summary

This chapter foregrounded the immigration policies that create transnational families and threaten the emotional well-being of immigrants. With the use of case studies we illustrated the intergenerational legacies of migration that can manifest as parent-child misunderstanding and conflict. An intersectional analysis of families and the impact of policies helps us understand the diversity of experience among Latinx migrants and the need for cultural attunement and humility in the delivery of services to Latinx.

HOMEWORK ASSIGNMENT

- Reflecting on the movie *Mi Familia*, identify the micro- and macroaggressions experienced by the male protagonists. In what way, if at all, do these differ from those experienced by women?
- Reflect on any of the migration stories you have heard in your family as you answer the following questions:
  - What are the major challenges mixed-status families encounter in accessing education or health care? (Draw on readings, lectures, films you may have seen.)

- o In your family, what are the major intersectionalities affecting young people?
- o What are additional stressors/challenges queer immigrants may face? (Draw on additional readings and previous chapters to answer this question.)

KEY TERMS

Attachment problems: Characterized by difficulty forming emotional bonds to others. Limited experience of positive emotions. Difficulty with physical or emotional closeness or boundaries. Anxiety. Mood changes. Intense reactions to changes in routine or attempts to control. Engaging in high-risk behaviors such as substance abuse.

Borrowed power: Power dynamics among couples and how this is negotiated and performed depending on the circumstances, agreements, and distribution of tasks and roles.

Companionate marriages: A union in which the partners decide not to have children, reserve the right to divorce amicably with mutual consent, and in which neither party would have any financial or economic claim on the other.

Mara Salvatrucha: Commonly known as MS-13, this is an international criminal gang that originated in Los Angeles, California, in the 1970s and 1980s. Originally, the gang was set up to protect Salvadoran immigrants from other gangs in the Los Angeles area.

Mask of culture: The justification of behaviors and expectations based on cultural values but that are actually a reflection of injustice in the family.

Mestizo: A person of combined European and Indigenous American descent, regardless of where the person was born. The term was used as an ethnic/racial category for mixed-race *castas* that evolved during the Spanish Empire.

MS 18: 18th Street, also known as Calle 18, Barrio 18, Mara 18, or simply La 18 in Central America, this is a multiethnic transnational criminal organization that started as a street gang in Los Angeles.

Pochos: Pejorative term used in Mexico to refer to U.S. born children of Mexicans who do not speak Spanish well and who "act" like Americans.

6

Psychological Impact of Undocumented Status

Nobody is going to return the dead and the disappeared to their families. What can and must be publicly restored [are] the victims' names and their dignity, through a formal recognition of the injustice of what has occurred, and, wherever possible, material reparation. (Martin-Baro, 1990, pp. 184–186).

I n the previous chapter, we provided an overview of the impact of immigration policies on Latinx families. In this chapter, we offer an in-depth analysis of how living in the shadows and in fear of parental deportation creates undue stress for all family members. However, for children and youth such adversities increase the risk for mental and physical health throughout the life span (Harris, 2018). Family separation due to the **deportation** of a family member also increases the risk for children and youth, particularly if the U.S. citizen or legal resident parent experiences depression or other mental health problems as the result of the removal of the spouse or partner. Lastly, we will provide a review of the new diaspora, immigrants and **asylum seekers** from Central America.

Mixed-Status Families

Mixed-status families are those where one or both parents is undocumented and older siblings brought as children to the United States also lack status, resulting in some family members having legal rights in the United States while others do not. According to the National Center for Institutional Diversity (Rodriguez, 2018), there are approximately 16 million people in mixed-status families in the United States. According to the same report, between 2010–2012 the United States deported more than 200,000 parents of U.S.-citizen children. Despite the stated policy that only high-risk individuals (those who had committed crimes) would be deported, the Obama Administration's massive deportations resulted in the break-up of extremely high numbers of families, most of them Latinx. At the end of the Obama Administration, deportation rates started to decrease and remained relatively low into the Trump Administration. In the early years of the Trump Administration, the deportations slowed. However, the Department of Homeland Security reported 12,464 deported immigrants who had at least one U.S. citizen child in the first half of 2017 alone. A key promise of Trump's campaign was to build a wall between the United States and Mexico and stop undocumented immigration from the region. Furthermore, he promised to rid the United States of what he labeled the rapists, criminals, and thieves that Mexico sent. The hateful, racist rhetoric of his administration instilled fear among immigrants, particularly those who had no legal status. Clearly, such rhetoric adversely affected the well-being of all family members, regardless of status.

The American Psychological Association's (2012) Presidential Task Force on Immigration outlined the challenges experienced by immigrants to the United States, and in particular the psychological effect of **living in the shadows**, that is having to negotiate the reality that a parent or sibling could be deported at any time. U.S.-citizen children often become the family representatives, burdened with engaging with larger systems (making phone calls for the parents, being interpreters for the family, supporting younger siblings who have academic difficulties, etc.). These children often are afraid to bring friends to their home or disclose their parents' nativity for fear that the disclosure could lead to their detection and deportation. These children often enter adolescence with the expectation to succeed, yet may face pressure to enter the workforce after high school since mixed-status families often face financial hardship due to the limited work opportunities of the parents. In addition, such families face health disparities since parents typically do not have jobs that provide health insurance; thus, eligible children likely will have some form of government insurance while their undocumented siblings or parents will not, except in case of an emergency or pregnancy. Many youth in mixed-status families feel guilt over their more privileged status and may experience jealousy and resentment from siblings born abroad.

Rodriguez Cassandra (2018) argues that the United States penalizes immigrants for the very policies that helped create mixed-status families headed by undocumented parents because "US foreign policy fosters conditions in foreign countries that make migration and settlement in the United States necessary for survival. Returning to a country of origin, in some cases, means certain violence, and even death" (p. 7). U.S. policies have actually encouraged Mexican undocumented immigrants to stay in the country, instead of participating in historical patterns of seasonal migration. The militarization of the border that began full force in the 1980s and 1990s altered seasonal Mexican labor migration. This caused migrants to consider permanent settlement in the United States.

Family Separation

In April of 2020, the Trump Administration has used COVID-19-related health concerns to justify aggressively restricting immigration. According to a *New York Times* report (Rogers et al., 2020) even before the administration's indication that by executive orders the issuance of new visas would be stopped for 60 days, Trump had expanded travel restrictions, slowed visa processing, and moved to swiftly bar asylum seekers and undocumented immigrants from entering the country. Stopping the visas of adults who are eligible to work in the United States under the guise of protecting U.S. workers is seen as his continuing effort to cease immigration. His immigration ban, however, does not include "guest workers"; an Associated Press (Colbin, et al., 2020) report indicates that exceptions to the ban include temporary workers, doctors and nurses, spouses, and children of citizens. How and to what extent his policies will be implemented remain to be seen and to what extent Latinx immigrants will be restricted from obtaining visas, even if they qualify. What is clear is that the immigration policies adversely affect Latinx families.

Psychological Implications of Family Separations

According to a report from Physicians for Human Rights (PHR) (Habbach et al., 2020), between 2017 and 2020 more than 5,000 children were separated from their families and more than 2,000 were under the age of 10. The same report documented the serious and damaging psychological effects experienced by those children being in detention who were in shock, terrified, and grieving the loss of their parental figures. The evaluating PHR clinicians reported that children presented the following symptoms: being confused and upset, crying a lot, not eating well, having nightmares, being preoccupied, having severely depressed moods, overwhelming symptoms of anxiety, and physiological manifestations of panic, despair, and hopelessness, among others. Children exhibited reactions that included "regression in age-appropriate behaviors" and "loss of developmental milestones."

Family separation is a traumatic experience with short- and long-term consequences for children and families who in many cases have already experienced traumatic experiences before and during the migration process. Studies show that disruptive changes and traumatic experiences increase the risk for emotional and behavioral stress in those children (Canino & Alegría, 2009; Falicov, 1998; Gonzales et al., 2009). Prolonged separations after a migration, separation, or divorce also increase the risk for subsequent mood and anxiety disorders, academic underachievement, and adolescent conduct problems (Flores, 2011). The images of children and youth caged at the border, living in subhuman conditions, not receiving medical treatment, among other human rights violations, have been well documented and highlights the inhumanity of the current U.S. administration. A recent study of children in detention under the current Trump Administration (MacLean et al., 2019) revealed that children who had been separated from their parents experience high levels of mental health distress, separation being more detrimental for younger children. The study alerts of the need for these children to receive comprehensive mental health interventions and culturally responsive and trauma-informed treatments. However, the follow-up on providing support, especially for those children who were deported to their countries of origin, is still unknown, and the psychological damage of these prolonged separations may be carried for the rest of their lives.

The New Diaspora: Central American Asylum Seekers in Detention

Migration patterns have dramatically changed in recent years where more females and unaccompanied children cross borders. In the past few decades, many women from Mexico and Central America migrated to the United States, leaving their children with relatives

(Flores, 2011). The majority of unaccompanied children and families who have migrated since 2012 come from a region of Central America known as the **Northern Triangle**, where high rates of violence and homicide in Honduras, Guatemala, and El Salvador have resulted in limited economic opportunities. Likewise, fear of the possibility of being kidnapped, raped, or murdered has resulted in significant migration from the region (Restrepo & Garcia, 2014; Sidun & Flores, 2020). The majority of these children left their countries of origin seeking to be reunited with family members in **El Norte** or traveling on their own to find a better future and job opportunities, in most cases, to help their families back home. In their countries of origin, they witnessed crimes and family deaths, faced separations, escaped *maras*, and encountered numerous hazards through their journeys, such as human trafficking, violence, and multiple traumatic experiences (Ataiants et al., 2018; Sidun & Flores, 2020). The flux of immigrants from Central American escaping violence continues being a border "issue" perpetuated by the current anti-immigrant rhetoric.

The international crisis of the **Caravan** meant the displacement of more than 7,000 Central American immigrants mainly coming from Honduras. More than half of those migrants were undocumented and 2,500 of those migrants were children in need of asylum and international protection (Montes, 2019). According to Doctors without Borders (2020), despite international and national obligations to protect people seeking asylum, the migration policies adopted by the U.S.'s current government criminalizes people seeking safety, detaining and deporting them to the same violent conditions that they were trying to escape.

The migration journey and traveling through Central America and Mexico exposes migrants to multiple dangers and fatalities. The train called *La Bestia* (The Beast) is taken by thousands of migrants, mainly from El Salvador, Guatemala, and Honduras, in their attempt to reach the U.S. border. The journey often ends with fatalities, taking the lives of many migrants or causing them injuries, losing body parts such as arms or legs. Migrants travel under extreme conditions, such as on the top of this train, which is meant to transport merchandise but not human beings (Tello et al., 2017). However, in a small town in the state of Veracruz, since 1995 a group of volunteer women called *Las Patronas* (The Patrons) assist migrants with water and food provisions as well with other initiatives to help migrants and their families. These women help find migrants who have disappeared, were killed, or were kidnapped. The *Patronas* have received multiple recognitions for their support of the human rights of migrants crossing Mexico (Sorrentino, 2016). Indeed, the journey can be traumatic and tragic for migrants and their families. Migrants experience constant psychological and physical struggles: abuses from *coyotes* or smugglers who bring migrants across the border, institutional mistreatment from authorities in different countries, and assaults and robberies. In providing therapy to migrants who crossed the border and listening to their journey narratives, author Torreiro-Casal observed that often the migrants created a narrative of the journey focusing on the positives and their accomplishment getting to the final destination rather than the extreme conditions and vicissitudes that they encountered. This selective recollection of memories acted as a psychological protective mechanism.

Joaquin, a 17-year-old asylum seeker from Guatemala recounted to author Flores during his psychological evaluation that he left home because *maras* had killed an older brother and his life was threatened. He stated that he was happy to be in the United States despite the challenges of finding work and a place to live. It was not until the third interview that he was able to disclose what had happened during the journey. Author Flores invited Joaquin to talk first about his family left behind, the family that initially hosted him, and his experiences in school and with peers. Once trust was established, she proceeded to ask him about his time in detention, how he was treated, and how he was able to convince the asylum officers and judge that his claim was credible. Joaquin described the *hielera*, being given half-frozen white bread and processed cheese sandwiches three times a day. Initially, he stated, he was allowed to play soccer with other youth, but then a stricter officer banned the activity. But he argued, he was treated well. He was grateful to the people who tended to him. Lastly, he was able to describe his journey, riding atop *La bestia*, seeing other youth fall and not knowing if they had survived. It took many therapy sessions for Joaquin to fully describe the trauma of the journey and the violence he endured prior to his departure. For Joaquin, as for many other youth, focusing on the positive allows them to face the multiple challenges of adjusting to a new social context. It is often during the asylum process, when asked to recount over and over the reasons for their departure, that they begin to speak of the horrors they have survived.

Eloy, an Honduran 27-year-old male, came to the United States after a 10-year separation from his mother who fled Honduras after a neighbor who was reputed to be a drug trafficker murdered her brother and vowed to do away with the entire family. Eloy left after the murder of three of his cousins by the same individual who murdered his uncle. The journey to the United States was harrowing. Eloy left with a backpack and no money after the murder of his cousin Javier, to whom he was very close, and after the murderer pointed a gun at him from a vehicle and mouthed, you are next. Eloy stated that in his country Narco traffickers commit crimes with impunity. He walked and hitched rides from Honduras to the Mexican border where he hopped on *La Bestia*. He had sores on his legs and feet from walking and witnessed other males, mostly boys, fall from the train and die on the tracks. He entered the United States near San Antonio, Texas, and was apprehended. Eloy described the 32 days he spent in the *hielera* as traumatizing. One hundred men were housed in a room with the air conditioning at an extremely low temperature, hence the nickname freezer. They were fed mush; Eloy stated he never knew what he was being fed. Daily officers threatened them, told them they were scum and would be deported. All the men were forced to shower together. There was no privacy. Eloy stated that the *hielera* is designed to humiliate and convince detainees that they would be better off deported, even if it meant certain death. He was repeatedly told he was lying about his fear of persecution and death. He asked repeatedly to speak to a judge and was denied. One morning Eloy received a document that he was being granted an audience with a judge. He was being readied for deportation and he showed the letter to an agent, who told him, "You are in luck asshole, you won't leave today." Eloy did not know that his mother had been contacted by immigration officials. His mother is a legal U.S. resident. The immigration officer who called her threatened her with removal if she had paid a *coyote* to bring her son. She was convincing in her shock to hear her son was in detention, as he had not told her he was fleeing Honduras. After his hearing with the judge, he was granted bail and, once in California, began to solicit asylum. Unfortunately, his mother and stepfather hired an attorney who was extremely abusive and traumatized him further. He was denied asylum at the hearing and was remanded to court for a deportation hearing, which will occur in January of 2021. His new attorney is kind, compassionate, and ethical in her treatment of clients. Eloy is a very traumatized man, a hard worker, and now the father of a U.S. citizen child. Of all the horrors he has experienced in his life, detention in *la hielera* ranks high in his list.

The Asylum Process and Unaccompanied Minors

The majority of the Latin Americans immigrants seeking asylum in the United States are escaping from wars, persecution, violence, or natural disasters. According to the American Immigration Council (2020) asylum is a protection granted to foreign nationals already in the United States or at the border who are considered by law refugees; and this applies to children and adults with special considerations for protecting minors.

The Office of Refugee Resettlement (2020) reported that in 2017, of the unaccompanied minors entering the United States, 17% were between 0 and 12 years of age, 13% were between 13 and 14 years of age, 37% between 15 and 16 years of age, and 32% were 17 years old. In 2019, U.S. Customs and Border Protection (2020) reported that immigration authorities apprehended 76,020 **unaccompanied alien children** (**UACs**) and recounted the entrance of more than 473, 000 **family units** of parents or legal guardians traveling with children; many of those family units were apprehended and separated when they reached the southern border. In 2018, a zero-tolerance policy for border crossing separated thousands of children from their parents and reclassified them as UACs. Requirements set forth by the **Flores Settlement Agreement** in 1997, the Trafficking Victims Protection Act of 2000, and the TVPRA of 2005 and 2008 intended to guarantee children human rights as the U.S. government responsibility for meeting those agreements. However, the Trump Administration has also proposed regulations to replace Flores and allow ICE to detain parents and children indefinitely (Kandel, 2016). These children have been separated from families without adequate protection, screening, custody, and basic human rights. Many of these minors ended up in detention centers or *hieleras* (Cantor, 2015). These conditions and the inhumane treatment of these migrants, especially children, was reported by different organizations and media, requesting services to meet the legal, health, and psychological needs of these minors. (Linton et al., 2017). However, this inhumane treatment was ignored and justified by the current anti-immigrant rhetoric and implemented policies.

Santiago

Santiago, a student from the University of California (UC) Davis anonymously and voluntarily shared his journey to the North to document and contribute to the knowledge of others. Santiago is about to graduate with a bachelor's degree; he wants to pursue a career in the medical field and is considering being a physician assistant. Santiago was one of those thousands of unaccompanied minors who came to the United States to be reunited with his undocumented family. His narrative is an example of resilience, strength, and determination. It documents the narratives of those families who risk their lives, of families who work hard to overcome challenges and see the *frutos* or results of their sacrifices when children access higher education in the United States.

Santiago was born in Guatemala in a small town close to the Mexican border. His paternal uncle was the first family member to migrate to the United States; then his dad crossed the border, and when Santiago was 7 years old, his mother attempted to cross the border for the first time and ended up being deported. A week later, she tried again, and this time she succeeded, leaving Santiago back home with his *abuelita* or grandmother, and soon after Santiago moved to live with his aunt, whom he considered a mother as well. At the age of 13, Santiago's parents arranged "the journey" to the North as an unaccompanied minor. First, Santiago crossed the border to Mexico with a group of other migrants on a bus. Santiago shared how the border officer in Mexico was friendly and let him enter Mexico, even though he smiled and commented on Santiago's identification indicating that Santiago was 19 years old. The journey through Mexico was unclear to Santiago; he stated that it seemed like a hiding game, sharing rooms and beds with other immigrants, staying at different places along the way. Santiago shared that it was also very confusing for him to understand the implications and dangers of the journey until he took *La Bestia*. He realized how he could have easily fallen from the top of the train or been a victim of assaults as a minor traveling alone. He remembered the lack of food and proper clothing for the hard weather conditions. Santiago remembered the comments other immigrants made about him traveling on his own and how they would never let their children do so; he remembered people giving food and selling food to the migrants through the journey. He also remembered being picked up by the *coyotes* on a truck. Santiago stated that they drove like crazy on the roads in Mexico, dropping him and a group of migrants by the Rio Grande.

By the river, Santiago stated he felt physically small when he saw that he had to jump into the flotation devices. He mentioned he was the only child in that group. Once he managed to cross the river, he struggled to run through the desert before reaching the truck, which brought the group of migrants to another location. The trip was harsh, and Santiago's legs felt numb when they had to run again. Santiago stated that he could no longer run and the border police detained him. They turned him over to ICE who took him to a detention center in the state of Texas. Santiago mentioned that border police told him that since he was a minor he could not go with the others; the officer had the obligation to report him to the authorities. Santiago stated that in that center there were children of all ages and from different countries, some of them lacking any type of family contact. He said that the children who arrived first were isolated for a period; they were forced to wear masks and get multiple vaccines. Santiago was able to speak regularly with his family but for no longer than 5 minutes. His family started the petition to claim his stay in the United States and begin with the asylum process. He also commented how at that time he could go out to the playground for an hour to play with other children. During his stay, he remembered learning American history and geography. He stated that when he left the detention center, he knew the names of all the 50 states and got a certificate for his learning accomplishments. Santiago spent 6 weeks in this detention center and then he could finally reunite with his family in California.

The C. Family

Javier and Gladis are a Mayan couple who fled Guatemala after their 14-year-old daughter, Amapola, was sexually assaulted by a *Mara*. The couple also feared that their 11-year-old son, Luis, would be recruited by the local gang members. Gladis has a past history of sexual violence; she was raped by landowner of the farm in which she worked, when she and her older siblings fled to Chiapas, Mexico, after their parents were murdered by Guatemalan military. During the journey to the United States, the family experienced significant hardship but managed to remain together. When they arrived at the U.S.-Mexico border, they turned themselves in to immigration officials. Gladis and her son were sent to a detention facility. Javier was sent to another, and Amapola was separated from both of her parents, triggering a severe traumatic reaction. Gladis begged and pleaded for her daughter and was told to shut up by an immigration agent and threatened with deportation. For several days, Gladis and Luis were kept in a *hielera*. Luis became ill; Gladis pleaded for medical attention, which was not given. Instead, immigration officials visited her daily and insisted she sign a voluntary departure, with threats that if she didn't, she might be held in detention for months if not years. Gladis was terrified but refused to sign until she was told where her daughter was. When she appeared before the immigration judge, he found her credible and accepted her petition for asylum. Her uncle had reached out to his church when he heard of his sister's plight in Guatemala. He had found a local family in the San Francisco Bay Area who offered to sponsor Javier and his family. This family paid the bond for Javier first; he was then allowed to fly to California. Once with the host family, the sponsor found an immigration attorney who obtained the release of Gladis, Luis, and Amapola.

Author Flores conducted an asylum evaluation for the whole family. During the course of the evaluation, the family disclosed the multigenerational history of violence they faced in their country due to being Maya, their hopes for being able to stay in the United States, and their fear of the immigration system. In addition to the evaluation, author Flores provided family therapy to assist the family in the adjustment process to a new culture, to provide the youth with educational support and Amapola with trauma-informed therapy to address the sexual trauma and the trauma of being separated from both parents and her brother during detention. The asylum process for this family has been ongoing for 3 years. At the beginning of the 3rd year, Javier obtained a work permit and began to work at a restaurant. He was grateful for all the help he received from his faith community and at the time of this writing had been able to rent an apartment where he, his wife, and children could live independently. In one of the first evaluation sessions, Gladis talked about how she missed the sewing and embroidery work she used to do. With the help of colleagues, author Flores provided Gladis with a sewing machine and wool to get started. She found healing in her ability to sew and embroider again. Recently, Javier's final court hearing where his asylum petition would be heard was postponed due to the court closure from the COVID-19 pandemic. It is not clear when the hearing will be rescheduled. Until then, the family will remain in limbo; however, their resilience is fully manifest in myriad ways. This family, as many others, have been fortunate to find sponsors, immigration attorneys, and mental health professionals who support and provide indefinite services at a reduced fee or pro bono. Once asylum is granted, hopefully the family will need to remain in therapy, as the asylum process often reopens historical wounds and triggers trauma symptoms, as petitioners have to retell their traumatic histories multiple times (Sidun & Flores, 2020), and as they are trying to resettle and create family life and some degree of normalcy for their children.

Healing for Families After Separation: Reunification

Families and minors will continue to migrate to the United States; mental health service providers and educators will need to identify collaborative approaches to facilitate the adaptation of these children and increase the likelihood of good health and educational outcomes. In assessing children with emotional and behavioral problems, it is critical to evaluate a prior history of separation and migration history. The stress of reunification can be alleviated by conveying to communities and families information regarding the impact of migration on adult and child mental health and by offering support for families with histories of migration (Flores, 2011). Under the current anti-immigrant rhetoric, often undocumented and mixed-status families hesitate to ask for help or go to government offices for fear of being mistreated or reported (Cervantes et al., 2018). Recent policies on denying residency to individuals who **were public charges** also has precluded families from seeking assistance, including medical and mental health support. Building the trust of the community requires a collective and community effort, reaching out to these families with programs specifically targeted for those communities and delivered by health providers who can build trust (see Manzo et al., 2020).

Family psychologist Celia Falicov (2014) has developed a comprehensive psychological model in working with immigrant families. Her model includes different domains of intervention addressing challenges and opportunities in working with family members nationally and transnationally, as well as the community where immigrants live, and building on a strong therapeutic relationship. Some of the interventions include utilizing the community as a support system (churches, English classes), nurturing the relationship and communication of transnational family members after separation by using technology such as Skype to maintain contact. Other therapeutic interventions provided by culturally sensitive providers include, for instance, "catching up narratives" that allow family members to share their lived experiences and hear each other's stories about the time they were apart as part of the healing process.

Summary

In this chapter we have examined the psychological implications of living in the shadows, as undocumented or mixed-status families. We have contextualized their experiences under anti-immigrant policies that deny fundamental rights and impact transnational families. These policies alienate immigrants, create a sense of insecurity and fear for authorities, and explicitly limit their access to services despite their contributions to society. We have also illustrated the journey of immigrants seeking better opportunities, escaping violence, facing dangers, and surviving under extreme conditions. These narratives reflect some of the thousands of children and transnational families who are victims of global imperialisms, social injustice, and cruelty. The current anti-immigrant rhetoric dehumanizes their experiences, disregards their suffering, and excludes them from society. The situation of those families waiting for asylum, those who have been deported, separated, and live as undocumented, requires different levels of coordinated work and efforts. These families are in great need of psychological, health, and educational support. It is very important to reach out to those families in their safe spaces in their communities and consider their national and or Indigenous origin, language preferences, and migratory process. This work also includes policy changes and collaboration among nonprofit organizations nationally and transnationally to affect change in immigration laws, particularly if there is a new government after the 2020 elections. The trauma of child and adult immigrants, asylum seekers, and mixed-status individuals who are facing family unemployment and disproportionate rates of COVID-19 infection and death will need to be addressed with cultural humility and appropriate treatment interventions once the pandemic ebbs and children return to school.

HOMEWORK ASSIGNMENT

1. What are your family's migration narratives and separations?
2. What are some of the ecological and systemic considerations affecting immigrant families?
3. What are some of the psychological implications for children and families who are undocumented?
4. What are some of the venues to support undocumented families?

KEY TERMS

Abuelita: Grandmother but in Spanish is used with a diminutive to express higher levels of affections.

Asylum seekers: Persons who fled their home country because of war or other factors harming them or their family and who apply for asylum or international protection in another country. A refugee is a displaced person who has been forced to cross national boundaries and who cannot return home safely.

Caravan: The Central American migrant caravans, also known as the *Viacrucis del Migrante* (Migrant's Way of the Cross), are migrant caravans that travel from the Guatemala-Mexico border to the Mexico–United States border. The largest and best known of these were organized by Pueblo Sin Fronteras that set off during Holy Week in early 2017 and 2018.

Deportation: The expulsion of a person or group of people from a place or country; often used as a synonym for deportation, though expulsion is more often used in the context of international law, while deportation is more used in national (municipal) law.

El Norte: "The north," also is used commonly in Mexico and Central America to refer to the United States and Canada, which lie to the north.

Flores Settlement Agreement: This was as a U.S. Supreme Court case that addressed the detention and release of unaccompanied minors. The Court ruled that the Immigration and Naturalization Service's regulations regarding the release of alien unaccompanied minors did not violate the due process clause of the Constitution.

Frutos: Literally means fruit but in Spanish is associated with the results or outcomes of work or sacrifices performed by someone.

Hielera: Means freezer or icebox and refers to the facilities or holding cells in the United States for migrants who are in detention. These facilities are extremely cold, frequently overcrowded, and without beds, and migrants there lack adequate food, water, and medical care.

La Bestia: Also known as *el tren de la muerte* (the death train) and *el tren de los desconocidos* (the train of the unknowns), it refers to a network of Mexican freight trains that are utilized by U.S.-bound migrants to more quickly traverse the length of Mexico.

Las Patronas: A group of volunteer women of the *La Patrona* community, from the town of Guadalupe in the municipality of Amatlán de los Reyes, Veracruz in Mexico. Since 1995 the group has provided food and assistance to migrants on their way north through Veracruz.

Living in the shadows: Refers to those individuals and families with undocumented status, lacking protections and any rights and experiencing fear and discrimination.

Maras: Plural for *mara* (or *marabunta*); a form of gang originating in the United States, which spread to Central American countries such as El Salvador, Honduras, and Guatemala.

Mixed-status families: A family whose members include people with different citizenship or immigration statuses. One example of a mixed-status family is one in which the parents are undocumented and the children are U.S.-born citizens. The number of mixed-status families is growing.

Northern Triangle: The three Central American countries of Guatemala, Honduras, and El Salvador. The term is used with respect to the countries' geographical and economic situation and their shared challenges, including widespread poverty, violence, and corruption, which have prompted many to become refugees fleeing the three nations.

Public charges: A new rule that limits the number of legal immigrants living in or entering the United States by penalizing those who depend on food stamps, among other public assistance. Low-income immigrants would be denied green cards (permanent legal status) if it's determined they will be relying on the federal safety net.

Reunification: Family reunification is a recognized reason for immigration in many countries because of the presence of one or more family members in a certain country, enabling the rest of the divided family or only specific members of the family to immigrate to that country as well.

Unaccompanied alien children (UACs): U.S. government classification for children in immigration custody. The term designates unaccompanied minors who are immigrants and asylum seekers and have been apprehended upon their entry in the U.S. territory. Children separated from their parents under the Trump Administration's family separation policy were referred to the UAC program.

7

Separation, Divorce, and Blended Families

Latinx families, as individuals from other ethnic groups, face divorce, separations, and the formation of newly **blended families**. Families are exposed to societal changes, migration patterns, and demographic changes that have shaped their composition and life cycles. Patterns and longitudinal changes for Latinx families will be available after data collection and reports are generated and finalized from the 2020 Census. Previous data on Latinx families indicated relevant variations and changes in the composition, marriage, divorce rates, and separation among them. Immigration patterns, policies, and recent political changes have dramatically impacted Latinx families, especially immigrant and transnational families (Landale et al., 2006). In the 2000 Census, 7.4% of Latinx aged 15 years and older were divorced while the national average was 9.7%. Latinx are following national trends in both marriage and divorce rates (Teachman et al., 2000). For Latina women aged 40–44, divorce rates rose from 20 to 27% between 1980 and 1990, and the 2000 Census reported the overall rate for Latina females who are divorced or separated was 21.5%. This group of Latina women seems to present a similar percentage of divorce and separation rates to their White counterparts; the national average is 21.1% for all divorced or separated families (Teachman et al., 2000). Among Latinx groups, Mexican and Puerto Ricans present lower divorce rates than other Latinx. However, the longer that they live in the United States, those patterns seem to change, becoming similar to the U.S. average (Falicov, 2014).

According to the U.S. Census Bureau (2019), 74.7% Latinx live in family households, and 47.5% of those are married couples; 8.9% are male householders and 18.3% are female householders. In addition, nearly one in four (24%) Latinx households were found to be food insecure when compared to White American households where just one in ten (11%) were food insecure (Gundersen & Ziliak, 2014). The majority of the Latinx families in the United States are composed of immigrant adults; many are transnational families with members in more than one country. In 2016, 34% of the Latinx population was foreign born, and 19% of Latinxs under the age of 35 were also foreign born (Lopez et al., 2018). Immigration and its ecological considerations shape the realities of the majority of the Latinx families and couples in the United States. It may determine when couples get married, cohabit, or remarry. Further, the migratory process disrupts the family life cycle. Often families are separated temporarily or indefinitely, increasing family stress levels and bringing economic hardships and despair to many of these families. Immigrant families and couples also have to adapt to a new culture, encountering language barriers and multiple challenges navigating systems (Falicov, 2014).

In this chapter we will cover some of the changes Latinx families have undergone in this century. We will describe marriage among Latinx from a traditional and contemporary perspective. We will also focus on intermarriage, separation, and divorce and their implications for families and children from an ecological and psychological perspective. In addition, we will illustrate this with *testimonios* and our own personal and clinical experiences.

Latinx Families and Marriage

Marriage for Latinxs is frequently tied to the cultural values of **familism** and **collectivism** and the value of having children (Falicov, 1988, 2014; Flores, 2011). When a couple marries, parenthood is prioritized, and children become central to the functioning of the newly formed family (Harris et al., 2008). Studies also show that collectivism prioritizes familial relationships to marital relationships, and marriage is seen as more important than the autonomy of individual spouses. Therefore, family needs are expected to be above individual needs (Flores et al., 2004; Oropesa & Gorman, 2000). Marital stability has usually been higher among Latinxs than other racial and ethnic populations in the United States, partially because of their cultural values and beliefs (Bramlett & Mosher, 2002; Fu & Wolfinger, 2011). For instance, religion, in particular Catholicism, still plays a significant role in the lives of Latinx families. For the Roman Catholic Church, divorce is not accepted, and marriage is considered a life commitment (Jenks & Woolever, 1999).

Research on Latinx marital relations also emphasizes the role of *machismo* and *marianismo* as two cultural values embedded in Latinx couple's gender roles. According to these cultural constructs, women are expected to be self-sacrificing mothers, inspired by the Catholic tradition of the Virgin Mary, and men are expected to act as authoritarian patriarchal heads of the household (Ginorio et al., 1995). However, feminist researchers have also focused on expanding restrictive views on Latinx families and couples, highlighting that these families displayed a much greater diversity of gender roles and patterns than the traditional views assigned to Latinx families (Ramirez & Arce, 1981; Zavella, 1989). In her clinical work with Latinx transnational couples, Falicov (2014) reveals that gender ideologies are in cultural transition in Latin America and the United States. Indeed, family and couple dynamics reflect societal changes, presenting a much larger scope of roles than the **archetypal** representations of Latinx men and women in U.S. society. These changes in roles and views on marriage have been influenced by the increase of divorce rates in Latin American countries and **cohabitation** before marriage (Seltzer, 2004). **Consensual unions** and cohabitation, including families with children, were also common in Latin American societies among couples with limited resources (Landale & Oropesa, 2007). In addition, women's participation in the workforce has contributed to the incorporation and adaptation of new roles among Latinx families (Pesquera, 1993). Access to more educational opportunities for Latina women has opened venues for changing couple and family expectations. In our clinical and teaching experiences, new generations of Latinxs share how they voice their disagreement with some family expectations on gender roles, showing less adherence to those traditional gender roles.

Intermarriage has been considered an important indicator of more flexible racial and ethnic boundaries and exchanges between different social groups (Rosenfeld, 2002). Laws restricting interracial marriage for African Americans, Asian Americans, and Native Americans have historically limited these exchanges in the United States. However, these views on interracial marriage have changed, and more Americans are open to it, with Asian Americans and Latinx groups presenting the highest numbers of intermarriage (Livingston & Brown, 2017). According to Stevens and Tyler (2002), intermarriage is determined by group's preferences for marrying in-group versus out-group members. Several factors contribute to intermarriage, for instance the size of the groups, demographic characteristics including language, religious affiliations, residential location, and generational differences. Mexican Americans present a higher level of **endogamy** than all other Latinx groups; this is explained by migratory patterns but also by the large presence of Mexicans in the United States. Further, different patterns are present among Latinx subgroups. For instance, foreign-born Latinx are less likely to marry a non-Latinx, but Latinxs living in new immigrant destinations are more likely to intermarry than those living in traditional Latinx **enclaves**. Furthermore, Latino men with higher education levels are more likely to intermarry, and Latina women who married at older ages or who are employed outside the home are more likely to intermarry a non-Latinx (Qian & Lichter, 2018). Intermarriage is also considered the result of assimilation. However, this process seems to be more challenging for Latinx immigrants from lower socioeconomic status; this is partially attributed to the negative reception, discrimination, and restrictions that they experience to be accepted into mainstream society (Oropesa & Landale, 2004). Indeed, in our classes, students share how some of them grew up in families with intermarried couples, having parents who are from different countries and parents from different racial and ethnic groups and religions. Many of those students share how these multicultural and multiethnic families shape and define cultural values and traditions and how students identify with one or another identity and values.

According to Falicov (2014), intermarried couples face **cultural losses** that may impact their well-being. Couples may share, to a greater or lesser extent, similar characteristics that include language preference, religious views, or cultural practices. Couples may present interethnic, interracial, interreligious, interclass, or a combination of those dimensions. Depending on these similarities and differences, the couple will have to adjust, negotiate, and balance the implications of those differences and similarities. Couples can highly benefit from those differences complementing each other or could face increased stress due to those differences (Falicov, 1995). Author Torreiro-Casal met her partner from the Netherlands in Spain when they were both undergraduate students. They spoke different languages, came from different cultures, grew up in different countries, and had very different personalities. These differences were an opportunity to learn from each other, overcome multiple challenges, learn to respect differences, and raise a child within a multicultural foundation. The couple's transition from living in two very distinctive northern and southern European countries to live in the United States helped them develop a stronger sense of their similarities. Both spoke each other's language, and Spanish and Dutch were spoken at home. The child born of this relationship identifies as Californian, speaks three languages, and his appearance gives him privilege in the United States, which he uses to help and defend other Latinx peers at school who often experience discrimination at school from whom he calls *los gringos*. Indeed, as Falicov (1995) mentioned, a couple with different backgrounds can highly benefit each other and their children. Author Torreiro-Casal's views on diversity and multiculturalism are consonant with this and she considers that the end of her marriage is attributed more to an existential crisis suffered by her partner rather than their cultural differences.

Author Flores's first marriage was to a U.S.-born Chicano who grew up in Texas. Both shared a bicultural identification, as author Flores had migrated to the United States as an early adolescent. Her command of Spanish was higher than his; thus, in their marriage, his Spanish language fluency increased. Although they shared similar family values, his gender views were more traditional than hers. Nevertheless, he supported her academic aspirations and was instrumental in her early career success. Together they raised two children. He was often the one who cooked and, with the help of author Flores's parents, picked up the children from school while she worked at and commuted to the university at least 4 days a week. The end of the marriage was centered primarily on their different views on childrearing and differences in life cycle stages, as he was 14 years older than Dr. Flores. Her second marriage was to a Central American man who was binational, as she was. Their shared history, values, and immigrant experiences brought them together. It was their life cycle differences, as he was younger, and different long-term life goals that failed that marriage. In both marriages, however, author Flores experienced a lack of family support for her choices, which contributed to stress and conflict. As a highly educated, financially independent woman, author Flores had the option to divorce, unlike many Latina women who feel bound to remain married for religious, cultural, or financial reasons.

Separation and Divorce

There are multiple reasons why couples divorce or separate, including marital disagreements, family conflicts, infidelity, abandonment, domestic violence, loss of a child, or a combination of those. Some couples may separate but still be legally married until the couple decides to get divorced by following the necessary legal steps to dissolve the marriage. A divorce or separation can occur by mutual agreement or once one member decides to leave the relationship. In each situation, family members cope differently with the pain, financial stress, and consequences that a divorce or separation brings to the family unit and especially to children. According to Padilla and Borrego (2006), approximately half of all marriages in the United States end up in divorce. Divorce seems to be more accepted for most Americans than Latinx families who may see it as a calamity and as a negative stigma for the extended family, creating additional stress for both sides of the family who may have had strong bonds and ties. Latina women may feel it is a failure to go through a divorce or separation, hiding their situation from family members. Author Torreiro-Casal was in shock when her partner of 20 years abandoned her and their son for a younger woman. It was heartbreaking and embarrassing; it took the author a long time to openly share her divorce with others, including her parents. She thought she married for the rest of her life as her family members did. She did not want to worry her parents back home in Spain, who ended up showing unconditional support for her and her son. Being an immigrant added extra stress, and it had multiple implications and meanings. Further, she was unfamiliar with the legal system, alone without any family, in an insecure job situation, and most importantly dealing with the deep pain that made her question whether to remain in the United States. The inner strength to overcome the barriers and challenges came from a very strong desire to survive for her child and the need to protect and minimize the pain. The support received by friends, colleagues, and family was fundamental to overcome the ongoing suffering of a belligerent divorce process due to her ex-husband's lack of willingness to follow the child support and alimony laws.

Author Flores's second divorce was equally unexpected and devastating. Her first divorce occurred after her children were out of high school to minimize the disruption in their lives. When she decided to divorce her first husband, author Flores did not tell her extended family for some time. When she did, one of her aunts crossed herself and fell on her knees to pray. When she chose to marry a much younger man the second time, she knew the transgressive nature of the union and the reduced likelihood of success. However, when she entered her second marriage, she hoped and expected to remain married. Nevertheless, she did not tell the extended family about it, as she expected to hear negative feedback. She did not disclose the information until relatives were coming to visit from Costa Rica. Indeed, her cousin loudly stated, *Estás loca* (You are crazy). Author Flores's son did not speak to her for a year when she told him about the marriage. When her second husband announced he was no longer in love, the pain and shame "of not having known better" led to depression and a decision never to fall in love again. The support of her friends, daughter, colleagues, and privilege of a secure job and homeownership facilitated her recovery from the grief and anger about the divorce.

Despite the implications of less acceptance of divorce among Latinx, divorce rates among Latinx have increased. According to Oropesa and Landale (2004), Latinxs tend to show similar numbers in divorce rates to White Americans when the Latinx has been in the United States longer and when they have better job opportunities, educational attainment, and English proficiency. However, those Latinxs who married before migration or first married at an older age are less likely to be divorced. The numbers for remarried couples are still lower compared to White Americans. In 2012, six in ten divorced White Americans remarried, compared with 51% of Hispanics, 48% of Blacks and 46% of Asian Americans. These numbers are lower when the marriage happened at least twice before, showing that 10% of White adults remarried compared with 6% of African Americans, 4% of Latinx, and just 2% of Asian Americans (Livingston, 2014).

Marianas's Case

This story shows how a Mexican woman in her 40s overcomes and survives multiple systems of oppression. It also reflects the intersection of culture, socioeconomic status, gender roles and expectations, intergenerational family patterns, and domestic violence.

In addition, Mariana is an educated Latina, but her case shows how challenging it still was for her to navigate systems and get support.

Mariana is the oldest of four siblings born to a migrant farmworker family from Mexico. The family spent some time living in Mexico when Mariana was in middle school. As the oldest female sibling, Mariana had to take care of her siblings while her parents worked in the fields. The youngest male sibling was born with Down syndrome, and due to her parent's lack of insurance, he was not properly diagnosed when he was born. Mariana had to help her parents interpret and get the services for him. Mariana expressed that she never felt valued by her parents for all the burdens and responsibilities that she had on her shoulders. Mariana also stated that she experienced the issues of living in an affluent wine country area where migrant farmworkers were not welcome at schools, forbidding them from speaking in Spanish. Mariana stated that she felt safe around "her people" and when having little interactions with White Americans. Mariana grew up near her extended family, and she had a very strong bond with her *tías*, spending the summer picking up fruit in the fields with her relatives in what she called her "summer camp." She stated that her *tías* and *tíos* were close to her in age, and she felt supported by them; she was also allowed by her parents to visit and go to places with them.

Mariana reported that growing up with a very strict mother with strong Catholic views made it impossible for her to socialize with other peers during her high school experience. Mariana's mother opposed letting her go to college, arguing that she will turn into a *puta* or whore, but thanks to a *tío* who was already in college, they convinced her parents to let her go. In college, Mariana became forever friends with other Mexican peers with similar backgrounds and who were also getting a degree in engineering. Mariana stated that without them it would have been impossible for a Mexican female to graduate as an engineer and overcome all the institutional discrimination that she faced. She also met her husband while organizing the graduation for Latinx students. They started dating, and Mariana helped him to complete his degree because he was not good at math. They married, and Mariana started working as an engineer for the state. Soon after getting married, their first son was born. However, Mariana realized that something was different about her son. She found out that her child was on the autism spectrum; he was rejected from regular daycare, and she had to find help to take care of him. It was not until her *prima* (cousin) came to live in the area with her family that she was able to manage work, family, and house demands. Mariana stated that her husband only cut the *zacate* (grass) in the backyard at the house that they bought and left all the other responsibilities to her. Mariana stated that her husband was acting like her father-in-law, a lower SES White American who married a Mexican woman and abused her and her children physically and psychologically.

When Mariana got pregnant with her second child, she realized that her husband was cheating on her with a colleague from work. At that time she wanted to save the marriage, and she forgave him. However, his abuse started to be more explicit, putting her down verbally and emotionally more often. Mariana stated that while growing up her family did the same to her, especially her mother. She thought it was normal to treat other family members like this. Mariana had very strong values about family and marriage as a Catholic; she believed that she married for the rest of her life. Mariana began to attend therapy, and she learned about her life narrative, family dynamics of abuse, and gender issues. The relationship continued to experience more conflicts as her husband started to manifest other aggressive behaviors. On one occasion, Mariana called the police for fear of her children being hurt as well. Her husband was taken to jail, but later Mariana removed the charges against him. It was in her 40s when she found out that her husband was cheating again with another woman. In the meantime, Mariana was being harassed at work by her male boss; Mariana complained about it following the advice of other female coworkers, and she was transferred to another position. This work situation cost her much psychological stress but also helped her to initiate her divorce process. Mariana felt strong about her decision, but her husband made it hard for her. Custody rights were given by law to both parents, but Mariana found out that her ex-husband physically abused her children. The child on the spectrum reported this at school, and **Child Protective Services** (**CPS**) started an investigation; however, after his dad threatened him, he denied everything to them. On the contrary, the youngest child reported to the police that she did not feel safe with her dad, and after the investigation a restraining order was delivered. Mariana experienced the consequences of a painful divorce, the difficulties of navigating systems, and the lack of support from therapists, police, and court to get full custody of her children. It cost an enormous amount of time to make some progress and for Mariana to be able to share with other family members. This experience is still a secret in her family. Mariana mentioned that sometimes her mother still makes comments about her former marriage, saying that at some point, they may *arreglarse* (make up). Maria feels free now, and as a successful professional engineer she has been able to move on with her life, although she stated that she is aware that divorcing an abuser does not end the abuse when the marriage is over, and the trauma remains.

Divorce and Separation Through Psychological Cultural Lenses

Divorce and separation within the context of family functioning have been extensively addressed in the psychology literature by family system theorists and clinicians (Bowen, 1978; Gottman, 2014; Minuchin, 1974; Boszormenyi-Nagy, 1987). These theories and clinical modalities have explored what contributes to the good functioning of a marriage: the dynamics of the relationship, the life cycle of the relationship, and each individual's personal growth and values about marriage. The feminist perspective on couple's therapy has also expanded the attention to gender differences, differential access to power, and expectations regarding intimacy and autonomy in heterosexual and gay couples. Multiculturalism has provided the base for couple's therapists to broaden their understanding of the diversity of couples by addressing race, ethnicity, religion, social class, sexual orientation, age, and geographic location (Gurman, 2008). However, the majority of these models do not conceptualize Latinx families and couples from a cultural, intersectional, and ecological approach. Chicanx and Latinx clinicians and researchers have added cultural lenses in working with Latinx couples. For instance, some work has considered family injustices as a result of domestic violence or substance abuse (Flores-Ortiz, 1993, 2000). Others focus on Latina women's roles and expectations in the context of their families and intimate relationships (Chabram-Dernersesian & de la Torre, 2008) as well as the multiplicity and borderlands of multicultural Latinx couples (Bacigalupe, 2003).

The MECA model developed by Falicov (2014), described in previous chapters, addresses couple's therapy work as well. This multidimensional ecosystemic comparative approach or MECA model also assesses Latinx couples. The model considers the couple's current life cycle stage, migration narratives, and ecological context. The model also includes the integration of the **migration relational stress** experienced by immigrant couples and how those immigrant couples negotiate and adapt to the new contextual realities of living in a different country. It also considers how the couple negotiates transnational relationships with other family members and how, for instance, they raise bicultural children. The model also takes into consideration intermarriage among Latinxs, considering their strengths and personal enrichments. Finally, Latinx families going through a divorce or remarriage or becoming part of a stepfamily are assessed within those cultural and multidimensional approaches. Author Torreiro-Casal experienced the implications of being married to a partner from Northern Europe with a Catholic background as well but from a more individualistic society. She always considered it a good relationship with the capacity to negotiate and adapt to the multiple changes that the couple encountered, such as living in different countries. However, as a self-identified Latina woman, author Torreiro-Casal made the sacrifices of leaving her country of origin and moving to the Netherlands, supporting her partner's career, learning a new language, and adapting to a new country. Initially, her sacrifices were considered part of being in love; years later, this was interpreted as *la sufrida*, who has to *aguantar* (put up) with everything for the benefit of the family.

Often women who decide to divorce unfaithful or abusive partners are regarded by family members to be selfish; they are accused of prioritizing their well-being over the happiness of the children. Often extended family members are not aware that the toxic environment of an unhappy home endangers the children's mental health, particularly if there is violence in the relationship. Less culturally traditional couples may find more understanding and support from peers than family members. Lack of support at the time of a painful separation or divorce adds to the psychological distress of the divorcing partners. Author Flores waited to leave a marriage that no longer worked until her son graduated high school to avoid a custody battle and to maintain the family unit together. Neither he nor his sister, in retrospect, felt it was a good idea for their mother to make that sacrifice. They saw her unhappiness as palpable, and the parents' lack of love was painful for them. The extended family explained Author Flores's decision to leave a marriage to a man who, in their eyes, was a good provider and did not drink or abuse her as resulting from too much education and acculturation. No family members ever asked her directly why she was seeking a divorce.

Blended Families

For the past decades, **blended families** have become increasingly common family units in the United States (Teachman & Tedrow, 2008). With the growing number of **stepfamilies**, there has also been an increase among Latinx stepfamilies (Lamidi & Cruz, 2014). Approximately half of all remarriages bring at least one child from a prior relationship to the new blended family (Kreider, 2008). For Latinx families in remarriages, cohabiting relationships and those with children in these relationships face unique challenges (Teachman & Tedrow, 2008; Vespa et al., 2013). Despite the increase in divorce among Latinx, there is limited psychological literature on the impact of divorce on the couple and the children. When the original family is dissolved, some Latino parents may cut all communications with each other. Once a parent has left home, the parent may no longer be considered part of that family unit. Latinx immigrant families might have one of the biological parents still living in their native country (Adler-Baeder et al., 2010). The characteristics, circumstances, and meaning of a blended family may substantially be different from non-Latinx families. Also, Latinx families tend to live with multiple generations and other family members, blood related and not. For instance, author Torreiro-Casal lives with her son, brother, nephew, and niece. These types of family units and arrangements may seem peculiar to non-Latinx families. However, many of our students from Latinx families also report living with multiple generations and family members. In Spain, like in Latinx countries, the priority is the well-being of the family as a unit and especially children, helping them develop a sense of security and having family members around them whom they can relate to, learn from, and learn to value and respect . As professor Angie Chabram-Denersesian mentioned to author Torreiro-Casal after her divorce, Latinx families have the strength to reunite and support each other in times of adversity, building new families after unexpected ruptures and disruption. Further, often Latinx families have *tías* (aunt), *tíos* (uncles), and *comadres* who are not blood related but who are considered part of the family and contribute to the well-being of the family with their support. Indeed, Latinx families are very diverse in terms of colors, structures, and compositions; they also show values of solidarity, as well as resilience, and when families encounter ruptures, these characteristics and values highly contribute to their adaptability.

Author Flores lives in a multigenerational household with her daughter, son-in-law, and their three children. As a young couple, her daughter, husband, and baby daughter had moved to Florida to be near his divorced mother. However, when author Flores told them that her second marriage was ending, her son-in-law insisted on returning to California to support her. Despite author Flores's protestations that such a move was unnecessary because she had the support of her network of friends, her daughter and family returned and moved in with her. Author Flores's son-in-law felt strongly that his mother-in-law should not live alone and deal with the trauma of divorce without their support. He is a second-generation Latino who still holds traditional values. A few years later, his son, by a previous relationship, also joined the household. The blended family he created after his son joined his new marriage has been cohesive. As a child of divorce himself, he understood the importance of providing security to all the children and the women who often are affected adversely economically by divorce, even though that was not the case with his mother-in-law.

Implications of Divorce and Separations

The dissolution of a marriage or a couple's rupture has short- and long-term effects, and without the necessary support and healing the consequences can be more damaging. Children and teenagers may become sad, vocal, and angry about the separation and divorce

(Falicov, 2014). In situations of domestic violence, drug-related issues, or litigations on custodial rights, the interactions with the court system and other institutions may last for years, and children may suffer from those. Those families must receive help and support from institutions providing counseling and guidance. In our clinical experiences, we encountered situations where clients needed multidisciplinary support to find out about their legal rights, immigration options, and parental rights. When author Torreiro-Casal worked with domestic violence survivors, many of these clients were women who did not have an income. For these women separating, divorcing, or leaving the relationship was much more difficult, especially for those who were undocumented. Women are still dealing with gender and power dynamics that interfere with their decisions. Clinicians working with populations encountering these situations need to advocate, help coordinate systemic support, and utilize available resources in the communities where clients live. For instance, in working with Latinxs, the support from family members, *amistades* (friends), and other resources in the community that is accessible and culturally congruent are often very helpful. Healing takes time, and for a family to transform their realities, available resources are crucial for mitigating the consequences of changes in the family composition and structure.

Summary

In this chapter, we have addressed some of the characteristics of divorce, separations, and the formation of blended families for Latinxs and how the dissolution of a marriage has multiple cultural and social implications for family members. An intersectional understanding of the challenges posed by intermarriage, as well as the stress resulting from the rupture of marriage, is critical to identify the supports needed by the family. Likewise, identifying the family member's strengths and cultural resources is necessary to mobilize their resilience and support their recovery.

HOMEWORK ASSIGNMENT

1. Why do you think Latinxs respond and adapt differently to divorce and separations?
2. How would you describe divorce and separations in the context of your family?
3. What are your values and beliefs about marriage and divorce?

KEY TERMS

Aguantar: To keep up with something; also associated with the value of being strong and accepting reality as it comes.

Archetypical: Refers to an original form or a main model which other statements, patterns of behavior, and objects copy or emulate.

Blended families: A step, bonus, or instep family where at least one parent has children not biologically or adoptively related to the other spouse or partner. Either parent, or all, may have children from previous relationships.

Cohabitation: An arrangement where two people are not married but live together. They are often involved in a romantic or sexually intimate relationship on a long-term or permanent basis.

Consensual unions: A situation when two persons belong to the same household and have a relationship with each other but are not married or in a registered partnership with each other.

Collectivism: A value that is characterized by emphasis on cohesiveness among individuals and prioritization of the group over the self.

Enclaves: When referring to ethnic enclaves where people live, those geographical locations offer stronger social networks.

Endogamy: The practice of marrying within a specific social group, caste, or ethnic group, rejecting those from others as unsuitable for marriage or other close personal relationships. Endogamy is common in many cultures and ethnic groups.

Familism: A social value where the needs of the family are more important and take precedence over the needs of any of the family members.

Intermarriage: Marriage between people of different religions, tribes, castes, ethnicities, or racial groups.

La sufrida: The one who suffers; associated with values of *Marianismo* and women sacrificing for their families.

Los gringos: Plural of *gringo* or *gringa*; refers to someone considered a foreigner, especially form the United States of Canada, from the perspective of Spanish- and Portuguese-speaking countries in Latin America.

Migration relational stress: Psychological strain or distress responses to immigration-related challenges that an individual, couple, or family encounter as they adapt to life in a new country. Immigration stress is a multidimensional construct consisting of functionally related behaviors, attitudes, processes, and experiences.

Stepfamilies: Families formed on the remarriage of a divorced or widowed person and that include one or more children.

Testimonios: Plural of *testimonio*, or testimony. It is generally defined as a first-person narration of socially significant experiences in which the narrative voice is that of a typical or extraordinary witness or protagonist who metonymically represents others who have lived through similar situations and who have rarely given written expression to them.

8

LGBTQ Couples and Families

As a mestiza I have no country, my homeland cast me out; yet all countries are mine because I am every woman's sister or potential lover. (As a lesbian I have no race, my own people disclaim me; but I am all races because there is the queer of me in all races.) I am cultureless because, as a feminist, I challenge the collective cultural/religious malederived beliefs of Indo-Hispanics and Anglos; yet I am cultured because I am participating in the creation of yet another culture, a new story to explain the world and our participation in it, a new value system with images and symbols that connect us to each other and to the planet. (*Anzaldúa, 1987, pp. 102–103*)

In this chapter, we focus on **LGBTQ** (lesbian, gay, bisexual, transgender, queer or questioning) Latinx couples and their families from the lens of Latinx psychosocial and family models (Falicov, 1998, 2014; Flores, 2001, 2013). We describe the unique characteristics of LGBTQ Latinx communities from a cultural, historical, and socioecological perspective. We also acknowledge the multiplicity of identities and challenges experienced by LGBTQ Latinx individuals, and we recognize their strengths navigating multiple identities and spaces. Anzaldúa (1987) described the "borderland" as *el sitio* (the place or space) between being gay/lesbian and Chicanx. She refused to privilege a single identity; she developed a hybrid sense of self, a woman of the borderlands, as she found this place or *sitio* as a source of strength and creativity. The dominant Anglo or European American culture's views on minorities are often unidimensional and rooted in deficit perspectives (Garcia & Guerra, 2004). This reductionist approach overlooks the ecological realities experienced by sexual, racial, or ethnic minorities and neglects to contemplate their **cultural** and **social capital** as sources of strength (Yosso, 2005). For instance, a study conducted by the National Council of La Raza addressing issues on tolerance and acceptance of LGBTQ individuals among Latinx showed that contrary to some of the deficit beliefs and assumptions about Latinx, they are as accepting and supportive, if not more accepting, of LGBTQ individuals than the general population in the United States (Dutwin, 2012). Therefore, it is very relevant to conduct more studies and develop programs for LGBTQ Latinx and their families from a strength-based perspective and through Latinx and Chicanx lenses. Indeed, in working with LGBTQ Latinxs fundamental differences exist compared to other LGBTQ groups, for instance different value systems and the importance of family (Flores, 2015). In this chapter, we will discuss Latinx families with LGBTQ youth members, LGBTQ Latinx couples and those **same-sex couples** raising children, as well as LGBTQ Latinx immigrants. We will explore some of the ecological and intersectional realities experienced by LGBTQ Latinx within the broader U.S. **queer** and straight communities. We will also illustrate some of these realities with *testimonios* of those who anonymously and voluntarily shared their narratives.

Demographics

There are approximately 1.4 million LGBTQ Latinx adults representing 4.3% of the Latinx population in the United States; 146,100 of those are in same-sex couples, and 29.1% of those couples are raising children. LGBTQ Latinxs tend to live in areas where there are already high concentrations of Latinx individuals. One third of same-sex Latinx couples live in New Mexico, California, and Texas (Williams Institute, 2013). Latinx individuals in same sex couples are 1.7 times more likely to be raising children than White same-sex couples. Twenty-six percent of all Latinx same-sex couples have completed a college degree or more, compared to 14% of Latinx individuals in different-sex couples. The subpopulations of same-sex couples experiencing more socioeconomic vulnerability are Latinx female same-sex couples, couples raising children, and couples where one or both partners are noncitizens (Gates & Kastanis, 2013). Literature addressing LGBTQ Latinx couples raising children in the United States is still very limited, which is attributed partially to the fact that gay marriage in the United States only became legal at the federal level in 2015 (Masci et al., 2015). Until recently, many LGBTQ Latinx couples had lived in the shadows or without the legal rights available to straight couples. Many of these couples face similar issues as straight couples do, for example domestic violence situations. However, they may lack access to resources and professionals specialized in intimate partner violence and LGBTQ Latinx. Therefore, it becomes more challenging for LGBTQ Latinx individuals to report and seek help. The Network La Red in Boston, founded by former survivors and allies, is an example of the very few organizations with specialized services for LGBTQ Latinx communities and their intersectional identities.

From a family perspective, another relevant subgroup of LGBTQ Latinx are **millennials**, those between the ages of 18 and 34 who identify as lesbian, gay, bisexual, or transgender. A recent study showed that Latinx LGBTQ millennials tend to be more open to disclosing their sexual orientation than other ethnicities in the United States (Cohen et al., 2018). However, despite legislative changes and more openness in society, LGBTQ Latinx youth still encounter multiple systemic barriers and increased health disparities compared to other groups. For instance, overall poverty rates among Latinx LGBTQ are higher than in most other races or ethnicities (Albelda et al., 2009). Poverty indeed contributes to health disparities and the lack of access to health services, prevention, and treatment. Indeed, HIV cases are alarming among Latinx **gay** and **bisexual** males (Gruberg et al., 2018). Additionally, another important group are the LGBTQ Latinx immigrants who often encounter linguistic barriers in accessing and navigating systems. The Williams Institute (2013) at the UCLA School of Law reported that approximately

904,000 LBTQ Latinx immigrants are coming mostly from Central and South America and at least 267,000 of them are also undocumented; 75,000 of those are LGBTQ Latinx DREAMers, including 36,000 who have participated in the Deferred Action for Childhood Arrivals (DACA) program.

One of the most vulnerable groups among Latinx LGBTQ immigrants are Latinx **transgender** women who experience very high rates of violence and abuse (Issuu, n.d.). It is noted that mental health resources and services to provide adequate emotional support and advocacy for immigrant transgender women are very limited (Quintero et al., 2015). In 2008, the National Center for Transgender Equality (NCTE) and the National Gay and Lesbian Task Force conducted a nationwide study of anti-transgender discrimination in the United States (Issuu, n.d.). One of the most important findings of this study was that the combination of anti-transgender bias with structural and interpersonal racism resulted in devastating levels of discrimination for transgender and **gender-nonconforming** LGBTQ Latinx. In the same report, findings also showed that Latinx transgender and gender nonconforming respondents who attended kindergarten through 12th grade expressing a transgender identity or gender nonconformity reported high numbers of harassment (77%), physical assault (36%), and sexual assault (13%) at school, resulting in high dropout rates for these LGBTQ Latinx students. Respondents who were harassed and abused showed worse health and increased numbers of suicide than those who did not experience such abuse. Finally, the report indicated that those Latinx transgender and gender nonconforming respondents who were accepted by their families were much less likely to face discrimination. In conclusion, each Latinx LGBTQ subgroup encounters similar but also specific challenges. Therefore, it is necessary to provide specialized psychological counseling, legal and medical services, as well as family and individual support at multiple settings, including schools, clinics, and nonprofit organizations.

Mona

Mona was born in Morelos, Mexico. Her preferred **pronouns** were all, and in this *testimonio*, Mona uses he, she, they, zie, among others. Her mother raised Mona as a single mother until she met Mona's stepfather. Mona shared that they were very close to their mother, whom they described as a very resilient woman who got pregnant with her as the result of rape. In 2002, when Mona was 7, they crossed the border through Tijuana, Mona by car with another family and her mother on foot. Both ended up in the Central Valley, where his undocumented stepdad already worked as a taxi driver under a Social Security number that was previously provided. Mona described both parental figures as very hardworking individuals. Mona stated that being raised in a California **Bible belt** town was very limiting and difficult for her. In growing up, they remembered being curious about their mom's eyeliner. Mona started shaving her legs as a teen, justifying to her parents that it was for athletic performance. Mona remembered that at home they had some conversations about **LGBTQ rights**. However, he added that religious beliefs seemed to limit those conversations. On one occasion, their parents brought up a conversation about the possibility of Mona having children in the future, and their parents asked Mona if they maybe were gay. Mona remembered becoming very defensive about that question and strongly denying it because of deeply instilled religious beliefs. He later thought that he internalized shame and toxic masculinity as the result of living in a very rigid and conservative environment. She also echoed the sentiment that maternity gives mothers an extra sense to feel and understand their children, and that probably her mother knew more about Mona than she thought. At school, Mona was often bullied, but they indicated that it was not because of their feminine-coded mannerisms or suppressed identities. The constant bullying was intolerable for Mona; he fought back, getting in trouble because his perpetrators accused him of planning to bring a gun to school. The school district classified **zir** as being a threat to other children and pushed them to a community middle school for students with behavioral issues. There was a "trial" and the school district requested that the high school district honor their decision for a 1-year punishment even though it was out of their jurisdiction. The high school district honored it. Luckily at the school **zie** reintegrated into there was an academic counselor whom Mona mentioned: "*Me salvó la vida*" (He saved my life) during very hard times when zie also felt depressed. The academic counselor came from the same town and studied at both Berkeley and Harvard. He encouraged students to access higher education to get involved in the community and apply to prestigious schools. Following zir's counselor's advice, Mona started working as a volunteer in a local hospital and zie started dating Estrella. Mona described Estrella as someone from a middle-class Catholic family, and she attended a local Catholic school. Estrella and Mona dated for 7 years on and off, even though they ended up going to different colleges.

Mona was accepted to a UC far from her town, and she started double majoring in aerospace and mechanical engineering and minoring in Spanish. During their freshman year, they mentioned escaping from the trauma at home. He also described not "**coming out**" yet to anyone, behaving as bien *macho* and as a "lady's man" and performing his masculinity with his girlfriends in what he recalled as codependent relationships. Mona stated that zie was repressing and having a distorted image of **zirself**. Her mother's health continued to deteriorate, and Mona withdrew from the university with intentions of taking care of her. Mona ended up on academic probation that year. He then went back home to take care of his mother who suffered from renal agenesis and diabetes. Mona's parents were no longer together; their mother was already separated from her partner due to his multiple affairs and other disputes. Mona's mother died that year, and Mona's stepfather a few months after that. Mona worked in town, and he started to socialize and make new friends. On one occasion, zie was invited to a party where there were some of zir coworker's gay friends, and Mona also met a trans woman for the first time. She stated that she felt very uneasy, finding her weird due to what Mona described as her internalized shame and religious beliefs. Years later, Mona considered that encounter as very revealing of their process integrating their **androgyny**. Mona spent 2 and a half years back at home before going back to UC to continue with his studies. Mona shared that when Trump took over the administration, as a DACA recipient, zie panicked over the fear of being deported, and they considered marrying zir girlfriend. Mona stated that later she disregarded this idea because she considered it very selfish.

Eventually, they broke up because Mona cheated on her with a coworker. Mona stated that she felt justified because at the time she "felt so betrayed by her saying no to marrying [her] after going through so much together." Mona started attending therapy because of the several "super toxic" and abusive relationships that followed. Mona started attending therapy and initiating her transition from what she described as a masculine cisgender body into a more feminine archetype and presentation. As Mona mentioned, this needs to be navigated carefully on how trans women are perceived. The rhetoric that trans women are trapped in men's bodies is not only wrong but also problematic and dangerous. Mona stated that she managed to start hormonal treatment under their insurance. However, zie was disappointed that only one doctor was specialized in transgender care. As a trans woman, Mona started to experience life at UC very differently; in some spaces, he felt safe, in others very unsafe since often people stared at them. Zie had to face and encounter rejection in classroom settings. She also mentioned that on several occasions her identities felt oppressed when she had to ask for help from teaching assistants and professors who were unwilling to address them with their correct pronouns. Mona spoke out in class on one occasion, and they ended up at the judicial affairs office, as zie mentioned because "no soy *pendeja*" and "I don't take any shit." Fortunately, the judicial affairs staff member's coworker was the former director of the LGBTQIA center on campus, and they helped Mona. Mona also shared how supported she felt at the AB540 and Undocumented Center, the LGBTQIA center, and the groups that she attended. Mona stated that as a Brown trans woman, they feel more comfortable around **POC LGBTQ**, zir undocumented peers, and **non-POC LGBTQ** folx.

Mona stated that his future after graduation is still unclear. They came out to their family in the United States and Mexico. She mentioned that she has a very good relationship with a couple of cousins who live in Mexico. Zie is also considering going back to her town in the Central Valley as their mentor did, but he stated that this would be an uphill battle. Additionally, her DACA status limits her choices, and she is considering applying for asylum. At UC, she feels supported but somehow alienated from academia due to some concerns of performative inclusiveness. In terms of intimate relationships, Mona brought up her uncertainty yet openness for future partners. Mona has openly stated that they are **pansexual**. As Mona shared *un anarquismo de género no haría de mal*, gender anarchism would not be a bad thing. Zie is a Mona Lisa of the 21st century in the United States, painted by the colors of the queer Mexican flag that zie has in zir room. Zie is a Mona Lisa of the borderlands; zie represents hybridity, as UndocuQueer, as Mexicanx, as Chicanx as all and beyond because as Mona stated zie embraces all identities. They are all in one, as they said: *Lo mío es la fusión* (My thing is fusion). Indeed, Mona's *testimonio* shows their extraordinary resilience despite all the barriers that her intersectionality creates.

Intersectionality and Ecological Realities for LGBTQ Latinx Individuals and Families

The ecological realities of Latinx LGBTQ as members of three marginalized communities on the basis of ethnicity, gender, and sexuality result in an increased risk of experiencing multiple systems of oppression and barriers. For instance, LGBTQ Latinx immigrants are often in need of comprehensive services that cover legal, health, employment, and educational access and that are culturally and linguistically competent (Gruberg et al., 2018). The inequality suffered by LGBTQ Latinx involves barriers in accessing educational and working opportunities, experiencing discrimination against their ethnicity, **sexuality,** and **gender**. It is well reported that minorities in the United States experience high rates of harassment and alarming hate crimes perpetrated against them. The Pulse nightclub shooting in 2016 in Orlando, Florida, during Latin night is one example of a hate crime perpetrated against LGBTQ and Latinx individuals (Torres, 2016). Individuals with intersectional minority identities are some of the most vulnerable to those attacks and often fear reporting hate incidents or seeking help from institutions. The concept of intersectionality developed by Crenshaw (1989) captures how minorities in the United States identify with multiple intersecting identities, which influence their positionalities and power in the United States.

Scholars have pointed out the need for queer intersectional family theory coming from the "borderlands" to better attend to the lived experiences of LGBQ Latinx (Acosta, 2018). In addition, there is a great need for clinicians who are culturally responsive, racially conscious of marginalized identities, systemic inequities shaping client's lives (Adames et al., 2018). For instance, Morales (1989) developed the model of sexual identity formation for minority queer and gays as an alternative to Anglo models of the "coming out" process. This model captures the integration of multiple identities and the particular realities of LGBTQ Latinx where culture, community, and family are integrated. The importance of family as a support system and protective factor is prevalent among Latinx, and for LGBTQ Latinx "coming out" in the context of their families is more complicated than, for instance, LGBTQ individuals from individualistic cultures. Latinxs may be marginalized from their families and communities, which are both critical sources of support, especially for immigrants (Espín, 1993). Clinicians lacking cultural knowledge and sensitivity may neglect to consider those sources of support and invalidate LGBTG Latinx cultural values, their struggles, or their hesitation "to come out." As Espín (2012) notes, Latinas who are lesbians, transgender, queer, or questioning often feel torn between maintaining a connection with family members who are not accepting of their sexual identity or losing the extended family support. Likewise, queer Latinxs must negotiate the racism prevalent in queer White communities, where their sexual identity may be affirmed but they may be discriminated based on language, culture, and/or color.

Literature and research addressing LGBTQ Latinx from an ecological and intersectionality framework are still very limited. Several reports and publications generated from different governmental and nonprofit organizations on LGBTQ Latinx have incorporated those ecological considerations and call for the importance of understanding and supporting their intersectional identities. They also emphasize the significance of advocating, informing, and providing resources for LGBTQ Latinx and their families. Their guidelines suggest, among others, being intentional in creating inclusive and safe spaces for all identities, have those spaces available at work placements and schools, providing culturally and linguistically appropriate support to LGBTQ individuals and their families, and promoting ally training and policy changes. Finally, these resources call for training health and mental health clinicians to deliver adequate services for LGBTQ Latinx (Human Rights Campaign, 2018). In author Torreiro-Casal's clinical experiences working with queer families and LGBTQ Latinx individuals at community mental health clinics and university counseling centers, she learned that their lived experiences and realities were very different from the cultural norms and expectations of U.S. society or the realities encountered by other non-Latinx LGBTQ clients. Some of these realities are illustrated in this book. For instance, in Chapter 2, the case of Mariluz and Eva documents the "coming out" process of a couple as a life process, happening in the context of their complex realities (Flores, 2013). Their powerful story captures intersectional and ecological realities where identity, immigration, legal system, political activism, gender issues, family dynamics, intergenerational issues, trauma, rejection, and historical aspects all collide. Mariluz and Eva's case illustrates different intersecting realities in their "coming out" process. For Mariluz, as an immigrant woman married with two children, the "coming out" process meant difficult decisions that affected her, her children, and her relationship with her partner and ex-husband. Mariluz and Eva's love and beliefs showed their strength to overcome the difficulties. They encountered a challenging situation, fighting for their rights during a time there was a legal vacuum on LGBTQ rights and limited legal protection. Luckily, their children showed acceptance and understanding, showing how new generations of Latinx children may be more accepting and seem to have more progressive views than previous generations. On the contrary, Mariluz's ex-husband's rage brought the family into a turmoil situation. His reactions reflect gender and power dynamics in couples as well as how conservative beliefs may thwart an individual's freedom to express their identities and love, which can be cast as nonnormative or "deviant." Furthermore, Mariluz's mother represents another generation in the family who went through her own process in accepting the relationship. In this case, the multiple Latinx identities and the intersection of classism, skin color, and privilege shaped her acceptance of this new relationship. Mariluz and Eva are some of those first Latinx LGBTQ couples who are an example of the complexity of being LGBTQ Latinx and coming out for their families and society. The couple described next encountered similar and unique ecological and intersecting realities. They were both immigrants with undocumented status, they both had a previous history of domestic violence and abuse, and they both had children from those previous relationships. Maria and Ana lived their realities in the "shadows," navigating systems, surviving, and finding meaning to their existence as a couple.

Author Torreiro-Casal worked with Maria and Ana at a community health clinic that primarily offered services to parents and residents from a school district in the South Bay Area of Northern California. The clinic offered a comprehensive model of delivering services to the community, including insurance for undocumented clients, medical services, and counseling and parental support through different programs. Maria and Ana migrated from Mexico and attended couple's therapy as former domestic violence and sexually assaulted survivors. They both identified as women, they were both undocumented, and they both worked in the cleaning sector. In therapy sessions, they shared some of the abuses they both experienced in their previous relationships and at their work placements. Maria had two children; the oldest was born after being raped by a stranger in Mexico, where he was still living with Maria's mother. Ana was previously married to a male and had two children from that abusive relationship. They expressed that they were two women loving each other, but in session they never identified as lesbians and never expressed the need for "coming out" to society. They were both Catholic, but in therapy they never brought up religion as an issue that interfered with their love, and they never shared any concerns about their respective family's rejection. In fact, when Maria's mother had the opportunity to visit them in the United States, they openly shared the relationship with her. Author Torreiro-Casal states, "In my role as a therapist, I did not work on convincing them 'to come out,' but I tried to understand the realities they faced and respect their personal choices in describing and defining themselves. In one therapy session, they shared that two individuals were coming regularly to their house to talk about faith and the Mormon Church. I asked Maria and Ana if those visitors were aware that they were a couple. They shared that these visitors knew about their relationship. However, they told Maria and Ana that their situation could be easily forgiven by God and be solved with strong faith. Maria and Ana shared that they had no intention to give up Catholicism. In addition, they stated that they were very happy with these two visitors coming to their house because besides talking about religion, they were helping with cleaning and organizing the house. I consider this couple an example of resistance, in their own terms and within their own realities as undocumented women, survivors of domestic and sexual violence. They lived their life as they wished within the limitations of their migratory status." This couple's relationship illustrates how they managed to survive and how they healed from their past in the context of the new family that they formed.

In consideration of other intersectional identities, recent research pointed out the dual identities of individuals self-identified as **UndocuQueer**, those who are undocumented and DACA recipients who identified as queer (Gruberg et al., 2018). In author Torreiro Casal's clinical post-doctoral fellowship at UC Davis's AB540 and Undocumented Center, she worked with students who shared their UndocuQueer identities and their unique challenges navigating systems, as well the lack of services sensitive to their complex realities and multiple identities. Indeed, more research and scholarly work need to be expanded to capture the multiplicity of the LGBTQ Latinx experience, including Indigenous conceptualizations of gender and sexuality. For instance, LGBTQ Latinx heritage and views can be traced back to pre-Columbian times before colonization and Christianity. Sexual practices, acceptance of homosexuality, and same-sex relations are well documented in the Maya civilization and other Indigenous groups (Sigal, 2003). Many of those Indigenous populations in Latin America have traditions of two-spirit people considered to be a third gender. Nonbinary individuals are often celebrated and respected in those communities, for instance the **Muxe** people in Oaxaca (Mirandé, 2017). Many Latinx individuals come from or belong to families with Indigenous roots who may have different conceptualizations of gender (two spirit) and sexuality as well, thus showing more acceptance of LGBTQ individuals than other families. Additionally, the representation of LGBTQ Latinx through history and media has evolved. For instance, Latinx artists and writers like Frida Kahlo, Alex Sanchez, Julio Salgado, and Ricky Martin have shared their stories and intersectional perspectives through their work. Chicana and Latina lesbian writers (Anzaldúa, 1987; Espín, 2012; Perez, 2015; Trujillo, 2003) have expanded the literature on gender, sexuality, and cultural expectations from a Chicanx/Latinx perspective. A more comprehensive socioecological, historical, and intersectional view on LGBTQ Latinx from a Latinx psychological paradigm also needs to be expanded to inform clinical practices and programs that serve LGBTQ Latinx.

LGBTQ Latinx: Religion and Faith

According to the Pew Hispanic Center and Pew Forum on Religion & Public Life on religions believes among Latinx (Pew Research Center, 2007) almost 68% of Latinx identified as Catholic; for many LGBTQ Latinx, reconciling sexuality, religion, and culture may not be possible. However, the letter to the Catholic bishops on the pastoral care of homosexual persons (Ratzinger & Bovone, 1986) claimed that the fundamental human rights of homosexual persons must be defended, eliminating any forms of injustice, oppression, or violence against them. However, the Catholic Church's position on homosexuality is still not accepting and inclusive of LGBTQ identities. This position has implications for LGBTQ Latinx who identify as Catholics or their families who may reject LGBTQ Latinx family members due to their religious views. At the community level, some initiatives directed toward the LGBTQ and Latinx community have taken place, for instance the "A La Familia" initiative is a comprehensive, multifaceted, and bilingual program geared toward Latinx Christian communities in the United States. This program aims to facilitate conversations around the intersections of faith, sexual orientation, gender identity, ethnicity, and family. It involves community and faith leaders who wish to engage Latinx participation in civic discourse, leading to LGBTQ inclusion (De La Torre et al., n.d). Indeed, religious beliefs may interfere with the family acceptance and coming out process of many LGBTQ Latinx. The guilt or *culpa* embedded in cultural and religious beliefs may stop LGBTQ Latinx to come out. Additionally, they may fear being rejected by their family members and communities, which often are their only sources of support.

In our classes, students bring out some of their lived experiences. Some shared how their families rejected them because of their religious beliefs. This rejection forced them to find other sources of support or what they considered their nonblood-related new families. In class discussions, students who openly identify as LGBTQ Latinx and consider themselves religious claim their right to profess their religion and venerate, for instance, the Virgin of Guadalupe. In class presentations, students who attend art classes at our Chicana/o department at UC Davis or are part of "El Taller del Arte del Nuevo Amanecer" share their work with other students and talk about their identities through the representation of "queer" versions of the Virgin of Guadalupe. These queer visual representations of significant icons of the Catholic religion created by our self-identified LGBTQ Latinx students integrate multiple identities and constitute new forms of religious syncretism. Ultimately, we witness how these spaces and artistic tools help Latinx LGBTQ students deconstruct religious icons, represent intersectionality, contribute to de-marginalizing LGBTQ Latinx individuals, and turn out to be healing practices. The following *testimonio* or narrative captures the fear of potentially being rejected by family members.

Ana

In her words: I have yet to tell anyone in my immediate family about my sexual orientation, and I don't think I ever will in fear of rejection. Whenever I overhear their comments on same-sex couples, my heart breaks a little more each time since they don't know their own daughter is bisexual. As I hear those comments, I feel myself getting disrespected even though it is not personally about me. Their argument to support their beliefs is "God created a man and woman for a reason. He didn't create two women or two men." I dislike not being able to be myself around my family, but I would dislike it even more to possibly being not accepted if I do tell them the truth. On the other hand, I do not mind that my peers or friends know about my sexuality since I do not hold that fear of rejection strongly. This shows how family plays such an important role in the life of an

LGBTQIA Latinx. If I do decide to share my sexuality with my family, I am debating when that would be. I always had the idea that I would only tell them if I get in a serious relationship with someone of the same sex. However, I am worried the more time I wait to tell them, the more they could feel betrayed or feel lied to for so long. This could cause even more tension as they have to both adjust to the news of my sexual orientation while meeting my significant other. Therefore, I know it would be a better choice to tell them before I become serious with anyone, but I am very hesitant and nervous about doing so. Many people do not realize that "coming out" could be exhausting as it is not a singular moment but rather a series of moments. LGBTQIA people find themselves explaining their sexuality every time they meet new people. Therefore, coming out of the closet is not a Band-Aid one rips off once but rather repeatedly. I wish someday homosexuality would be normalized in a way that heterosexuality is. There should come a day where same-sex couples will not get stared at or judged for holding hands or kissing in public as straight couples do. That way there wouldn't be a need for people to necessarily "come out" anymore since it would be a norm in society.

"Coming Out" in the Context of Latinx Families

For LGBTQ Latinx, the coming out process can be more challenging to navigate than other ethnic groups in the United States. LGBTQ Latinx youth may experience more burdens than other LGBTQ youth and may not have the same access and choices as non-Latinx LGBTQ due to immigration status, SES, systemic barriers, and health disparities. LGBTQ Latinx also have to navigate and negotiate different identities and prioritize, in many cases, the health of the family to their own and often feel as if they have to choose between their cultural community and sexual community (Flores, 2013). The coming out process also presents generational differences and religious considerations, being more compli-cated for those who belong to religious groups (Espín, 1987) as discussed. Furthermore, one of the most difficult problems facing LGBTQ Latinx youth is the persistent negative responses of their families to their LGBTQ identity despite the increasing acceptance by some family members (Kane et al., 2012). Therapists and those in the helping professions need to contextualize and understand the unique experiences of LGBTQ Latinx youth and how important families are for Latinx individuals before "advising" or "encouraging" them to come out.

As faculty members perceived as allies, we have been, at times, one of the first people to whom disclosure is made by LGBTQ students. Likewise, as clinicians, it has been our privilege to support clients who are questioning or who are exploring the potential impact of coming out to family and family members attending therapy to support their family members. Frequently, our clients and students share how alienated they felt at school settings, in counseling sessions, or with educators and providers who were unaware of the meaning and complexity of coming out for LGBTQ Latinxs. Latinx families may also have difficulties in understanding their children's coming out process, and this can be further exacerbated by language barriers and limited access to information. Further, often LGBTQ terminology used in different languages vary, making it impossible to find equivalent words to describe LGBTQ identities and experiences without sounding insulting; for instance words used by Latinx families may refer to gay and lesbian using terms as *joto, jota, mariposa*, or **homosexual** (Del Castillo & Güido, 2014).

In working with LGBTQ Latinx and their families, often parents disclosed feeling guilty or unfamiliar with the coming out process. Furthermore, they may have a limited understanding of what it means to identify with a particular term or multiple terms to refer to sexual and gender orientation as well as sexual practices and preferences. In our classes, college students share stories of parental and family rejection or experiencing families who initially rejected them but later showed unconditional love and, in some cases, became allies to support other Latinx families with LGBTQ members. Indeed, very few studies have addressed how to work with Latinx families from a strength-based perspective considering their cultural values and beliefs and building on the importance of family bonds (Abreu et al., 2020). Schools also play a fundamental role in supporting LGBTQ Latinx youth and their families. The National School Climate Survey (Kosciw et al., 2018) included some recommendations for schools to develop more inclusive school environments by having supportive educators and LGBTQ-inclusive curriculum and sex education and promoting student activism and parent advocacy.

A.'s Testimonio

This *testimonio* is from a former undergraduate student who conducted an undergraduate honors thesis on LGBTQ Latinx and HIV. We call the student "A." Their preferred pronouns are he/him/they/theirs. A. shared that conducting research in this area was relevant for him/them. A. stated that faith, cultural aspects, family relationships, and internalized expectations shaped his/their sexuality and identity. A. shared that "being closeted" does not allow queer and **trans youth** to explore their sexual orientation until later in life and often in a "hypersexual way." A. also stated that LGBTQ Latinx might internalize **heterosexism** through the curriculum at schools around gender that are based on a binary model. A. considered that these ecological and intersecting realities created a "disassociating" experience and contributed to A.'s health outcomes and the health outcomes of other LGBT Latinx experiencing similar circumstances. A. is currently working in a nonprofit on health prevention for LGBT Latinx and minorities. The following testimony shows different stages of the "coming out" process for a Latinx LGBTQ college student raised as Catholic.

In his/their words: I always had the top bunk while my elder brother had the bottom bunk. After getting ready for bed, I would climb all the way up and put aside my stuffed animals. After the nightly conversations with my brother, I'd stare straight up at the ceiling and pray. Our Father, Hail Mary, Glory Be and finally a short prayer expressing gratitude to God and asking for a blessing. I always began with "Dear God, please bless my mom and dad, brothers, *tías, tíos* and cousins. My **nino** and **nina** (godparents) and everybody else in the world." The last blessing I had always asked for was for myself, and it was to not be gay. Some nights involved tears and some nights involved holding them back so that my older brother would not hear me crying. I didn't want to be gay and wished God would take the sin that I was ashamed of away from me. I felt like I couldn't control my thoughts and behaviors and wondered why my God made me the way I was. While my peers were whispering about my sexuality and making assumptions, I put up defenses that involved sexualizing girls so that they would stop. As I got a little older, my mother showed my four brothers and I a movie about a teenage couple having an unexpected pregnancy. She told me this is what would happen if I had unprotected sex with a girl. The idea of a baby and sex with a girl scared me, and I knew I had to avoid both of these things. However, in order to avoid being called gay, I forced myself to participate in sexual activity with my girlfriend. It damaged me emotionally, but it was worth it to me during that moment in time. During high school, I knew I wasn't straight and started to accept it when I started having relations with one of my friends. While having a girlfriend, I started having sexual relations with another guy and had never thought of using protection because I couldn't get him pregnant. We kept our relationship a secret for all of high school. By the time I got to college, I knew I was gay but was left with feelings of loneliness and no experience of what it was like to be with other guys romantically. I started engaging in hypersexual behavior while trying to balance my studies. It was very exciting for me. I was desired by so many men and started learning my likes and dislikes. This meant I could also freely explore my gender especially because I was away from my family.

My first year of college ended and I returned to my family's house for the summer. One day, I found myself lying on the emergency room table unable to eat or drink anything. My mom was next to me very concerned about my health since I had lost almost 10 pounds in a week. Even though my mom was next to me, I asked the nurse for an HIV test. To my surprise, she scoffed and told me it would have to be done on my own time. Her words stung me and made me embarrassed that I asked for one, especially while in front of my mom. I wondered what she had thought. I wondered if she thought I was going to hell for loving other men. She knew I was gay but asked me to not talk about it. I felt isolated from the care I was receiving and the person I loved most. A month after I returned to school, I listened to a voicemail that asked me to come in and talk about my test results. Immediately after, I called my best friend and told them that I thought that I had HIV. There were only two people I had ever had unprotected sex with, but I knew there could have been a chance I contracted it. My heart ached because I had just learned what PrEP was. Wondering how I contracted HIV became a starting point in my life filled with disassociation and the worsening of psychological symptoms that I had previously experienced in my life.

Recommendations for Working With Latinx LGBTQ and Family Members

LGBTQ Latinx communities and families present their own particular realities, as we have explored in this chapter. Indeed, in working with Latinx LGBTQ and their family members, ecological realities and intersecting identities need to be addressed with more research and guidelines to provide the appropriate support for these families. For instance, it has been reported that parents of LGBTQ youth experience emotional reactions that include anger, sadness, despair, feelings of guilt, and even depression when their children "come out" (Phillips & Ancis, 2008). The experiences of Latinx parents and families with LGBTQ children are minimally explored in the literature. In addition, the available materials or programs delivered to LGBTQ Latinx and families often do not fully capture and address their ecological realities. Information is simply translated into Spanish without considering the population's demographic and cultural characteristics. This perpetuates the gap rather than building a bridge to reach out to these members. The psychological work in providing services to LGBTQ Latinx and their families should incorporate a Latinx perspective, considering their values, intergenerational differences, immigration narratives and status, language of preference, gender dynamics, communication styles, levels of oppression, and other historical and geographical factors. It is also vital to utilize culturally appropriate tools and promote the resilience that these families already have. The delivery of services, the ones delivering the services, and the reception of those services may vary based on geographical locations, characteristics of the Latinx families, and their access to those. Coming out is a process not only for LGBTQ Latinx but also for their families. The different phases and processes encompass psychoeducational aspects, understanding of individual members' process, individual fears, guilt, religious beliefs, available support systems, and safety issues. Considering families from a strengths-based perspective and their protective factors, including their cohesion, solidarity among members, collectivism, and other values, as well their resilience and networks, could benefit this process (Falicov, 2014). We also need to consider different venues for establishing communication between family members and the important role of those family allies who can facilitate those conversations and initiate the acceptance of other LGBTQ family members and their identities and sexual orientations. Parents can also seek advice and guidance on sexuality and identity at school settings where their children attend schools.

Families also should seek services at organizations that are congruent with their cultural values and offer a safe space for them. An example of a nonprofit organization providing services for LGBTQ Latinx and their families is called *Somos Familia*, located at East Bay in Northern California. It is an example of a comprehensive model that is inclusive and culturally and linguistically sensitive. This agency offers online materials and resources congruent with the needs of the LGBTQ Latinx community and their families. For instance, on their website, they have a list of resources available to help LGBTQ families and communities. This organization has created a series of **novelas** or videos addressing issues on LGBTQ Latinx coming out to their families and other relevant topics. They also included *testimonios* of parents in Spanish and English as well as other resources for families on how to initiate conversations, how to seek help, and how to become an ally. Other initiatives to involve and support LGBTQ Latinx families include providing information at places that are accessible to those families, for instance schools, local organizations, and local markets.

Summary

In this chapter we offer some of the uniqueness of the LGBTQ Latinx and their families. We have addressed the lack of research and literature on the topic, the different LGBTQ Latinx groups, and the lack of services and specialized programs for them. We have also reviewed the most prevalent issues affecting the LGBTQ Latinx community: immigration, linguistic barriers, health disparities, discrimination, and difficulties navigating systems. We have described intersecting and ecological realities and future directions for supporting LGBTQ Latinx and their families.

HOMEWORK ASSIGNMENT

1. Reflect on your sexual and gender identity. How do you think those identities have evolved throughout your life and how do you think others accept your identities?
2. What are some of the ecological and intersecting realities when addressing the coming out process for LGBTQ Latinx reflected in the chapter's testimonies?
3. What are some of the considerations in working and supporting LGBTQ Latinx and their families?

KEY TERMS

Androgyny: The combination of masculine and feminine characteristics into an ambiguous form. Androgyny may be expressed with regard to biological sex, gender identity, gender expression, or sexual identity. When androgyny refers to mixed biological sex characteristics in humans, it often refers to intersex people: a person with a gender that is both masculine and feminine or in between masculine and feminine.

Bible Belt: An informal region in the Southern United States in which socially conservative evangelical Protestantism plays a strong role in society and politics and church attendance across the denominations is generally higher than the nation's average.

Bisexual: A sexual identity whose primary sexual and affectional orientation is toward people of the same and other genders or toward people regardless of their gender.

Come out or coming out: Coming out is the process of voluntarily sharing one's sexual orientation and/or gender identity with others. This process is unique for each individual, and there is no right or wrong way to come out.

Gay: Often used to refer to a sexual identity, lifestyle, and same-sex erotic preference.

Gender: A social construct used to classify a person as a man, woman, or some other identity. Fundamentally different from the sex one is assigned at birth.

Gender nonconforming: People who do not subscribe to societal expectations of typical gender expressions or roles. The term is more commonly used to refer to gender expression (how one behaves, acts, and presents themselves to others) as opposed to gender identity (one's internal sense of self).

Hate crime: A criminal offense against a person or property, motivated in whole or in part by an offender's bias against a race, religion, disability, sexual orientation, ethnicity, gender, or gender identity. Victims of hate crimes can include institutions, religious organizations, and government entities as well as individuals.

Heterosexism: The assumption that all people are or should be heterosexual. Heterosexism excludes the needs, concerns, and life experiences of lesbian, gay, bisexual, and queer people while it gives advantages to heterosexual people.

Homosexual: Term used to describe a sexual orientation in which a person feels physically and emotionally attracted to people of the same gender. Historically, it was a term used to pathologize gay and lesbian people.

Joto/jota: Spanish terms used to refer to LGBTQ people with an associated derogatory connotation.

Lesbian: A woman whose primary sexual and affectional orientation is toward people of the same gender. However, some nonbinary people also identify as lesbians.

LGBTQ: An abbreviation for lesbian, gay, bisexual, transgender, and queer or questioning.

LGBTQ rights: Includes legal and human rights for individuals to live their sexual and gender identity openly. Many places around the world present a huge variety of legal rights, for instance gay marriage, recognition of the third gender or lack of those, with legislation in same countries threatening the life of those individuals even with the death penalty.

Macho: Associated with those who express their masculinity in an aggressive or hypersexualized way.

Mariposa: Meaning butterfly, it is used as a derogatory term to refer to LGBTQ identities.

Millennials: People who belong to the generation of people born in the 1980s or 1990s.

Muxe: An individual part of the Indigenous Zapotec group in Mexico who identifies with a third gender identity.

Niño/niña: Girl or boy in Spanish.

Nonbinary: A gender identity and experience that embraces a full universe of expressions and ways of being that resonate for an individual, moving beyond the male/female gender binary. It may be an active resistance to binary gender expectations and/or an intentional creation of new unbounded ideas of self within the world.

Novelas: The direct translation is novels but the term refers to Latinx soap operas.

Pansexual: Term used to describe people who have romantic, sexual, or affectional desire for people of all genders and sexes.

Pendeja/o: A Spanish profanity word with multiple meanings depending on the context; one translation could be "dumbass" or "asshole" in many situations, though it carries an extra implication of willful incompetence or innocent gullibility that is ripe for others to exploit.

POC: An acronym used to denote people (or a person) of color.

Pronouns: Linguistic tools used to refer to someone in the third person who identifies as nonbinary. Examples are they/them/theirs, zie/hir/hirs, she/her/hers, he/him/his.

Queer: A term that is also used as gay for an umbrella term encompassing the LGBTQ community. Not all LGBTQ are comfortable with the use of this term for it was used as a derogatory term because one definition of queer is abnormal or strange.

Questioning: The process of exploring one's own gender identity, gender expression, and/or sexual orientation. Some people may also use this term to name their identity within the LGBTQIA community.

Same-sex couple: A relationship between people of the same sex and can take many forms, from romantic and sexual to nonromantic homosocially close relationships. The term is primarily associated with gay and lesbian relationships.

Same-sex marriage: The institutionalized recognition of such relationships in the form of a marriage.

Sexual identity: How one thinks of oneself in terms of to whom one is romantically or sexually attracted.

Sexuality: Components of a person that include their biological sex, sexual orientation, gender identity, sexual practices, and so on.

Social capital: The networks of relationships among people who live and work in a particular society, enabling that society to function effectively.

Testimonio(s): First-person narration of socially significant experiences in which the narrative voice is that of a typical or extraordinary witness or protagonist who may represent others who have lived through similar situations and who have rarely given written expression to them.

Tías/Tíos: Aunts and uncles in Spanish.

Trans youth: Underage transgender people.

Transgender: A term used to describe people whose gender identity differs from the sex they were assigned at birth.

UndocuQueer: Term used by people who are undocumented immigrants and identify as part of the LGBTQIA community.

Zie/zir/zirs/zirself: Gender-neutral pronouns that are used instead of "she" or "he" and could be someone's pronouns. It is also acceptable to use singular they (they/them/their/themselves) instead of (he/his/him/himself, she/hers/her/herself) when referring to someone who has not expressed a clear pronoun choice.

9

(Re)building Healthy Families

In the preceding chapters we have described the multiple challenges that migration, acculturation, and discrimination in all its forms can present to Latinx families. We have also reviewed several theoretical models that inform clinical work with Latinx families in distress, specifically Celia Falicov's MECA model developed in the 1990s and refined and updated in 2014, Ivan Boszormenyi-Nagy's contextual intergenerational model, Sal Minuchin's structural model, and the just therapy and narrative approaches developed in Australia and New Zealand. Although the latter methods of understanding and treating families were not specifically developed for Latinxs, as was MECA, they have applicability because they take into consideration the context of families and the threats to family well-being that emerge from injustice and disparities.

In this chapter the focus is working with families who want to heal from injustice that may be historically rooted and intergenerationally transmitted or from present-day policies, such as immigration laws and discriminatory practices that reflect colonial, patriarchal, and hegemonic views. The first section provides an overview of clinical work with trauma survivors; by utilizing a case example of a family affected by war, intimate partner violence, and histories of genocide, we underscore the importance of mobilizing systems of support and identifying culturally appropriate healing practices. The next section offers narrative-based strategies for rescripting narratives of pain in clinical work with couples in distress. The third section offers strategies to rebalance intergenerational accounts in families affected by substance abuse and violence. Lastly, a discussion of the importance of promoting justice within the family closes the chapter.

Healing From Trauma

Amoridolor, a term coined in the 1970s by Chicanxs in Texas, reflects the fact that many of us love so deeply we "feel the pain from the suffering of our generations" as well as the Earth, writes Inés Hernández Ávila (2014, p. xiii–xx). Indeed the pain created by historical oppression and injustice may be coded into our DNA and influence how we experience and deal with contemporary trauma.

This *amoridolor* may manifest as impatience, despair, depression, *nervios*. We may cope through prayer, avoidance of the memories, dissociation (separation of mind/body/spirit), and become susceptible to outrage and rage that explodes into violence. We may also feel that we are unlucky and undeserving of being loved in respectful and healthy ways. After she was raped at a college campus by another Chicano, a young woman wept and stated, "I am one more, one more in the long chain of victimized women in my family. It goes back to when the *españoles* came. *Siempre seremos las chingadas* (We will always be the violated ones)." Her despair was augmented by the knowledge that her victimizer was a *carnal*, a "brother." She understood that he too was a victim "of the system," which made it all the more difficult to report the crime.

As stated in earlier chapters, historical trauma weighs on the generations that follow, creating risk factors for family injustice and individual-collective suffering. In collectivist cultures, when one suffers, everyone feels the pain. Thus, individual pain reverberates throughout the family system. While individual family members may respond differently to the trauma, to varying degrees everyone experiences it. Therefore, healing often best occurs in family and in community; this was at the root of the *cultura cura* (culture heals) consciousness of the 1970s and 1980s that informed the movement to provide culturally attuned and responsive services (Flores, 2013).

Central to healing from intergenerational trauma is to *know* the history in order to *understand el por qué* (why things happened) and then to *change* the legacies. In our work with families we mobilize storytelling. We invite the adults to tell the story of how they became a couple/family and then each tells the other and their offspring how their own families of origin came to be. If grandparents or other elders are available, they too are invited to share their stories. In this way the younger generations begin to learn not only their family's history but also their cultural/national/racial/class origins. Then together they do a family tree. The genealogy is begun in the office but continued at home. We usually tell families that every family system has a genealogist and invite them to inquire who in their extended family holds that role. This is particularly helpful when the family in treatment knows little of their origins. Someone always knows something and is waiting to be asked. If long-term disconnections have occurred, We invite the family, especially if they have U.S.-educated children, to do some research about the town, city, and country, from which their ancestors came. We invite them to read novels and hold family meetings to share what they have learned. In this way, communication increases, elders feel valued because they are included, parents feel their history is validated, and younger ones become more rooted into their culture of origin, which is an antidote to the psychological homeless caused by discrimination and racial oppression in the United States.

By analyzing their genealogy, family members begin to visually observe when the "problems" or injustices began among their ancestors. They also can identify patterns of resilience. If suddenly someone begins to manifest problematic drinking, the family is asked to hypothesize what might have happened to cause it. Family members become researchers and chroniclers of their own family history. Key questions are explored: Who has held the role of identified patient in earlier generations? Does the current holder of that role manifest similarities in birth order, gender, sexuality, and color to those who previously held those roles? In families that have migrated, I ask family members to identify migration-related roles. Who is the mourner? Who is the over- or underacculturator? Who in the family is expected to continue the legacies of success and of suffering? As the MECA model suggests, family dysfunction may be related to changes in meaning systems' post-migration losses, mourned and not, as a result of leaving the homeland, intergenerational and value conflicts as a result of migration; the loss of cultural niche and difficulties forming or integrating into a new one. These challenges are manifested primarily among immigrants while depression and anxiety disorders may be more prevalent among the children of immigrants (Flores, 2013; Sluzki, 1979).

The treatment goal is to make the invisible visible (which is a contextual therapy technique). In this way, family grand narratives or organizing principles are made visible to all. Often there is an "aha" moment, when the family members begin to make sense of previously puzzling family patterns or beliefs.

Author Flores states:

> "My mother had a saying that echoed throughout my childhood and adolescence: 'Once we were rich, once we were White, once we were French, but because men mess up everything they do, we are now poor and colored.' As I got older, I wanted to know what she meant by that. Her grandfather Antoine Perigault had migrated from France with his young wife in the late 1800s to work on building the Panama Canal. She quickly succumbed to malaria and died. He then met a young woman in Panama who was of German ancestry, Ana Nücher. They married and had two children, Alfonso and Antonia Perigault Nücher. Antoine and Ana gave their children Spanish versions of French names. Overtime Antonio became a successful business owner of bars and gambling houses. Antonia became educated and married an Afropanamanian man who became a famous writer. Alfonso worked in his father's businesses but had a penchant for drinking the profits and womanizing. He married a *mestiza/mulata* woman, Maria de las Mercedes Medina, whose father was a Spaniard and whose mother was Black and Indigenous. Alfonso carried his parents' unresolved migration traumas and histories of losses and abused alcohol. In an alcoholic state he was often violent. Some of my mother's childhood memories are of his rages, wherein he would destroy the sewing his wife had worked on to sell in order to help the family economy because Alfonso's drinking and gambling made him a poor provider. My mother cowered in fear, full of love and pain— *amoridolor*—for this man. My maternal grandmother was a strong woman who fought back against her husband's rage; but my mother became a sad, quiet, anxious child. Her parents' marriage was volatile; her parents often separated but quickly reconciled until her father died when my mother was 7 years old. My grandmother, Maria de las Mercedes Medina, had known nothing of the business and was left destitute. Therefore, she put my mother in convent school and worked full time to support herself and her two children, a 9-year-old boy who also went to work. Therefore, my mother grew up alone, mistreated by racist Spanish nuns who disliked poor children. Mother developed a grand narrative that men were not accountable and reliable. Therefore, women must study to be financially independent. She became a teacher and married young. She was unaware that her first husband, who fancied himself a poet, was also a gambler. After she had two sons with this man, she left him and went to live with her brother and his wife.

Author Flores continues:

As I grew older I called into question my mother's views of men because my father, her second husband, had been the perfect financial provider. It was not until I learned the story of Alfonso that I fully understood her views. But her grand narrative invisibly influenced my life decisions: with whom I partnered, how I lived my marriages, and how I left and was left by men I loved. Although I taught my children their family history, the power of the legacy has continued. My daughter married the son of a mixed-raced couple. My son-in-law's father is Afro-Caribbean and German. While my mother minimized her German and African roots, my grandchildren carry a German surname and are proud to be Afro-Latinas. They represent the racial tapestry of the Americas; the eldest looks Indigenous Mexican, like her mother and maternal grandfather. The middle child looks more Afro-Latina, like her paternal grandmother; the youngest, a boy, is the lightest of the three with golden curls. As they grow up in the United States, my grandchildren will undoubtedly face the colorism[1] that affects Latino families and is a direct legacy of conquest, colonization, and racial mixing.

"As a graduate student I studied my own family history to uncover the secrets and mysteries that had invisibly affected my generation. It became obvious to me why I had chosen psychology as a profession and how I had ended up working in substance abuse services and family violence programs: I have been trying to heal wounded men and thereby understand and exonerate the pain of my maternal grandfather. My life work has been with immigrant families and their children. This is a legacy of the *amoridolor* of my family.

"Both as an educator and a practicing psychologist I view the problems families present in treatment as rooted in historical legacies; consequently, understanding one's history is paramount in order to heal and to change dysfunctional patterns of behavior. Thus, in treating trauma I utilize primarily the contextual intergenerational model. As stated in earlier chapters, family problems must be understood through a contextual analysis of the families' historical realities, migration and its legacies, the particularities of an individual's experience, the psychological sequelae of the legacies, and the unique experiences of the family members, as well as how the individual gives meaning to their experience and historical realities. Likewise, it is also essential to understand the family's cocreated scripts and roles (mourner, overacculturator, etc.). I see family problems often as psychological manifestations of historical facts."

These psychological manifestations occur at both the individual and family system level. As noted in previous chapters, families in distress typically manifest parentification, triangulation, imbalanced levels of involvement (either cutoffs or overinvolvement), as well as cultural freezing and problems in adaptation to life cycle changes, migrations, separations, and so on. "Problems" often become visible after a life cycle transition, such as marriage, birth of a child, divorce, or death of a loved one. Moreover, trauma often is

---

1 Skin color in Latinx and other families of color is important. In some families White skin is preferred over Brown, Black or darker shades. Myriad terms are used in Spanish to denote colorism. Among Mexicans *huera* is used to refer to light-skinned people and is considered a compliment. *Morena* refers to brown skin and *prieta* to darker shades of brown. Discrimination on the basis of skin color is prevalent among Latinxs.

rooted in relational justice—exploitation, family or intimate partner violence, infidelity, and economic control. In turn relational injustice is rooted in legacies of miscegenation, oppression and pain, legacies of migration, imbalances in debits and merits, over- or underentitlement and destructive entitlement, and lack of reciprocity.

Thus the goal of treatment is first to understand the historical roots of the problem and how these legacies affect each and every family member; second, to address the individual needs of family members and promote their individual healing, particularly of the identified patient; third to encourage systemic change to improve family relations and create greater balance in debits and merits and promote reciprocity and to mobilize compassion and forgiveness within the family. Lastly, to promote *concientización* (consciousness raising) within the family so that through their actions and efforts at change a new legacy is created for future generations. Author Flores' work with the Luna family helps illustrate this approach.

Elba and Nestor Luna were a couple in their early 30s who sought therapy because Nestor was having "anger management issues." She had insisted on therapy as a condition to remain in the marriage. Elba is a U.S.-born third-generation Latina of mixed parentage. Her mother immigrated from Ecuador as a teenager with her mother and four sisters. She became an educator and married a second-generation Chicano Vietnam-era veteran. They had Elba but divorced because her father had "difficulty being married." Elba's father was a mental health professional. Elba's mother remarried "a very nice Peruvian man" who was also an immigrant. Elba also became educated and married an immigrant from El Salvador who was a political refugee and whose immigration status was pending.[2]

Since the early days of the marriage the couple had cultural and linguistic conflicts. Elba felt more comfortable speaking in English and Nestor preferred Spanish. He was very supportive of his wife's educational aspirations and career plans, partly because due to his forced migration he had been unable to pursue his studies. However, Elba felt unsupported, because in her view her husband had unrealistic expectations of her, which were culture and gender based. He was neat and liked an organized home. He could not tolerate the chaos that her piles of paper and children's toys created in their home. She did not prioritize having a clean home and felt that working, going to school, and parenting were enough work for one person to do. Although her husband helped with housework, he became frustrated when she did not keep up with his efforts at cleanliness and organization. He felt she did not respect him; she felt he did not understand her. They also had conflict because Nestor and his in-laws disagreed on parenting practices once their son was born.

Elba temporarily separated when during an argument Nestor punched the wall and made a hole. She became "terrified of his violence" and moved in with her parents. The separation from his son and wife was devastating for Nestor, who sought individual treatment for his "anger issues." They did not want to divorce. As a child of divorce, Elba did not want to end the marriage; she wanted him to change. She felt strongly that his behavior was unacceptable and that she needed to protect her son from his father's rigidity and aggression. After a few months, they reconciled and Nestor moved in with his wife. However, the conflicts regarding parenting amplified once they lived with the in-laws.

---

2   Nestor had applied through **the Nicaraguan Adjustment and Central American Relief Act,** or **NACARA,** a U.S. law passed in 1997 that provides various forms of immigration benefits and relief from deportation to certain immigrants who are eligible to apply for political asylum.

Nestor felt that his mother-in-law was undermining his authority; he viewed her as overly permissive and that she and his wife were spoiling his son. They expressed concerns that his authoritarian discipline was too harsh for a young child.

Elba also complained that Nestor was too rigid. He had to go to bed early because he began work at 5:00 a.m. She liked to stay up and socialize with her parents. Therefore, he would put their son to bed and go to bed alone while she stayed with her parents. He felt rejected. She thought his feelings were ridiculous. Another source of conflict was that Nestor liked to eat quietly and her family used dinnertime as a coming together and socializing opportunity. Thus, Elba became anxious every day at dinnertime because Nestor ate quickly, did not talk, and left to their room as soon as he was done eating. They often argued about this. On one occasion, their son was making too much noise and Nestor yelled at him at dinner. Everyone was shocked. Elba was ashamed about her husband's behavior in front of her family. She began to consider divorce, discouraged about his "unwillingness to change."

At face value the "problems" of this family did not seem serious or related to intergenerational trauma. The treatment could have focused on resolving couple conflicts. While it was important to understand their couple conflicts and their feelings of being unsupported and not understood by the other, the extended family involvement, migration histories, and losses related to divorce needed to be addressed. We began by exploring their family histories and paying attention to the historical realities each partner brought to the marriage. Elba shared how her parents' divorce left her feeling insecure. She described her father as very self-absorbed and not really able to "connect emotionally." As he was a war veteran I inquired about the presence of trauma symptoms. Elba had not really thought about that, as he did not like to speak of the war. She had been born post-Vietnam and had not learned much about that war in school. After the session, she asked her mother about whether her father had had any PTSD symptoms. Her mother confided that during their brief marriage she lived in fear of his moods and that her worries about feeling unsafe had motivated the divorce. Her mother really did not understand his political views or his focus on Chicanxs either. She was Latina and comfortable in her identity; she could not understand her ex-husband's "chip on his shoulder" about his ethnicity.

Nestor did not like to talk about himself, his family, or his migration. He was reluctant to talk about his life in El Salvador; when he did, he disclosed a difficult childhood. His parents were married but lived apart. His father liked living in the country on his farm where he raised animals. His mother liked the comforts of the city. She ran a small business and was rarely home. Nestor ate alone in the kitchen with the maid. This was the root of his discomfort with family meals at his in-laws. He was a sullen child, by his own account, but enjoyed visiting his father in the country. His father was a man of few words, so when together they spent their time in quiet companionship. Nestor had learned to be a man by observing his father's isolation, strong work ethic, and quiet presence.

When Nestor was studying at the university he had friends who were politically active. As a result of his association, he began to be followed by police who suspected most young university students to have leftist leanings. During the civil war, both the military and the guerrilla targeted Nestor. He refused to join either group. Fearing for his life, his parents insisted that he migrate to the United States. Nestor had a few relatives in southern California, so he agreed to join them there. Nestor denied experiencing any violence directly but witnessed the detention and disappearance of friends. He was cut off from any feelings related to this. In one session he noted, "*Yo no puedo pensar en eso, abriría una fuente interminable de dolor*" (I can't think about any of that; it would open an interminable fountain of pain).

I encouraged Elba to consider the similarities in her husband's and her father's experience with war-related violence and invited them to explore how these experiences had influenced their individual psychology and their family relations. Elba suddenly realized that she carried a great deal of fear, which manifested as anxiety that was related to her mother's fear of her first husband's potential violence. Her fear of Nestor's potential violence was connected to that historical reality. She realized she had married a man very similar in psychological make-up to her father but wanted him to act and be more like her more "modern, progressive, calm" stepfather. Nestor had married a woman "totally unlike his mother" as he perceived Elba to be overinvolved and overprotective of their son while his mother was physically and emotionally absent for most of his childhood and adolescence. What Nestor had not consciously realized was that by being a loving demonstrative mother and due to their conflicts Elba was treating him in a more cool and detached way, as his mother had during his childhood.

Moreover, Elba also had a history of trauma in her genealogy. Her mother's migration to the United States had been the result of multiple family tragedies. Elba's grandmother had three sons who had all died suddenly, accidentally or violently. Elba's grandmother could no longer bear to live in Ecuador and moved with her surviving children, all girls, to the United States. Little was known of Elba's grandfather. The legacy of unreliable men had begun long before in South America and was affecting Elba's relationship to her husband. Moreover, Elba's grandmother was a strong matriarch who exemplified for the daughters and granddaughters the strength required of women to make it in the world. The early losses were not talked about, but the family valued interdependence and frequent contact, unlike Nestor's family of origin that was more disengaged. In therapy they explored how their own family histories of trauma had nuanced family life.

Nestor loved his wife and child, but he seemed uncomfortable with showing his affection, as he had not experienced the *cariño* (caring tenderness) that his wife so freely showed their son. The *amoridolor* he felt for his own childhood was interfering with his desire to be a good husband and father. He was too stern, unable to balance his love with his desire to shape his son into a strong and noble man. By exploring how their respective family legacies intersected and shaped their relationship style, they became more conscious of their family dynamics. Elba struggled to balance her fears with her trust in her husband. Nestor struggled to be emotionally present when overwhelmed with the sounds of family life.

In order to change how they related as a couple and as parents, Elba and Nestor needed to critically examine their history and cultural practices. Elba was more acculturated than Nestor who wanted to recreate life in his country in a setting that required far more of him: emotional presence, high contact with extended family, less authoritarianism. To accomplish this, he needed his wife to support his masculinity and his contributions to their family. Elba was often critical of everything he did and had difficulty pointing out her husband's contributions. Her anger at her father was unfairly directed at her husband. Elba needed to understand how his social position as an unauthorized immigrant marginalized him and led to feelings of disempowerment. He needed to feel valued and important at home. Instead he felt overly criticized and devalued by his wife and her family. His anger was fueled by his marginalization within and outside his home.

Both felt profoundly disloyal to their families of origin when they began to change and engaged in self-sabotaging behaviors. Elba knew how to trigger his anger and he knew how to erode her trust in him. This dangerous dance needed to stop for their benefit and that of their son. Extensive reconstructive dialogues (Flores, 1998) were encouraged so that each partner could be accountable for his and her part in their problems and commit to mindful coupling and parenting. They both wanted their son to grow up feeling loved and secure, to develop the ability to trust that his parents had his best interests at heart and behaved accordingly. By shifting the focus to the well-being of their child, both parents could feel less guilty about changing. They examined the gifts they had received from their parents, as well as the burdens, and became more conscious of how their parenting could promote emotional balance in their son.

The couple's cultural differences were also addressed. Elba came to acknowledge that she fell in love with Nestor's *Latinidad*. She loved the sound of Spanish as the words smoothly rolled off his tongue while simultaneously feeling ashamed that her Spanish was too Americanized. She wanted her son to be bilingual. Nestor resisted speaking English because he felt insecure due to his accent and lack of fluency. His legal status in the United States and his accent interfered with his ability to feel that he belonged in his new country. Moving into a bilingual household where both languages were spoken fluidly triggered Nestor's feelings of belonging and loss. We spoke about how living in the borderlands is challenging but also provides the opportunity for cocreating multiple flavors of *Latinidad*. Their son was Ecuadorian, Salvadoran, Chicano, and American. We discussed what that meant to each of them, what cultural gifts could come from such rich cultural legacies. As immigrants and children of immigrants, as direct survivors and witnesses of traumatic experiences, each partner showed and had great resilience. Given the complex world in which we all live, home could be the site of sustenance and love as well as protection. Elba and Nestor were invited to imagine a home and family life where they did not fight other people's wars; instead they could live in peace.

It was critical to convey to this couple that change is a lifelong process. While "symptoms" or problems may diminish in intensity, being Latina and Latino in the United States will present daily challenges. Therefore, it is essential to learn more adaptive ways to deal with stress, manage microaggressions, and be emotionally present. Ultimately, both Elba and Nestor needed to feel that they deserved to have a loving marriage; they did not need to divorce to find peace and balance in their lives. Nestor could be loyal to his parents without sacrificing himself. He could be a husband and father who was both physically and emotionally present. Elba could support her husband and be a strong, independent woman. She need not exonerate her father by pushing her husband out of their marriage. They could both create peace at home.

Rescripting Narratives of Pain

Couples often present with stories embedded within multiple stories; that is the complaints they bring to treatment reflect the stories and narratives of others important to their life (e.g., extended families, in-laws), as well as historical issues of justice/injustice. The goal is to develop a collaborative relationship with the partners by posing questions to help externalize the problem in order to deconstruct and reconstruct it. The therapist is less directive in narrative approaches than in other modalities of couple therapy and needs to be aware of social justice considerations, including cultural/familial-embedded stories that oppress (e.g., *el que dirán*, a preoccupation of what others will think). In such cases the couple does not own the story. The story owns them. A treatment goal would be to shift to *cómo lo diré o cómo lo diríamos* (the couple owns the story) (Flores & Rivera-Lopez, 2013). The therapist also ought to listen to narratives of disempowerment and despair, as discussed in earlier chapters. The following vignette may illustrate these issues.

Marcos and Elena were both highly educated second-generation Chicanx professionals in their early 30s; both were children of working-class Mexican immigrants. After 6 years of marriage she had separated because of his "sexting" to a female friend. She moved out and continued with her master-level studies while working full time. Despite the separation, they saw each other occasionally and were often sexually intimate during those meetings. She had agreed to come to a few sessions as long as he was accountable and "fessed up" to how he had ruined her love for him and their marriage.

Elena was ambivalent about divorce but furious at Marcos's behavior. Moreover, she described him as financially immature; despite his good education, he mismanaged money and she often had to bail him out. She stated that she could no longer be married to a man who could not be financially responsible and who was morally corrupt as well. Marcos described his wife as rigid, angry, and unwilling to negotiate. Over the course of three meetings, both admitted to infidelity. Marcos was particularly wounded because Elena had invited her lover and not him to a family dinner in honor of her graduation. She responded that he had gone away for a weekend with his lover when he proclaimed to be trying to work on their relationship. They were at an impasse, full of *amoridolor*.

Since Elena had only agreed to a few sessions and had decided to file for divorce between our second and third meeting, the focus of treatment was on ending their relationship well by understanding how things went awry. This was challenging as neither saw the usefulness of exploring their families of origin or how these had any influence on their relationship. I asked Elena how her husband had learned to be financially immature and seemingly unable to commit to the marriage. She quickly noted that his family was unable to rise from their poverty and seemed very comfortable in their "Mexican ways." Her family on the other hand, while still very Mexican, did not devalue success or acculturation. Marcos retorted how this description of his family was "typical" of his wife's demeaning treatment toward them. He added that his family had been unable to attend the wedding because Elena had insisted on getting married at a fancy Mexican resort, which his low-income earning family could not afford. Elena offered to pay for their expenses, but out of pride (according to her) they had refused. Thus, their marriage began on shaky ground; Elena did not feel accepted by his family. Her family on the other hand had initially been warm toward him; but after the sexting incident, her brother and sister-in-law had grown cool toward him. Marcos was grieving that he might not be able to see his niece and nephew, children of Elena's brother, once they divorced. He did not want to lose that connection.

Each held a view of their relationship and of each that appeared unchangeable. I inquired about Elena's hopes and aspirations when they first met and married. Her tone softened and she recalled fondly how she was impressed by his intelligence. She felt at home with him. However, she had become increasingly depressed by his behavior and had begun individual therapy to help her deal with his financial problems and his unacceptable behavior with other women. She had to "close [her] heart to him" in order to go to work, finish her master's thesis, and graduate.

She described her parents as kind and loving, supportive, and proud of her. Because her family, unlike his, she stated, was functional, she grew up believing that everything was possible—to be Chicana, educated, married, and happy. She had believed that Marcos wanted the same. However, he had a lot of educational debt to pay, which, in her view, he mismanaged. Moreover, he had lost a good job for not keeping track of client accounts. He seemed to have difficulty managing money. I asked Marcos what it meant to him to move out of the working-class through education. Feelings of disentitlement emerged. He also had great guilt that he did not have to work as hard as his father, who, ailing from diabetes, still had to work as a laborer. He described his mother as loving but stern, not unlike his wife.

Marcos was influenced by a grand narrative that he should not succeed and become "a better man" than was his father, which he equated with having more education and access to income. His problematic relationship with money made sure that he remained on the brink of financial disaster and functionally working class despite his professional career. When I asked him when he stopped being a husband and became a son to his wife, he blinked, held his breath and responded, "When she killed our baby in order to go back to school." She gasped and accused him of "hitting below the belt." They both wept. Elena had had a first-trimester abortion 3 years before prior to beginning her master's program; according to her she had made such a painful and difficult decision partly because she did not feel secure in the marriage. Marcos engaged in what she considered to be inappropriate text messaging with female friends. She accused him of being a sex addict. He acknowledged that her rejection and criticizing of him caused him great stress, which "fantasy sex games" with other women helped release. They continued to blame each other.

I invited them to consider what role if any their class position and status as multiple minorities had on their relationship problems. They both spoke of the routine microaggressions they experienced as Chicanxs and the feelings of disloyalty they had about "making it" out of the *barrio*. Although they had actualized their families' American dream, they still carried feelings of disentitlement. Marcos struggled with his masculinity and how to balance the internalized views of what it meant to be a *macho* with his ideals of how to be a well-balanced modern man. He engaged in sexting as a way to reduce tension, but also as way to be *macho* (in the negative sense) and to avenge the dishonor his wife's abortion caused. Elena struggled to balance her "soft mothering tendencies" with her Chicana warrior persona, which had served her well in her educational trajectory.

Both seemed unable, however, to form a healthy couple relationship. Elena refused to be a loyal, long-suffering wife/mother as the women in her family had been. She had the economic viability to move on and start a new relationship. They did not feel at home in either their professional world or their family's working-class world. Marcos wondered if he was Mexican enough; Elena was not certain that she could remain sufficiently Mexican with her new European American partner. At the end of therapy they worked on rescripting their cultural narratives to create more balance in their life; in so doing perhaps they might be able to have more satisfying relationships in the future.

Unlike some Hollywood movies, not all relationships end happily ever after. Elena justifiably could not trust that Marcos would not break her heart again. However, by entering another relationship before the marriage with Marcos had ended, she was repeating a pattern. She had been engaged when she met Marcos, and after a night with him, broke the engagement and moved in with Marcos. She appeared unable to end relationships without having another man as a life raft, despite her independence. She had internalized a cultural message that a woman without a man is not complete. She also struggled with the good girl/bad girl dichotomy and appeared to associate sexual freedom with being a strong independent woman without regard to how her infidelity might affect the marriage. Marcos struggled with how to be a man, as he had internalized very negative stereotypes of Chicano and Mexican men. I encouraged him to engage in individual therapy to work on these issues.

Elena and Marcos needed to heal their spirit and grieve for their unborn child and the death of their marriage. However, they left therapy as they left relationships, without closure but with more awareness of the social, cultural, and family narratives that influenced them.

Rebalancing Intergenerational Accounts

As stated in Chapter 5, sexual violence within the family often has intergenerational roots that create multiple forms of dysfunction. Histories of oppression create patterns of dysfunction as a result of unfairness, internalized oppression, and outrage. The psychological sequelae of sexual violence include psychological homelessness, symptoms of psychological distress, and unhealthy scripts for living. Furthermore, relational challenges and problems can be a result of historical unfairness.

Injustice affects the mind, the body, and the spirit. Thus, healing may begin mentally, emotionally, physically, or spiritually. Ultimately, the individual must (re)integrate mind, body, spirit, and heart. Healing generally begins in the sphere where symptomatology first manifests. Change can and sometimes must occur in how we think, act/behave, feel, and relate to others and ourselves. Treatment needs to address "the twin issues of helping patients," (a) to regain a sense of safety in their bodies and (b) to complete the unfinished past" (van der Kolk et al., 1996).

The foundation of treatment is the safety of the therapeutic relationship. To heal from sexual trauma often requires multiple modalities of treatment and the involvement of various healers. Natalia's story may elucidate these ideas.

Natalia sought treatment at the recommendation of her substance abuse counselor who did not feel she had sufficient training to deal with Natalia's psychological problems. The counselor feared that unless Natalia dealt with her trauma, she would continue to relapse. The counselor also felt that there might be cultural issues at play that she could not address as a European American woman. Natalia was 38 when she contacted author

Flores. She was a second-generation Nicaraguan woman who identified as lesbian. She also was a nurse who worked hospice. Day in and day out she helped men die from AIDS. The work was fulfilling but depressing, so Natalia began to use the narcotics prescribed to the men after the men died. She was afraid that if caught she would lose her job, her license, and possibly her freedom. Natalia had a couple of "close calls" and decided to deal with her addiction to morphine.

Initially in their work together author Flores focused on building trust. She stated that she had come to meet with author Flores to appease her counselor but really did not think that a psychologist could help with her addiction. Author Flores sensed that Natalia needed safety before she could disclose the roots of her depression and drug use. She was very curious about her origins, and when author Flores disclosed that she was Central American, she began to talk about her family.

Her maternal grandmother had been a successful businesswoman in Nicaragua but had migrated to the United States with her daughter and husband to join a sister who lived in the San Francisco Bay Area. When author Flores asked what might have invited or pulled her grandmother to the United States, Natalia stated she did not know. She became pale and appeared to dissociate. Author Flores encouraged her to stay in the present and to breathe. When author Flores asked what had just happened, Natalia could not explain. She said she just "left and went off somewhere." This was happening more often and had occurred prior to her drug use; therefore, she did not think it was related to it.

Author Flores then asked about her family composition in the United States. She stated that she lived alone, but her mother and grandmother lived together. She had a brother who was homeless due to alcohol abuse. When author Flores asked what she believed led to both she and her brother abusing substances, she dissociated once again. She did not want to speak any more. Over the next few weeks her drug use increased; she missed both work and her appointment with her counselor who then went to her home and found Natalia nearly unconscious from an overdose. The counselor and author Flores both recommended in-patient treatment but Natalia refused, as disclosure of the addiction to enter treatment would compromise her job. She agreed to go on medical leave for work-related stress and focus on recovery.

Natalia saw her counselor three times a week; she saw author Flores twice a week and went to Narcotics Anonymous daily for a period of 3 months. During that time period, we continued to explore the possible factors that led to her addiction. She recounted that her drug use had increased over the past year. Her grandfather had died and she found that she could not cry over his death. She felt guilty because she could not grieve. After his death, she had began to have flashbacks and physical sensations that she could not explain. When pressed her for details of these, she broke down and began to describe how her grandfather had sexually abused her from the time she was a small child. She had blocked these memories and wondered whether this man also had sexually abused her brother. When her grandfather died, the abuse memories began to surface as disjointed images and physical sensations.

She began to understand why she did not like to be touched and how she would not allow her lovers to make love to her. She had to be in control of the intimacy, and while she enjoyed giving pleasure she refused to be touched in her breasts or genitals. This often led to break-ups, as her partners wanted a more reciprocal relationship and complained that she was too controlling, even in bed.

When asked about the circumstances surrounding the abuse; she recalled that both her mother and grandmother left for work early in the morning and she and her brother were left in the grandfather's care. She did not know why he did not work. She wept and expressed great anger at her mother for leaving her with such a person.

Author Flores encouraged Natalia to invite her mother and grandmother to a session to fill in the memory gaps. Natalia wanted to know why he took care of the children, why he did not work, and why she was not protected. Her grandmother, age 70, and her mother, age 55, attended a therapy session, curious as to why Natalia was in therapy. Once formal introductions and a bit of *plática*[3] took place, Natalia told the women that she had been depressed for years and had become an addict because her grandfather had molested her. At the disclosure, her mother broke down and told us that he too had abused her. Natalia became enraged; how could her mother have left her with a perpetrator? What kind of mother was she that she handed over her daughter to the man who had abused her as a child? Her mother had no answers, only that she needed to work because Natalia's father had abandoned them. Working as a hotel maid she did not earn enough to pay a babysitter.

Both women then turned toward the grandmother and asked why they came to the United States. Appearing stoic, the grandmother said that her husband had been accused of raping children in their hometown and was about to be put in jail. Rather than suffer that humiliation, she left everything behind and came to the United States. He followed, and she forgave him, hoping that he would change. Both women were appalled. The grandmother stated, "*No se puede hacer nada; todos los hombres son así de mañosos*" (There is nothing one can do; all men have those bad habits). Both Natalia and her mother contested the grandmother's appraisal. All three women wept. Eventually, Natalia's mother begged her daughter for forgiveness and asked her what she could do to support her, how she could help. Author Flores suggested that from now on they could work on building an authentic relationship without secrets.

The grandmother spoke of how life was in Nicaragua during the Somoza regime, how the only way to survive was to be tough. She had to be strong not to be raped by soldiers. Gender violence was common and unpunished. Her own father had been military and had often beaten her mother. The three women were connected by a history of social and gender violence that began at the time of the conquest. They had survived and been resilient in the United States largely by blocking memories and developing "amnesia"; but Natalia and her brother had paid the price. They carried the unresolved trauma, guilt, suffering, and despair of previous generations. It was time to break the pattern.

Natalia tried to get her brother into treatment, but he refused. She continued to work on staying sober, and in therapy she began a lengthy process of healing mind/body/spirit. She wanted to return to work and wanted to manage her depression without drugs. Thus, we focused on healing the mind first. This entails changing the tapes and scripts learned, inherited or inserted into our consciousness. In cases of incest, such scripts reflect narratives of disempowerment and feelings of not deserving anything better than suffering. Cognitive behavior therapy (CBT), developed by Aaron Beck, is a Western practice that facilitates cognitive restructuring. The basic premise is that how one thinks about things influences behavior patterns and emotional responses to thoughts and external events.

---

3 Exchange of greetings and niceties many Latinxs engage in prior to getting to "the real issues" of the conversation.

CBT is considered a best practice in the treatment of depression, PTSD, and many other mental health problems (Rothbaum et al., 2000).

However, Natalia did not like doing homework and considered CBT not Latinx enough for her. She tried mindful meditation but would become too agitated as she tried to clear her mind. In therapy they talked about more Indigenous methods, such as rituals to cleanse from the trauma, *limpias* for soul retrieval to heal the wounded little girl that inhabited her body, and changing her agreements with self and others as articulated by Don Miguel Ruiz (1997). Natalia found the Toltec philosophy more compatible with her own worldview and began to practice following the agreements.

To heal her body from years of addiction and the trauma of abuse, Natalia needed to integrate mind and body. Mind/body integration can be achieved through Western psychotherapies, massage therapy, art, dance, or movement therapies. Natalia chose to engage in several forms of treatment. She did EMDR (eye movement desensitization and reprocessing) with her counselor who had recently obtained certification. EMDR is a psychological therapeutic technique used to desensitize and reprocess psychological trauma. It was developed by Francine Shapiro in 1987 and is considered best practice for the treatment of PTSD (Bisson et al., 2013; Shapiro, 1987).

Natalia also did family therapy work with author Flores. In their sessions she explored her cultural and sexual identity and how intergenerational trauma had derailed her for a time. Natalia also saw a body worker who helped her release the somatic manifestations of sexual trauma.[4]

After a year of sobriety, Natalia felt ready to heal her heart. Healing the heart entails gaining a deeper understanding of how violence affects emotions and, in turn, interpersonal relationships. Emotional healing can be achieved in many ways, including European and Indigenous therapies such as psychotherapy, art and movement therapy, writing, journaling, and giving testimony, that is breaking the silence about sexual abuse. Natalia began to speak out about her history and healing journey in both professional conferences and NA meetings. One day she noted that she had heard herself laugh; it had been years since she had experienced such joy. She rediscovered that the use of humor is essential for well-being.

To heal the emotions and the spirit sometimes it is helpful to hold perpetrators of injustice accountable by naming the offense and demanding redress while not really expecting to receive it. The redress can be symbolic. In one session, she screamed, yelled, and eventually softly spoke to her grandfather. She demanded that from the spirit world he protect her brother who was suffering still from his abuse. She would forgive him, she said, if he guided her brother into sobriety. She worked through the anger and disappointment toward her mother and grandmother by finding compassion for their own suffering. Some years later, when her grandmother became ill, Natalia nursed her until she passed. Her grandmother was able to die in peace because the secret had been revealed and her granddaughter had become healthy and functional in her chosen career.

---

4   In some cases healing the body after sexual trauma cannot occur until after the other forms of healing have occurred.

Once she felt more integrated in mind and body and feeling that she was more in control of her emotions, Natalia wanted to focus on healing her spirit.[5] Such healing can begin by becoming accountable and changing dysfunctional patterns. Externalizing the problem, blame, or dysfunction begins to deconstruct narratives of suffering and facilitates disidentifying with the oppressor and no longer engaging in self-destructive patterns. Natalia released guilt over her own victimization and focused on healing herself. As ancillary treatments to the "talking therapies," Natalia used prayer, meditation, guided imagery, and visualization. She found that she could take care of and heal her inner child by taking care of herself and spending time in nature or in quiet meditation. Given her profession and the demands of taking care of others, slowing down and staying in present time was essential. Healing the spirit also may entail finding a spiritual path. Natalia came to view her work as a nurse akin to that of traditional healers; she found balance in loving her patients and being present in their transition to the spirit world. After 2 years of therapy, Natalia "discharged herself," feeling quite healed and integrated.

A few years later author Flores and Natalia ran into each other at a conference. I was presenting on the treatment of trauma; she stopped and hugged and showed author Flores her sobriety pin. Natalia was in a healthy relationship and was taking care of her mother, who had severe arthritis and could no longer work. Natalia smiled and said she was happy. After years of suffering, depression, addiction, and despair, Natalia had regained a sense of safety in her body and had continued to complete her unfinished past.

Promoting Justice Within the Family

The scholar/activists of the Family Center of New Zealand tell us that the lives and relationships of people are shaped by the knowledge and stories that communities of color negotiate and engage in to give meaning to their experiences. These stories and the knowledge they impart have real consequences. They are not merely reflections or representations of our lives. They actively shape, constitute, and embrace our lives. In the preceding chapters we have seen how dominant stories of *amoridolor* influence the ways in which Latinxs form and live in families. Given the low utilization rates of mental health services by Latinos, unless these are culturally attuned and accessible, and the significant health disparities Latinxs face, it is imperative to promote justice within the family to strengthen family members within the home and inoculate them against microaggressions and institutionalized oppression.

In the last 20 years Chicano, Latino, and European American scholars have proposed prevention methods to strengthen Latinx families (Flores, 2013); moreover, since the 1960s Chicanx activists and scholars developed Chicana and Chicano studies programs that impart the knowledge of history, culture, and politics needed to promote self-esteem among Chicanx youth. In later decades, Latinx studies programs also were founded to address the realities and needs of the growing population of other Latinx groups in the United States. In the last few years, a backlash has attempted to ban these programs, arguing that they were separatists and a threat to the United States, although ample

---

5 Treatment could have begun with healing the spirit first, or the heart. Natalia chose where she wanted to begin. It was important that she direct the work to connect to her own agency and power.

evidence exists to the contrary.[6] Furthermore, in the past 20 years education, health, and government organizations have recognized the important role of ethnic pride and identification in the well-being of marginalized communities.[7]

Parents and educators can do much to promote justice in families and communities. Parental involvement in school and with their children's education is paramount for the academic development of the next generation of Chicanxs and Latinxs (see Manzo, 2014). Healthy, well-balanced families can guide, support, and root their children, promoting flexibility and bicultural identification, both of which are necessary to thrive in a multicultural context (Falicov, 2014). Jerry Tello's (1994) *Cara y Corazón: Face and Heart, a Family Strengthening, Rebalancing and Community Mobilization Process* offers culturally rooted tools to educators and family members. A similar program developed with his colleagues in 1991 specifically addresses strengthening families affected by substance abuse. Community education endeavors can strengthen families and thereby prevent myriad problems that arise post-migration for immigrant groups.

The Family Center of New Zealand offers us the journey metaphor as a tool to promote change:

- Moving from dominant stories about one's life to preferred stories is like making a journey from one identity to another.
- The provision of metaphoric maps of the sort of experiences, feelings, and pitfalls than can happen on this journey by other people who have already made it can play an important part in enabling people to move forward in their lives

This chapter has offered metaphoric treatment maps by telling stories of the lives of therapy clients who sought to rebalance relationships, heal from historical and contemporary wounds, and strengthen their families. In the conclusion of the book, we

---

6   The Mexican American studies, some of which were later renamed Chicana and Chicano studies programs, were created out of a federal desegregation case regarding equal education to all students. In 2010, the Arizona legislature passed the anti-ethnic studies law HB-2811, aimed at Mexican American studies. The law was written by state officials who argued that "such programs promoted racism against non-Hispanic whites, supported ethnic solidarity and endorsed the overthrow of the government." See Latino Voices (2013).

7   See, for example, the American Psychological Association's (1990) "Guidelines for Providers of Services to Ethnic, Linguist, and Culturally Diverse Populations," which include the following:

- Psychological service providers need a sociocultural framework to consider diversity of values, interactional styles, and cultural expectations in a systematic fashion. They need knowledge and skills for multicultural assessment and intervention, including abilities to
  - recognize cultural diversity;
  - understand the role that culture and ethnicity/race play in the sociopsychological and economic development of ethnic and culturally diverse populations;
  - understand that socioeconomic and political factors significantly impact the psychosocial, political, and economic development of ethnic and culturally diverse groups;
  - help clients understand/maintain/resolve their own sociocultural identification and understand the interaction of culture, gender, and sexual orientation on behavior and needs.

review the challenges that continue to face Latinx families and discuss community-based participatory action research strategies to promote family justice and well-being among rural and urban Latinx families.

HOMEWORK ASSIGNMENT

1. Identify and write about your dominant story. What sociopolitical and historical factors account for the development of that story?
2. Develop a preferred story.
3. In what ways can you promote justice within your family?

Conclusion

Toward the Future

To prepare for the future we have to look toward the past. We must know our story; understand our place in the world as Latinxs of diverse backgrounds, races, ethnicities, countries of origins, spiritualities, religious practices, abilities, political views, class positions, immigration status, and sexualities. We need to understand how our stories of migration potentiated trauma and mobilized resilience. We must remember that our ancestors built civilizations, explored the cosmos, and had advanced mathematical and medical knowledge thousands of years before the encounter with Europeans. We know now that cultural exchange and economic trade existed between Africa, Asia, and the Americas long before Columbus set sail and accidentally arrived on our shores. We have a rich cultural history that often is erased or silenced in U.S. educational institutions. We must pass this history and this knowledge to younger generations.

We also know that ancestral knowledge survived despite massive genocide during the conquest and the colonial period (Facio & Lara, 2014). As a people, Latinx are survivors. Over the past 50 years Latinxs from Central and South America have migrated in large numbers to the United States, joining the Mexicans, Mexican Americans, and Chicanx who had migrated previously or who had always been here. As stated in the introduction to this book and elsewhere (Flores, 2013), Latinxs are among the oldest inhabitants of and the newest immigrants to the United States. We have always been here, and we shall remain here.

As we write this book, hundreds of thousands of women, children, and youth have entered the United States fleeing gang violence in their countries.[1] The *Maras* (*Mara-Salvatrucha* and M-18) ironically were formed in the United States by disenfranchised offspring of Salvadoran refugees who experienced the marginalization commonly faced by Latino immigrants and children of immigrants (Wolf, 2012). They formed *familia* on the streets because their immigrant parents could not provide the guidance and the tools to deal with the disparagement and violence they faced at school and on the streets. As did Chucho in *Mi Familia*, these youth rejected their parents' culture without integrating

---

1   See U.S. Department of Homeland Security (2016) statistics and response to what has been termed a humanitarian crisis. https://www.cbp.gov/newsroom/stats/southwest-border-unaccompanied-children/fy-2016. Many argue that deportation of these children and youth back to their countries ensures a certain death because the Maras have been known to kill those who escape them. See Wolf (2012) and Arana (2005).

into the U.S. mainstream or forming their own hybrid culture, as did many Chicanxs. The police response to these gangs and the deportation of these youths back to El Salvador and Mexico led to the exportation of gang violence to their respective countries. Many of the deported youth had not lived in the country of their birth since childhood; they lacked the language and cultural knowledge to integrate back into their new homeland. As a result, they reconstituted their gangs, recruiting local youth who were economically disadvantaged or also deported from the United States. The *Maras* and similar gangs have expanded throughout the region, causing increased social violence in Honduras and Guatemala (Arana, 2014; Wolf, 2012). Some gangs have formed alliances with drug traffickers in the region and in Mexico, resulting in the U.S. Department of the Treasury (2012) declaring the *Maras* an international criminal organization that poses a threat to the security of the United States.

The unaccompanied minors who are allowed to remain in the United States will need culturally attuned and trauma-informed services to adjust to life in their new country without their families and support systems. What we know for certain is that these children will face great academic, social, and emotional challenges, not unlike those experienced by other Latinx, including the Cuban refugee children of the 1960s[2] and the repatriated Mexican Americans who were U.S. citizens but were caught in government raids during the depression (Ray, 2005). Mental health practitioners need to adapt their treatment strategies to respond to these children and youth. Mental health treatment must be grounded in social justice to be effective and respond to the needs of traumatized and marginalized Latinxs. Celia Falicov's work and the ideas presented in this book may be of immense help.

Latinx Families in the 21st Century

As we entered the second decade of the 21st century, Latinxs were no longer a minority in California and other states (U.S. Census Bureau, 2010), largely due to the growth of the Mexican-origin group. Most Latinx are now U.S.-born, and while overall the Latino population is young, many Latinos are now over age 60. It is expected that by 2050 the Latinx population will be 26%, nearly doubled what it was in 2010 (16.3%). Clearly Latinxs, especially Chicanxs or Mexican Americans, are no longer a minority in numbers. However, as stated earlier in this book, many Latinxs continue to face great educational and health disparities. Despite the barriers to educational and health care access, Latinxs continue to enjoy relatively good health and longevity. Latinxs have a life expectancy of 81.2 compared to non-Hispanic Whites' 78.8. This health paradox is partly explained by cultural protective factors, which, unless eroded, maintain the physical and emotional well-being of Latinos (Hayes-Bautista, 2004).

---

2   Cuban children were airlifted out of Cuba and brought to the United States through Operation Peter Pan, ostensibly to protect them from communist indoctrination. The children were granted political asylum and sent to live with American families throughout the United States; many children never saw their families again or returned to Cuba. For an excellent discussion of this program see González (2008).

Falicov (2014) lists some of the protective factors that maintain Latinx families' emotional and relational health:

- Family unity and protection of one another
- Help for those in need (interdependence or mutuality)
- A strong community orientation (collectivism)
- Preserving connection through the life span
- Valuing harmonious relationships (personalism)
- Teaching children the value of endurance and hard work
- Maintaining strong adult sibling bonds
- Dedication to protect and raise the next generation as productive and socially committed citizens
- Enduring separations from loved ones in order to improve everyone's lot
- A spirit of acceptance, struggle, and ultimate resilience against adversity
- A religiously or spiritually sustaining faith
- Deeply felt attachment to and pride in cultural traditions
- Respect for the dignity and wisdom of the older generations
- A celebratory spirit that affirms love, life, and joy in the midst of material deprivation

These are the strengths of Latinx families, which must be supported by social institutions, including schools and health programs. As Hayes-Bautista (2004) has noted, most second- and third-generation Latinxs identify as American Latinxs; they embrace a hybrid identity; they recognize their "Americanness" while maintaining adaptive Latinx cultural values and practices. Educational and social programs that promote and strengthen Latinx values can do much to ensure that Latinxs continue to thrive and maximize their opportunities because they will continue to face the challenges inherent in majority status within a racialized context that continues to stereotype, devalue, marginalize, and problematize them. A well-functioning family that maintains the strengths listed can facilitate the success of future generations.

The Chicanx and other social movements of the 1960s brought about a greater *concientización* and a reconnecting to ancestral knowledge(s) and spiritualities. To heal from trauma and unlearn social and gender violence, Chicano men formed men's circles. By sharing their stories, learning ancient ways, and being accountable these men sought to become *hombres nobles*, men in balance. Guided by the Mayan philosophy of the unity of all things and beings, which is reflected in the greeting *In Lak'Ech*, meaning *tu eres mi otro yo* (you are my other me), many Chicanx promote interdependence and accountability as well as healing in community. At the same time, many Chicanas and Latinas have reclaimed their Indigenousness and along with Indigenous women have begun to foreground their spirituality and spiritual activism (Facio & Lara, 2014). Through literature, the arts, and decolonial scholarship many Latinx and Chicanx began to seek culturally congruent ways to regain and remain in balance with themselves, each other, their *familias*, and the earth mother.

Role of Education and Mental Health in Family Health Promotion

As stated earlier, educational institutions and mental health professionals can do much to promote family well-being. Since the 1970s various Chicanx and Latinx agencies were created to provide psychological services to individuals and communities affected by various forms of trauma (see Flores, 2013), and mainstream groups such as the American Psychological Association have recognized the importance of culturally competent care. Much more remains to be done. As professionals, each of us is accountable to those upon whose shoulders we stood to get ahead. Those of us who have benefited from educational opportunities and have gained the privilege of an education can demonstrate that we did not stop being Latinx to get ahead. A commitment to social justice and spiritual activism is necessary for 21st-century scholarship.

We must contest dominant notions of assimilation, which attempt to erase the rich cultural dimensions of being Latinx. In her essay "Latinos and the Façade of Whiteness" Dana Torres (2014) notes,

> Therein lies the problem in the United States, whereby thriving is equated with assimilation into Whiteness. This plays into a fallacious ideology in which Whiteness signifies all that is right in the world, and thus, reinforces the idea that in order to be successful, we must let go of the things that make us non-White and "inferior." In other words, to be accepted and absorbed into the social construction that is Whiteness, we must accept a new pseudo-reality of racial and cultural ignorance.

She adds that "we are, as Latinx, also up against forces that do not want us to know who we are. The nation's history books do not document our achievements, tell us our history, nor our genealogical roots." And this is precisely what we must do to prevent psychological homelessness, outrage, and despair.

Instituted in the past decade at the University of California, Davis, the Center for Transnational Health (CTH), directed by Adela de la Torre, had as its mission "to enhance human capabilities through research-to-practice." A number of applied research projects have enhanced teachers' capabilities to work with children in immigrant communities (Flores & Manzo, 2013; Manzo et al., 2012) and a U.S. Department of Agriculture (USDA)– funded grant that utilizes community-based participatory research methods to reduce obesity among rural Mexican origin children (de la Torre et al., 2013). Understanding that health beliefs and practices are culturally nuanced, *Niños Sanos/Familia Sana* offered multimodal culturally attuned interventions to over 300 children and their families who participated in the research project in a rural Central California Community.

As coinvestigator in this grant, author Flores developed family well-being workshops for study participants who were members of the comparison communities and who therefore did not receive the nutritional intervention nor benefited from some of the enhancements offered to the treatment group. In collaboration with Dr. Rosa Manzo, Dr. Hector Rivera-Lopez, Marisol Reyna, and the project participants, author Flores developed a series of workshops aimed to support immigrant families' strengths and provide tools to negotiate life cycle challenges encountered while raising bilingual bicultural children in the United States. Workshop topics included "the impact of migration on family well being," "family violence," "male mental health," "parenting adolescents," "parenting bicultural children," "women's mental health" and "self-care." The goal is to train participants to become trainers themselves and deliver the workshops to community members. Dr. Manzo conducted a similar endeavor with families who participated in her education-focused workshops. The project also utilized the arts to engage the community and to demonstrate our appreciation. Two murals were created, and beautiful artwork was used to advertise the workshops. [3]

The workshops were developed based on topics generated by the project participants. We held focus groups and met with stakeholders and *promotores* from the communities to identify areas of need and topics of interest. Few mental health services are available to these families who live and work in rural, isolated communities. Thus, a community education model is useful in providing family psychology concepts that are culturally appropriate and can be utilized by the families on their own.

Projects such as these hold great promise for underserved communities because they are grounded on social justice ideals.[4] Academics, researchers, and practitioners can form partnerships with community members and stakeholders to potentiate research to practice. Such practices reflect Indigenous research methodologies as outlined many years ago by Manuel Ramirez III (1998) and more recently by Chela Sandoval (2013) and Bagele Chilisa (2019). This book, designed for an undergraduate course on psychological perspectives for Chicanx and Latinx families, has a similar goal: to provide students and young professionals with knowledge and tools to better understand their own and the families of others. It is offered in that spirit *In Lak'ech*.

---

3 See the CTH website for examples of the art team's work www.cth.ucdavis.edu

4 According to the RSA, Action and Research Centre the term 'social justice' implies fairness and mutual obligation in society. We are responsible for one another, and that we should ensure that all have equal chances to succeed in life. http://www.thersa.org/action-research-centre/ learning,-cognition-and-creativity/education/social-justice/what-social-justice-means. In other words, In Lak'Ech. For additional UC Davis projects grounded in social justice, visit the Social Justice Initiative funded by the Mellon foundation to address the trauma created by the infamous pepper spray incident on the campus on November 18th, 2011. http://socialjusticeinitiative.ucdavis. edu/2014/09/22/october-17-2014-launch-event-global-indigenous-identities-and-alliances/

References

AB540 and Undocumented Center. (n.d.). *Home page.* https://undocumented.ucdavis.edu/

Abraído-Lanza, A. F., Dohrenwend, B. P., Ng-Mak, D. S., & Turner, J. B. (1999). The Latino mortality paradox: A test of the "salmon bias" and healthy migrant hypothesis. *American Journal of Public Health*, 89(10), 1543–1548.

Abreu, R. L., Gonzalez, K. A., Rosario, C. C., Pulice-Farrow, L., & Rodríguez, M. M. D. (2020). "Latinos have a stronger attachment to the family": Latinx fathers' acceptance of their sexual minority children. *Journal of GLBT Family Studies*, 16(2), 192–210. https://doi.org/10.1080/1550428X.2019.1672232

Acosta, K. L. (2018). Queering family scholarship: Theorizing from the borderlands. *Journal of Family Theory & Review*, 10(2), 406–418.

Acuña, R. (2007). *Occupied America: A history of Chicanos* (6th ed.). New York: Pearson Longman.

Adames, H. Y., Chavez-Dueñas, N. Y., Sharma, S., & La Roche, M. J. (2018). Intersectionality in psychotherapy: The experiences of an AfroLatinx queer immigrant. *Psychotherapy*, 55(1), 73–79. https://doi.org/10.1037/pst0000152

Adler-Baeder, F., Robertson, A., & Schramm, D. G. (2010). Conceptual framework for marriage education programs for stepfamily couples with considerations for socioeconomic context. *Marriage & Family Review*, 46(4), 300–322.

Aguirre-Molina, M., & Betancourt, G. (2010). Latino boys: The early years. In M. Aguirre-Molina, L. N. Borrel, & W. Vega (Eds.), *Health issues in Latino males*, (pp. 67–82). Rutgers University Press.

Aguirre-Molina, M., Borrell, L. N., & Vega, W. (Eds.). (2010). *Health issues in Latino males: A social and structural approach.* Rutgers University Press.

Albelda, R., Badgett, M. L., Schneebaum, A., & Gates, G. (2009). *Poverty in the lesbian, gay, and bisexual community.* UCLA CCPR Population Working Papers. http://papers.ccpr.ucla.edu/index.php/pwp/article/view/CCPR-2009-007/238

Almedom, A. M. (2005). Social capital and mental health: An interdisciplinary review of primary evidence. *Social Science & Medicine*, 61(5), 943–964.

Almeida, R. V., Woods, R., Messineo, T., Font, R. J., & Heer, C. (1994). Violence in the lives of the racially and sexually different: A public and private dilemma. *Journal of Feminist Family Therapy*, 5(3–4), 99–126.

Alvira-Hammond, M. (2019). *Hispanic women are helping drive the recent decline in the U.S. fertility rate.* Child Trends. https://www.hispanicresearchcenter.org/wp-content/uploads/2019/08/Hispanic-fertility-trends-1989-20171.pdf

American Immigration Council. (2019). *U.S. citizen children impacted by immigration enforcement.* https://www.americanimmigrationcouncil.org/sites/default/files/research/us_citizen_children_impacted_by_immigration_enforcement.pdf

American Immigration Council. (2020, June 11). *Asylum in the United States.* https://www.americanimmigrationcouncil.org/research/asylum-united-states

American Psychological Association. (1990). *Guidelines for providers of services to ethnic, linguist, and culturally diverse populations.* https://www.apa.org/pi/oema/resources/policy/provider-guidelines

American Psychological Association. (2012). *Crossroads: The psychology of immigration in the new century: Report of the APA Presidential Task Force on Immigration.* https://www.apa.org/topics/immigration/executive-summary.pdf

American Psychological Association (2020). Division 43, Division of Couple and Family Psychology. www.apadivisions.org

Anzaldúa, G. (1987). *Borderlands/La frontera: The new mestiza.* Spinsters/Aunt Lute.

Anzaldúa, G. (1997). La conciencia de la Mestiza: Towards a new consciousness. In A.M. Garcia (Ed.), *Chicana feminist thought: The basic historical writings* (pp. 270–274). New York: Routledge.

APM Research Lab. (2020, August 19). *The color of coronavirus: COVID-19 deaths by race and ethnicity in the U.S.* https://www.apmresearchlab.org/covid/deaths-by-race

Arana, A. (2005). How the street gangs took Central America. *Foreign Affairs, 84*(3), 98–110.

Ataiants, J., Cohen, C., Riley, A. H., Lieberman, J. T., Reidy, M. C., & Chilton, M. (2018). Unaccompanied children at the United States border, a human rights crisis that can be addressed with policy change. *Journal of Immigrant and Minority Health, 20*(4), 1000–1010.

Barraza, C. (2016, March 15) *Hispanic homeownership on the rise. Housingwire.com* https://www.housingwire.com/articles/36524-hispanic-homeownership-on-the-rise/

Bacigalupe, G. (2003). Intercultural therapy with Latino immigrants and White partners: Crossing borders coupling. *Journal of Couple & Relationship Therapy, 2*(2–3), 131–149.

Becker, G., Castrillo, M., Jackson, R., & Nachtigall, R.D. (2006). Infertility among low-income Latinos. *Fertility and Sterility, 85*(4), 882–887.

Behar, R. (1995). *Bridges to Cuba = Puentes a Cuba.* Ann Arbor: University of Michigan Press.

Bermudez, J. M., & Mancini, J. A. (2013). Familias fuertes: Family resilience among Latinos. In D. S. Becvar (Ed.), *Handbook of family resilience* (pp. 215–227). Springer. https://doi.org/10.1007/978-1-4614-3917-2_13

Bernal, D. D. (2001). Learning and living pedagogies of the home: The mestiza consciousness of Chicana students. *International Journal of Qualitative Studies in Education, 14*(5), 623–639.

Bernal, G. & Alvarez, AI (1983). Culture and. Class in the Study of Families. In C. Falicov "Cultural Perspectives in Family Therapy," pp. 38. Aspen

Bernal, G., & Domenech-Rodriguez, M. M. (2012). Cultural adaptations in context: Psychotherapy as a historical account of adaptations. In G. Bernal & M. M. Domenech-Rodriguez (Eds.), *Cultural adaptations: Tools for evidence-based practice with diverse populations* (pp. 3–22). American Psychological Association.

Bernal, G., & Flores Ortiz, Y. (1982). Latino families in therapy: Engagement and evaluation. *Journal of Marital and Family Therapy, 8*(3), 357–365.

Bernal, G., & Flores-Ortiz, Y. (1984). Latino families: Sociohistorical perspectives and cultural issues. *Nueva Epoca, 1*(1), 4–9.

Bernal, G., & Flores-Ortiz, Y. (1991). Contextual family therapy with adolescent drug abusers. In C. Todd (Ed.). *Family therapy approaches with adolescent substance abusers,* 70–92. Allyn & Bacon.

Bernal, G., Flores-Ortiz, Y. G., & Rodriguez-Dragin, C. (1986). Terapia familiar intergeneracional con Chicanos y familias Mexicanas inmigrantes a los Estados Unidos. [Intergenerational family therapy with Chicanos and United States immigrant Mexican families]. *Cuadernos de Psicología, 8,* 81–99.

Bernal, G., Flores-Ortiz, Y., Rodriguez, C., Sorensen, J. L., & Diamond, G. (1990). Development of a contextual family therapy therapist action index. *Journal of Family Psychology, 3*(3), 322–331.

Bernal, R. (2018, July 22). *Latinos aren't reaching top military positions, study shows.* The Hill. https://thehill.com/latino/398139-latinos-arent-reaching-top-military-positions-study-shows#:~:text=The%20study%20by%20Casaba%20Group,to%2015%2C033%2C%20during%20that%20period

Bisson, J. I., Roberts, N. P., Andrew, M., Cooper, R., & Lewis, C. (2013). Psychological therapies for chronic post-traumatic stress disorder (PTSD) in adults. *The Cochrane database of systematic reviews,* 2013 (12), CD003388. https://doi.org/10.1002/14651858.CD003388.pub4

Boszormenyi-Nagy, I. (1987). Foundations of contextual therapy. New York: Brunner/Mazel.

Boszormenyi-Nagy, I., & Framo, J. L. (2013). *Intensive family therapy: Theoretical and practical aspects.* Routledge.

Boszormenyi-Nagy, I., & Krasner, B. R. (1986). *Between give and take: A clinical guide to contextual therapy.* Brunner/Mazel.

Boszormenyi-Nagy, I., & Spark, G. M. (1984). *Invisible loyalties: Reciprocity in intergenerational family therapy.* Brunner/Mazel.

Bowen, M. (1978). *Family therapy in clinical practice.* New York: Jason Aronson.

Bramlett, M. D., & Mosher, W. D. (2002). *Cohabitation, marriage, divorce, and remarriage in the United States.* Centers for Disease Control and Prevention. https://stacks.cdc.gov/view/cdc/6522

Brand, J. E., Moore, R., Song, X., & Xie, Y. (2019). Parental divorce is not uniformly disruptive to children's educational attainment. *Proceedings of the National Academy of Sciences of the United States of America,* 116(15), 7266–7271. https://doi.org/10.1073/pnas.1813049116

Brooks, V. R. (1981). *Minority stress and lesbian women.* Free Press.

Brown, W., & Oden, M. (2011, February 16). *Living across borders: Guatemala Maya immigrants in the U.S. South. Southern Spaces.* http://www.southernspaces.org/2011/living-across-borders-guatemala-maya-immigrants-us-south#sthash.c2BWVRSI.dpuf

Burciaga, J. A. (1993). *Drink cultura: Chicanismo.* VNR Verlag fur die Deutsche Wirtschaft AG.

Canino, G., & Alegría, M. (2009). Understanding psychopathology among the adult and child Latino population from the United States and Puerto Rico: An epidemiologic perspective. In F. A. Villarruel, G. C., J. M. Grau, M. Azmitia, N. J. Cabrera, & T. J. Chahin (Eds.), *Handbook of U.S. Latino psychology: Developmental and community-based perspectives* (p. 31–44). Sage Publications, Inc.

Cantor, G. (2015). *Hieleras (iceboxes) in the Rio Grande Valley sector.* American Immigration Council. https://www.americanimmigrationcouncil.org/research/hieleras-iceboxes-rio-grande-valley-sector

Cantu, M., & Najera-Ramirez, O. (Eds.) (2002). *Chicana life-cycle rituals in Chicana traditions: Continuity and change.* University of Illinois Press.

Cardoso, J. B., & Thompson, S. J. (2010). Common themes of resilience among Latino immigrant families: A systematic review of the literature. *Families in Society,* 91(3), 257–265. https://doi.org/10.1606/1044-3894.4003

Carter, B., & McGoldrick, M. (2010). The expanded family life cycle. Individual, family, and social perspectives (4th ed.). Allyn & Bacon.

Carter, B. E., & McGoldrick, M. E. (1988). *The changing family life cycle: A framework for family therapy.* Gardner.

Carter, E. A., McGoldrick, M., & Garcia-Preto, N. (Eds.). (1999). *The expanded family life cycle: Individual, family, and social perspective*s. Allyn & Bacon.

Carrillo, R., & Tello, J. (Eds.) (2008). *Family violence and men of color: Healing the wounded male spirit* (2nd ed.). Springer: New York.

Casey Family Programs (2010). *Foster care by the numbers.* fosteringsuccessmichigan.com

Castañeda, X. & Zavella, P. (2003). Changing constructions of sexuality and risk: Migrant Mexican women farmworkers in California *Journal of Latin American Anthropology,* 8(2), 126–150.

Castello, A. L. G. (2012). *Processing intergenerational trauma with EMDR* [Paper presentation]. 2nd EMDR Brazilian Congress, Brasilia, Brazil.

Centers for Disease Control and Prevention, (2019, November 12). *HIV and gay and bisexual men.* https://www.cdc.gov/hiv/group/msm/

Cervantes, J. M., Mejía, O. L., & Guerrero Mena, A. (2010). Serial migration and the assessment of extreme and unusual psychological hardship with undocumented Latina/o families. *Hispanic Journal of Behavioral Sciences,* 32(2), 275–291.

Cervantes, R. C., & Félix-Ortiz, M. (2004). Substance abuse among Chicanos and other Mexican groups. In R. J. Velásquez, L. M. Arellano, & B. W. McNeill (Eds.), *The handbook of Chicana/o psychology and mental health* (pp. 325–352). Lawrence Erlbaum.

Cervantes, W., Ullrich, R., & Matthews, H. (2018). *Our children's fear: Immigration policy's effects on young children.* Center for Law and Social Policy. (CLASP). https://eric.ed.gov/?id=ED582818

Cervantes-Pacheco, E. (2018). La inclusión del género en los estudios migratorios. El caso de los varones michoacanos con experiencia de migración hacia Estados Unidos [Gender inclusion in migrations studies. The case of the michoacano males with migrant experience to the United States]. In M. E., Rivera-Heredia & R. Pardo. (Coords.), *Migración: miradas y reflexiones desde la universidad* (pp. 103–120). México: Universidad Michoacana de San Nicolás de Hidalgo y Miguel Ángel Porrúa.

Chabram-Dernersesian, A., & de la Torre, A. (2008). *Speaking from the body: Latinas on health and culture.* University of Arizona Press.

Children's Bureau. (2013, December 17). *Child maltreatment 2012—Data tables.* https://www.acf.hhs.gov/cb/resource/child-maltreatment-2012-data-tables

Chilisa, B. (2019). *Indigenous research methodologies.* SAGE.

Chiu, B., Egyes, L., Markowitz, P. L., & Vasandani, J. (2009). *Constitution on ICE: A report on immigration home raid operations.* Cardozo Immigration Justice Clinic. https://larc.cardozo.yu.edu/cgi/viewcontent.cgi?article=1109&context=faculty-articles

Cohen, C. J., Fowler, M., Medenica, V. E., & Rogowski, J. C. (2018, June). *Millennial attitudes on LGBT issues: Race, identity, and experience.* Genforward. https://genforwardsurvey.com/download/?did=135

Collins, P. H (1990). *Black feminist thought: Knowledge, consciousness, and the politics of empowerment.* Routledge.

Collins, P. H. (2009). *Another kind of public education: Race, schools, the media, and democratic possibilities.* Beacon Press.

Colvin, J., Spagat, E., & Fox, B. (2020, April 22). *Trump bars new immigration green cards, not temporary visas.* AP News. https://apnews.com/81daf6cce6f75e385e9bb70c349f3995

COSSMHO. 1990. *Delivering Preventive Health Care to Hispanics: A Manual for Providers.* Washington, DC: The National Coalition of Hispanic Health and Human Service Organizations.

Crenshaw, K. (1989). "Demarginalization of race and sex: A Black feminist critique of antidiscrimination doctrine, feminist theory, and antiracist politics. *University of Chicago Legal Forum*: Vol. 1989: Iss. 1, Article 8.http://chicagounbound.uchicago.edu/uclf/vol1989/iss1/8

Cuéllar, I., Siles, R. I., & Bracamontes, E. (2004). Acculturation: A psychological construct of continuing relevance for Chicana/o psychology. In L. M. Arellano, B. McNeil, & R. J. Velasquez (Eds.), *The handbook of Chicana/o psychology and mental health* (pp. 41–60). Routledge.

Cuevas, C. A., Sabina, C., & Milloshi, R. (2012). Interpersonal victimization among a national sample of Latino women. *Violence Against Women*, 18(4), 377–403.

Cuevas, C. A., Sabina, C., & Picard, E. H. (2010). Interpersonal victimization patterns and psychopathology among Latino women: Results from the SALAS study. *Psychological Trauma: Theory, Research, Practice, and Policy*, 2(4), 296–306.

Cunradi, C. B., Caetano, R., & Schafer, J. (2002a). Alcohol related problems, drug use, and male intimate partner violence severity among U.S. couples. *Alcoholism: Clinical and Experimental Research*, 26(4), 493–500.

Cunradi, C. B., Caetano, R., & Schafer, J. (2002b). Socioeconomic predictors of intimate partner violence among White, Black, and Hispanic couples in the United States. *Journal of Family Violence*, 17(4), 377–389.

Dreby, J. (2012). The burden of deportation on children in Mexican immigrant families. *Journal of Marriage and Family*, 74(4), 829–845.

De Jesus, M., & Hernandes, C. (2019). Generalized violence as a threat to health and well-being: A qualitative study of youth living in urban settings in Central America's "Northern Triangle." *International Journal of Environmental Research and Public Health*, 16(18), 3465.

De la Rosa, M., Lambert, E. Y., & Gropper, B. (1990). Introduction: Exploring the substance abuse-violence connection. *NIDA Research Monograph*, 103, 1–7. https://archives.drugabuse.gov/sites/default/files/monograph103.pdf

De la Torre, A., Gomez-Camacho, R., & Alvarez, A. (2010). Making the case for health hardship: Examining the Mexican health care system in cancellation of removal proceedings. *Georgetown. Immigration. Law Journal*, 25 (1), 93–116.

De la Torre, A., Sadeghi, B., Green, R. D., Kaiser, L. L., Flores, Y. G., Jackson, C. F., Shaikh, U., & Schaefer, S. E. (2013). Niños sanos, familia Sana: Mexican immigrant study protocol for a multifaceted CBPR intervention to combat childhood obesity in two rural California towns. *BMC Public Health*, 13, 1033. https://doi.org/10.1186/1471-2458-13-1033

Del Castillo, A. R., & Güido, G. (2014). *Queer in Aztlan: Chicano male recollections of consciousness and coming out.* Cognella.

Diaz, M. A., & Lieberman, A. F. (2010). Use of play in child-parent psychotherapy with preschoolers traumatized by domestic violence. In C. E. Schaefer (Ed.), *Play therapy for preschool children* (p. 131–156). https://doi.org/10.1037/12060-007

Dreby, J. (2012). The Burden of Deportation on Children in Mexican Immigrant Families. *Journal of Marriage and Family*, Volume74, Issue4, 829–845.

Duran, E. (2006). *Multicultural foundations of psychology and counseling series. Healing the soul wound: Counseling with American Indians and other native peoples.* Teachers College Press.

Duran, E., & Duran, B. (1995). *Native American postcolonial psychology.* State University of New York Press.

Dutwin, D. (2012). *LGBT acceptance and support: The Hispanic perspective.* Social Science Research Solution. www.ncir.org/images/uploads/publications/LGBTAS_HispanicPerspective.pdf

Ennis, S. R., Ríos-Vargas, M., & Albert, N. G. (2010). *Census briefs: The Hispanic population 2010.* U.S. Census Bureau. https://www.census.gov/prod/cen2010/briefs/c2010br-04.pdf

Espín, O. M. (1987). Cultural and historical influences on sexuality in Hispanic/Latin women: Implications for therapy. In O. M. Espín (Ed.), *Latina realities: Essays on healing, migration and sexuality* (pp. 83–96). Westview.

Espín, O. M. (1993). Issues of identity in the psychology of Latina lesbians. In L. D. Garnets & D. C. Kimmel (Eds.), *Between men—between women: Lesbian and gay studies. Psychological Perspectives on Lesbian and Gay Male Experiences* (pp. 348–363). Columbia University Press.

Espín, O. M. (2012). An illness we catch from American women? The multiple identities of Latina lesbians. *Women & Therapy*, 35(1–2), 45–56. https://doi.org/10.1080/02703149.2012.634720

Facio, E., & Lara, I. (Eds.). (2014). *Fleshing the spirit: Spirituality and activism in Chicana, Latina, and Indigenous women's lives.* University of Arizona Press.

Falicov, C. (2014), *Latino families in therapy* (2nd Ed.). Guilford.

Falicov, C. J. (1988). Family Sociology and Family Therapy Contributions to the Family Development Framework: A Comparative Analysis and Thoughts on Future Trends. In C.J.Falicov (Ed.) In *Family Transitions: Continuity and Change Over the Life Cycle*, 3–51. Guilford Press.

Falicov, C. J. (1995). Cross-cultural marriages. In N. S. Jacobson & A. S. Gurman (Eds.), *Clinical handbook of couple therapy* (pp. 231–246). Guilford.

Falicov, C. J. (1998). *Latino families in therapy: A guide to multicultural practice.* Guilford.

Falicov, C. J. (2013). *Latino families in therapy* (2nd ed.). Guilford.

Falicov, C. J. (2014). Psychotherapy and supervision as cultural encounters: The multidimensional eco-logical comparative approach framework. In C. A. Falender, E. P. Shafranske, & C. J. Falicov (Eds.), Multiculturalism and diversity in clinical supervision: A competency-based approach (pp. 29–58). American Psychological Association. https://doi.org/10.1037/14370-002

Flores, E., Tschann, J. M., VanOss Marin, B., & Pantoja, P. (2004). Marital conflict and acculturation among Mexican American husbands and wives. *Cultural Diversity and Ethnic Minority Psychology*, 10(1), 39–52.

Flores, Y. (1998). Fostering accountability: A reconstructive dialogue with a couple with a history of violence. In N. Thorena & T. Terry (Eds.), *101 more interventions in family therapy* (pp. 389–396). Haworth Press.

Flores, Y. (2005). Parenting. In *Encyclopedia Latina: History, culture, and society in the United States*. In S. Ilan (Ed.). Scholastic Library. 316–322. Danbury: Scholastic Library.

Flores, Y. (2006). La Salud: Latina adolescents constructing identities, negotiating health decisions. *In Latina girls: Voices of Adolescent Strength in the U.S.*, 199–211. J., Denner & B.L, Guzmán, (Eds.). New York University Press.

Flores, Y. (2008). Embodying dementia: Remembrances of memory loss. In *Speaking from the body: Latinas on health and culture*. Chabram-Dernersesian & De la Torre (Ed.), 31–43. University of Arizona Press.

Flores, Y. (2013). *Chicana and Chicano mental health: Alma, Mente y Corazón.* University of Arizona Press.

Flores, Y. & Manzo, R.D. (2013). Preparing Teachers to Instruct Latino Students in U.S. Schools. *Teacher Education and Practice*, v.25, 4, 572–575.

Flores, Y. (2015). *Psychological perspectives for Chicano and Latino children and adolescents.* Sentia.

Flores, Y., Brazil-Cruz, L., Rivera-Lopez, H., Manzo, R., Sianez, M., & Cervantes Pacheco, E. (2019). Here in Confidence: Narratives of migration, mental health, and family reunification of Mexican immigrant men in the California Central Valley. In N. Deeb-Sossa (Ed.), *Community-based participatory research: Testimonios from Chicana/o studies* (pp. 153–178). University of Arizona Press.

Flores, Y., & Rivera-Lopez, H. (2013). *Couples therapy with Latinos* [Workshop presentation]. Strengthening Our Roots Conference, Visalia, California.

Flores, Y., & Valdez-Curiel, E. (2009). Conflict resolution and intimate partner violence among Mexicans on both sides of the border. In P. Zavella, D. Segura, & J. V. Palerm (Eds.), *Mexicans in California: Transformations and challenges* (pp. 183–216) X. University of Illinois Press.

Flores, Y. G. (2013). *Chicana and Chicano mental health: Alma, mente y corazón.* University of Arizona Press.

Flores, Y. G. (2015). *Psychological perspectives for Chicano and Latino children and adolescents.* Sentia.

Flores, Y. G., & Manzo, R. D. (2012). Preparing teachers to instruct Latino children in U.S. schools. *Teacher Education and Practice, 25*(4), 572–575.

Flores, Y. G., Rivera-Lopez, H., & Brazil-Cruz L. (2014). *Mental health and family well being among Mexican immigrant men in rural California.* Report of a PIMSA [*Programa de Investigación Migración y Salud*] funded grant. University of California.

Flores-Ortiz, Y. (1991). Psychotherapy with Latinos: A contextual approach. *The California Psychologist, 24*(4), 16–18.

Flores-Ortiz, Y. (1993). La mujer y la violencia: A culturally based model for the understanding and treatment of domestic violence in Chicana/Latina communities. *Chicana Critical Issues,* 169–182.

Flores-Ortiz, Y. (1997a). The broken covenant: Incest in Latino families. *Voces: A Journal of Chicana/Latina Studies, 1*(1), 48–70.

Flores-Ortiz, Y. (1997b). Voices from the couch: The co-construction of a Chicana psychology. In C. Trujillo (Ed.), *Living Chicana theory* (pp. 102–122). Third Women PR.

Flores-Ortiz, Y. (1998). Fostering accountability: A reconstructive dialogue with a couple with a history of violence. In T. Nelson & T. Trepper (Eds.), *101 more interventions in family therapy* (pp. 389–396). Haworth Press.

Flores-Ortiz, Y. (1999a). From margin to center: Family therapy with Latinas. In M. Flores & G. Carey (Eds.), *Family therapy with Hispanics* (pp. 59–76). Allyn & Bacon.

Flores-Ortiz, Y. (1999b). Injustice in the family. In M. Flores & G. Carey (Eds.), *Family therapy with Hispanics* (pp. 251–263). Allyn & Bacon.

Flores-Ortiz, Y. (1999c). Migration, identity and violence. *Breaking Barriers: Diversity in Clinical Practice,* (pp. 29–33). California State Psychological Association.

Flores-Ortiz, Y. (2000). Injustice in Latino families: Considerations for family therapists. In M. T. Flores & G. Carey (Eds.), Family therapy with Hispanics: Toward appreciating diversity (pp. 251–263). Allyn & Bacon.

Flores-Ortiz, Y. (2001a). Desde el diván: Testimonios from the couch. In Latina Feminist Groups (Eds.), *Telling to live: Latina feminist testimonios* (pp. 294–297). Duke University Press.

Flores-Ortiz, Y. (2001b). My father's hands. In Latina Feminist Groups (Eds.), *Telling to live: Latina feminist testimonios* (pp. 33–38). Duke University Press.

Flores-Ortiz, Y. (2003). Remembering the body: Latina testimonies of social and family violence. In A. J. Aldama (Ed.), *Violence and the body: Race, gender and the state* (pp. 347–359). Indiana University Press.

Flores-Ortiz, Y. (2004). Domestic violence in Chicano Families. In R. Velazquez, L. Arellano & B. McNeill (Eds.). *The handbook of Chicana/o psychology and mental health* (pp. 267–284). Lawrence Erlbaum.

Flores-Ortiz, Y. (2005). Why did he want to hurt me? All I ever did was love him: Understanding sexual violence in Latino marriages. In E. Buchwald, P. R. Fletcher, & M. Roth (Eds.), *Transforming a rape culture* (pp. 129–138) (2nd ed.). Milkweed Editions.

Flores-Ortiz, Y., & Bernal, G. (1989). Contextual family therapy of addiction with Latinos. Journal of Psychotherapy & the Family, G. Saba et. al. (Eds.), *Minority and Family Therapy* (pp. 123–142). Haworth Press.

Flores-Ortiz, Y., Esteban, M., & Carrillo, R. A. (1994). La violencia en la familia: Un modelo contextual de terapia intergeneracional. Revista interamericana de psicología. [Family violence: a contextual model of intergenerational therapy]. *Interamerican Journal of Psychology, 28*(2), 235–250.

Flores-Ortiz, Y., Valdez-Curiel, E., & Andrade Palos, P. (2002). Intimate partner violence and couple interaction among women from Mexico City and Jalisco, Mexico. *Journal of Border Health, 7*(1), 33–42

Flores-Ortiz, Y. G. (1991). Levels of acculturation, marital satisfaction, and depression among Chicana workers: A psychological perspective. *Aztlan: A Journal of Chicano Studies, 20*(1–2), 151–175.

Flores-Ortiz, Y. G. (1994). The role of cultural and gender values in alcohol use patterns among Chicana/Latina high school and university students: Implications for AIDS prevention. *International Journal of the Addictions, 29*(9), 1149–1171.

Fu, V. K., & Wolfinger, N. H. (2011). Broken boundaries or broken marriages? Racial intermarriage and divorce in the United States. *Social Science Quarterly, 92*(4), 1096–1117.

Fuentes, C. (1999). *The buried mirror: Reflections on Spain and the New World.* Houghton Mifflin Harcourt.

Gallardo, L. H., & Batalova, J. (2020, April 10). *Venezuelan immigrants in the United States.* Migration Policy. https://www.migrationpolicy. org/article/venezuelan-immigrants-united-states-2018

Garcia, S. B., & Guerra, P. L. (2004). Deconstructing deficit thinking: Working with educators to create more equitable learning environments. *Education and Urban Society, 36*(2), 150–168.

Gates, G., & Kastanis, A. (2013). *LGBT Latino/a individuals and Latino/a same-sex couples.* https://escholarship.org/uc/item/93mow231#author

Ginorio, A. B., Gutiérrez, L., Cauce, A. M., & Acosta, M. (1995). Psychological issues for Latinas. In H. Landrine (Ed.), *Bringing cultural diversity to feminist psychology: Theory, research, and practice* (pp. 241–263). American Psychological Association. https://doi.org/10.1037/10501-011

Gonzales, N. A., Fabrett, F. C., & Knight, G. P. (2009). Acculturation, enculturation, and the psychosocial adaptation of Latino youth. In F. A. Villarruel, G. Carlo, J. M. Contreras Grau, M. Azmitia, N. Cabrera, & T. J. Chahin (Eds.), *Handbook of U.S. Latino psychology: Developmental and community-based perspectives* (pp. 115–134). SAGE.

González Mandri, F. M. (2008). Operation Pedro Pan: A tale of trauma and temembrance. *Latino Studies 6,* 252–268.

Gottman, J. M. (2014). *What predicts divorce?: The relationship between marital processes and marital outcomes.* Psychology Press.

Gruberg, S., Rooney, C., McGovern, A., Mirza, S., & Durso, L. (2018, January 24). *Serving LGBTQ immigrants and building welcoming communities.* Center for American Progress. http://www.Americanprogress.org/Issues/Lgbt/Reports/2018/01/24/445308/Serving-Lgbtq-Immigrants-Building-Welcoming-Communities/

Guerin, P. (1976). *Family therapy, theory, and practice.* Gardner.

Guerin, P. J. (1996). *Working with relationship triangles: The one-two-three of psychotherapy.* Guilford.

Gundersen, C., & Ziliak, J. P. (2014). Childhood food insecurity in the U.S.: Trends, causes, and policy options. *The Future of Children,* 1–19. https://futureofchildren.princeton.edu/sites/futureofchildren/files/media/childhood_food_insecurity_researchreport-fall2014.pdf

Gurman, A. S. (2008). *Clinical handbook of couple therapy* (4th ed). Guilford.

Gurman, A. S., & Kniskern, D. P. (Ed.). (1991). Handbook of family therapy, volume II. New York:—Brunner/Mazel.

Habbach, H., Hampton, K., & Mishori, R. (2020, February 25). *You will never see your child again.* Physicians for Human Rights. https://phr.org/our-work/resources/you-will-never-see-your-child-again-the-persistent-psychological-effects-of-family-separation/

Hackman, M., Lazo, A., & Caldwell A. A. (2020, May 22). *Trump Administration changes rules for migrant children during pandemic. Wall Street Journal.* https://www.wsj.com/articles/trump-administration-changes-rules-for-migrant-children-during-pandemic-11590141601

Hardy, K. V., & Laszloffy, T. A. (2005). *Teens who hurt: Clinical interventions to break the cycle of adolescent violence.* Guilford.

Harris, N. B. (2018). *The deepest well: Healing the long-term effects of childhood adversity.* Houghton Mifflin Harcourt.

Harris, V. W., Skogrand, L., & Hatch, D. (2008). Role of friendship, trust, and love in strong Latino marriages. *Marriage & Family Review, 44*(4), 455–488. https://doi.org/10.1080/01494920802454041

Hawley, D. R., & DeHaan, L. (1996). Toward a definition of family resilience: Integrating life span and family perspectives. *Family Process, 35*(3), 283–298.

Hayes-Bautista, D., & Hsu, H. (2020). *The COVID-19 case rate and California's diversity: Patterns in coronavirus exposure.* UCLA: Center for the Study of Health and Culture. https://www.uclahealth.org/ceslac/work-files/Research/COVID19/The-COVID-19-Case-Rate-and-Californias-Diversity-Patterns-in-Coronavirus-Exposure.pdf

Hayes-Bautista, D. E. (2004). *La nueva California: Latinos in the golden state.* University of California Press.

Herman, J. L. (1992). *Trauma and recovery: The aftermath of violence—From domestic abuse to political terror.* Basic Books.

Hernández-Avila, I. (2014). Foreword: A meditation. In E. Facio & I. Lara (Eds.), *Fleshing the spirit: Spirituality and activism in Chicana, Latina, and Indigenous women's lives* (pp. xiii–xx). University of Arizona Press.

Hing, B. O. (2004). *Defining America: Through immigration policy.* Temple University Press.

Hirsch, J. (2003). *A courtship after marriage: Sexuality and love in Mexican transnational families.* University of California Press.

Homeland Security. *Humanitarian and Security Crisis at Southern Border Reaches 'Breaking Point'* (March 6, 2019) https://www.dhs.gov/news/2019/03/06/humanitarian-and-security-crisis-southern-border-reaches-breaking-point

Hughes, M. T., Valle-Riestra, D. M., & Arguelles, M. E. (2008). The voices of Latino families raising children with special needs. *Journal of Latinos and Education, 7*(3), 241–257.

Human Rights Campaign. (n.d.). *A la familia.* https://www.hrc.org/es/resources/a-la-familia

Human Rights Campaign. (2018). *Coming out: Living authentically as LGBTQ Latinx Americans.* https://www.hrc.org/resources/coming-out-living-authentically-as-lgbtq-latinx-americans

Hurtado, A. (2003). Theory in the flesh: Toward an endarkened epistemology. *International Journal of Qualitative Studies in Education, 16*(2), 215–225.

Hurtado, A., & Gurin, P. (2004). *Chicana/o identity in a changing U.S. society: ¿Quien soy? ¿Quiénes somos?* University of Arizona Press.

Issuu. (n.d.). *Injustice at every turn: Report of the National Transgender Discrimination Survey.* https://issuu.com/lgbtagingcenter/docs/ntds_report/4

Jan, T., & Clement, S. (2020, May 6). *Hispanics are almost twice as likely as Whites to have lost their jobs amid pandemic, poll finds. Washington Post.* https://www.washingtonpost.com/business/2020/05/06/layoffs-race-poll-coronavirus/

Jenks, R. J., & Woolever, C. A. (1999). Integration and well-being among Catholics—married, divorced, annulled. *Journal of Religion and Health, 38*(2), 127–136.

Johnson, K.R. (2004). *The "huddled masses" myth: Immigration and civil rights.* Philadelphia: Temple University Press.

Johnson K.R. (2009). The Intersection of Race and Class in U.S. Immigration Law and Enforcement, 72 *Law and Contemporary Problems* 1–36. https://scholarship.law.duke.edu/lcp/vol72/iss4/2

Johnson, M. P. (2008). *A typology of domestic violence: Intimate terrorism, violent resistance, and situational couple violence.* Northeastern University Press & University Press of New England.

Joseph, G. M., Henderson, T. J., Starn, O., & Kirk, R. (Eds.). (2002). The Mexico reader: History, culture, politics. Duke University Press.

Kandel, W. (2016). *Unaccompanied alien children: An overview,* Vol. 11. Congressional Research Service. https://fas.org/sgp/crs/homesec/R43599.pdf

Kane, R., Nicoll, A. E., Kahn, E., & Groves, S. (2012). *Supporting and caring for our Latino LGBT youth.* Human Rights Campaign.

Keefe, S. E., & Padilla, A. M. (1987). *Chicano ethnicity.* University of New Mexico Press.

Kosciw, J. G., Greytak, E. A., Zongrone, A. D., Clark, C. M., & Truong, N. L.. (2018). *The 2017 National School Climate Survey: The experiences of lesbian, gay, bisexual, transgender, and queer youth in our nation's schools.* Gay, Lesbian and Straight Education Network (GLSEN). https://www.glsen.org/sites/default/files/2019-10/GLSEN-2017-National-School-Climate-Survey-NSCS-Full-Report.pdf

Kreider, R. M. (2008). *Improvements to demographic household data in the current population survey: 2007.* U.S. Census Bureau. https://www.census.gov/library/working-papers/2008/demo/kreider-01.html

Kriel, M. (2020, March 3). New Trump administration policies fast-track some children's immigration court hearings, including video pilot in Houston. *Houston Chronicle.* https://www.houstonchronicle.com/news/houston-texas/houston/article/New-Trump-administration-policies-fast-track-some-15105573.php

Kuperminc, G. P., Wilkins, N. J., Roche, C., & Alvarez-Jimenez, A. (2009). Risk, resilience, and positive development among Latino youth. In F. A. Villarruel, G. Carlo, J. M. Contreras Grau, M. Azmitia, N. Cabrera, & T. J. Chahin (Eds.), *Handbook of U.S. Latino psychology: Developmental and community-based perspectives* (pp. 213–233). SAGE.

LaFromboise, T., Coleman, H. L., & Gerton, J. (1993). Psychological impact of biculturalism: Evidence and theory. *Psychological Bulletin, 114*(3), 395–412.

Lamidi, E., & Cruz, J. (2014). *Remarriage rate in the U.S., 2012.* National Center for Family & Marriage Research.https://www.bgsu.edu/content/dam/BGSU/college-of-arts-and sciences/NCFMR/documents/FP/FP-14-10-remarriage-rate-2012.pdf

Landale, N. S., Oropesa, R. S., & Bradatan, C. (2006). Hispanic families in the United States: Family structure and process in an era of family change. In M. Tienda & F. Mitchell (Eds.), *Hispanics and the future of America* (pp. 5). National Academies Press. https://www.ncbi.nlm.nih.gov/books/NBK19902/

Latina Feminist Group. (2001). *Telling to live: Latina feminist testimonios.* Duke University Press.

Latino Voices. (2013, August 1). *Mexican American studies may return to Tuscon, Arizona, kind of. Huffington Post.* https://www.huffpost.com/entry/mexican-american-studies-return_n_3690144

Lehavot, K., & Simoni, J. M. (2011). The impact of minority stress on mental health and substance use among sexual minority women. *Journal of Consulting and Clinical Psychology, 79*(2), 159–170.

Lewis, O. (1961). *The children of Sanchez: The autobiography of a Mexican family.* Vintage Books.

Linton, J. M., Griffin, M., Shapiro, A. J., & Council on Community Pediatrics. (2017). Detention of immigrant children. Pediatrics, 139(5), e20170483. https://doi.org/10.1542/peds.2017-0483

Livingston, G. (2014, November 14). *Chapter 2: The demographics of remarriage.* Pew Research Center. https://www.pewsocialtrends.org/2014/11/14/chapter-2-the-demographics-of-remarriage/

Livingston, G., & Brown, A. (2017, May 17). *Trends and patterns in intermarriage.* Pew Research Center, 18. https://www.pewsocialtrends.org/2017/05/18/1-trends-and-patterns-in-intermarriage/

Lopez, G., & Gonzalez-Barrera, A. (2016). Afro-Latino: A deeply rooted identity among U.S. Hispanics. Pew Research Center. http://pewrsr.ch/1LtW1qp

Lopez, M. G., Krogstad, J. M., & Flores, A. (2018, September 13). *Key facts about young, Latinos, one of the nation's fastest-growing populations.* Pew Research Center. https://www.pewresearch.org/fact-tank/2018/09/13/key-facts-about-young-latinos/

MacLean, S. A., Agyeman, P. O., Walther, J., Singer, E. K., Baranowski, K. A., & Katz, C. L. (2019). Mental health of children held at a United States immigration detention center. *Social Science & Medicine, 230,* 303–308. https://doi.org/10.1016/j.socscimed.2019.04.013

Madanes, C. (1990). *Sex, love, and violence: Strategies for transformation.* Norton

Madsen, W. (1964). The alcoholic Agringado. *American Anthropologist, 66*(2), 355–361.

Mahler, S. J., & Ugrina, D. (2006, April 1). Central America: Crossroads of the Americas. Migration Police Institute. https://www.migrationpolicy.org/article/central-america-crossroads-americas

Manzo, R., Cruz, L., Faltis, C., & De La Torre, A. (2012). Professional development of secondary science teachers of English learners in immigrant communities. *Association of Mexican American Educators Journal, 5*(1), 41–48.

Manzo, R., Brazil-Cruz, L., Flores, Y., & Rivera-Lopez, H. (2020). *Cultura y corazón: Decolonial approaches to research.* University of Arizona Press.

Manzo, R. D. (2014). *Pláticas de resistencia: An examination of the forms of parent involvement and negotiation of school-parent tensions in a farm working community in California's Central Valley.* University of California, Davis.

Manzo, R. D. (2016). Parent involvement practices of farmworking immigrant mothers in a rural community. *Association of Mexican American Educators Journal, 10.* https://www.semanticscholar.org/paper/Parent-Involvement-Practices-of-Farmworking-Mothers-Manzo/4b3ba69aea11046652a0772e762813005651b1c2

Martín-Baró, I. (1990). Reparations: Attention must be paid–healing the body politic in Latin America. *Commonweal, 117*(6), 184–186.

Masci, D., Sciupac, E., & Lipka, M. (2015, October 28). Gay marriage around the world. Pew Research Center's Religion & Public Life Project, 26. https://www.pewforum.org/fact-sheet/gay-marriage-around-the-world/

Massey, D. S. (2001, December 19). *March of folly.* American Prospect. https://prospect.org/economy/march-folly/

Masten, A. S. (1994). Resilience in individual development: Successful adaptation despite risk and adversity: Challenges and prospects. In M. C. Wang & E. W. Gordon (Eds.), *Educational resilience in inner-city America: Challenges and prospects* (pp. 3–25). Lawrence Erlbaum.

Masten, A. S. (2001). Ordinary magic: Resilience processes in development. *American Psychologist, 56*(3), 227–238.

McGoldrick, M. (1997) *You can go home again: Reconnection with your family.* Norton

McGoldrick, M. (2011). *The genogram journey: Reconnecting with your family* (revised ed.). Norton.

McGoldrick, M., Carter, E. A., & Garcia-Preto, N. (Eds.). (1999). *The expanded family life cycle: Individual, family, and social perspectives.* Allyn and Bacon.

McGoldrick, M., Giordano, J., & Garcia-Preto, N. (2005). *Ethnicity and family therapy.* New York: Guilford Press.

McGoldrick, M., Pearce, J. K., & Giordano, J. (1984). *Ethnicity and family therapy.* New York: Guilford Press.

McGoldrick, M., Giordano, J. & Garcia Preto, N., (Editors), Third Edition. (2005) *Ethnicity and Family Therapy.* Guilford.

McGoldrick, M., & Gerson, R. (1985). *Genograms in family assessment.* Norton.

McGoldrick, M., Gerson, R., & Petry, S. S. (2008). *Genograms: Assessment and intervention.* Norton.

McGoldrick, M., Carter, E. A., & Garcia-Preto, N. (2011). *The expanded family life cycle: Individual, family, and social perspectives.* Boston, Mass: Allyn & Bacon.

McGoldrick, M., & Hardy, K. V. (Eds.). (2008). *Re-visioning family therapy: Race, culture, and gender in clinical practice.* Guilford.

Médecins Sans Frontières/Doctors without Borders (MSF). (2020, February 11). *Report: No way out—The humanitarian crisis for Central American migrants and asylum seekers.* https://www.msf.org/report-no-way-out-central-american-migration

Minuchin, S., & Wiltwyck School for Boys. (1967). *Families of the slums; an exploration of their structure and treatment.* New York: Basic Books.

Minuchin, S. (1974). *Families & family therapy.* Cambridge, Mass.: Harvard University Press.

Miranda, J., Siddique, J., Der-Martirosian, C., & Belin, T. R. (2005). Depression among Latina immigrant mothers separated from their children. *Psychiatric Services, 56*(6), 717–720.

Mirandé, A. (2017). *Behind the mask: Gender hybridity in a Zapotec community.* University of Arizona Press.

Montalvo, B., & Gutierrez, M. (1983)X. The mask of culture. In C. J. Falicov (Ed.), *Cultural perspectives in family therapy* (pp. 15–30) X. Aspen Systems Corporation.

Montes, V. (2019). Fleeing home: Notes on the Central American caravan in its transit to reach the U.S.–Mexico border. *Latino Studies, 17*(4), 532–539. https://doi.org/10.1057/s41276-019-00214-x

Morales, E. S. (1989). Ethnic minority families and minority gays and lesbians. *Marriage & Family Review, 14*(3-4), 217–239.

National Center for Farmworker Health. (2018). *Indigenous agricultural workers.* http://www.ncfh.org/uploads/3/8/6/8/38685499/fs-indigenous_ag_workers_2018.pdf

National Center for Transgender Equality. (n.d.). *U.S. transgender survey.* https://transequality.org/issues/us-trans-survey

National Coalition of Hispanic Health & Human Services Organizations. (1999). *The state of Hispanic girls.* COSSMHO Press.

National Community Attitudes Towards Violence against Women Survey (2009). *Project Technical report.* Australian Government. Australian Institute of Criminology. https://www.vichealth.vic.gov.au/-/media/ResourceCentre/PublicationsandResources/PVAW/CATVAW_ProjectTechnicalReport2009.pdf?la=en&hash=1E24F73605599FC3FAAB0DBD64E9C9D0F7B58659

Nava, G. (Director). (1995). *Mi familia* [Motion picture]. New Line Cinema.

Nazario, S. (2006). *Enrique's journey.* Random House.

Nichols, M. P., & Schwartz, R. C. (1998). *Family therapy enters the twenty-first century. Family therapy: Concepts and methods* (4th ed.) (pp. 315–354). Allyn & Bacon.

Noe-Bustamante, L., Lopez M.H., & Krogstad, J.M. (2020, July 7). U.S. Hispanic population surpassed 60 million in 2019, but growth has slowed. *Pew Research Center.* https://pewrsr.ch/300Rezf

Office of Refugee Resettlement. (2020). *Facts and data.* https://www.acf.hhs.gov/orr/about/ucs/facts-and-data

Oropesa, R. S. , & Gorman, B. K. (2000). Ethnicity, immigration, and beliefs about marriage as a "tie that binds." In L. J. Waite (Ed.), *The ties that bind: Perspectives on marriage and cohabitation* (pp. 188–211). Aldine.

Oropesa, R. S., & Landale, N. S. (2004). The future of marriage and Hispanics. *Journal of Marriage and Family*, *66*(4), 901–920.

Padilla, A. M. (1980). *Acculturation, theory, models, and some new findings* (no. 39). Westview.

Padilla, A. M., & Borrero, N. E. (2006). The effects of acculturative stress on the Hispanic family. In P. T. P. Wong & L. C. J. Wong (Eds.), *Handbook of multicultural perspectives on stress and coping* (pp. 299–317). Springer. https://doi.org/10.1007/0-387-26238-5_13

Parker, A. (2020, February 10). The U.S. deported them, ignoring their pleas. Then they were killed. *Washington Post*. https://www.washingtonpost.com/opinions/2020/02/10/us-deported-them-ignoring-their-pleas-then-they-were-killed/

Parker, K., Menasce Horowitz, J., Morin, R., & Lopez, M. H. (2014, June 15). *Chapter 7: The many dimensions of Hispanic racial identity*. Pew Research Center. https://www.pewsocialtrends.org/2015/06/11/chapter-7-the-many-dimensions-of-hispanic-racial-identity/

Passel, J. S., & Taylor, P. (2010, August 11). *Unauthorized immigrants and their U.S. born children*. Pew Hispanic Center. https://www.pewresearch.org/hispanic/2010/08/11/unauthorized-immigrants-and-their-us-born-children/

Paz, O. (1970). *El laberinto de la soledad*. [The labyrinth of solitude] Penguin.

Paz, O. (2003). The sons of la Malinche. In G. M., Johnson & T. J. Henderson (Eds.), *The Mexico reader: History, culture, politics* (pp. 20–27). Duke University Press.

Peñalosa, F. (1968). Mexican family roles. *Journal of Marriage and the Family*, *30*(4), 680–689.

Perez, L. (2015). *El salon: The experience of idealized beauty constructs among Dominican women in Washington Heights, New York*. [Doctoral dissertation, The Wright Institute]. https://search.proquest.com/docview/1727739786?pq-origsite=gscholar&fromopenview=true

Pesquera, B. M. (1993). In the beginning he wouldn't lift even a spoon: The division of household labor. In A. De La Torre & B. M. Pesquera (Eds.), *Building with our hands: New directions in Chicana studies* (pp. 181– 195). University of California Press.

Pew Hispanic Center. (2007, April 25). *Pew forum on religion and public life. Changing faiths: Latinos and the transformation of American religion*. https://www.pewresearch.org/hispanic/2007/04/25/changing-faiths-latinos-and-the-transformation-of-american-religion-2006-hispanic-religion-survey/

Pew Research Center. (n.d.). *Hispanic Latino demographics*. https://www.pewresearch.org/topics/hispaniclatino-demographics/

Phillips, M. J., & Ancis, J. R. (2008). The process of identity development as the parent of a lesbian or gay male. *Journal of LGBT Issues in Counseling*, *2*(2), 126–158.

Portes, A., & Böröcz, J. (1989). Contemporary immigration: Theoretical perspectives on its determinants and modes of incorporation. *International Migration Review*, *23*(3), 606–630.

Portes, A., & Sensenbrenner, J. (1993). Embeddedness and immigration: Notes on the social determinants of economic action. *American Journal of Sociology*, *98*(6), 1320–1350.

Poverty rate of Hispanic families in the U.S. 2018 | Statista. www.statista.com

Public Policy Institute in California. (2017). *Poverty in California. Public Policy Institute of California*. https://www.ppic.org/publication/poverty-in-california

Qian, Z., & Lichter, D. T. (2018). Marriage markets and intermarriage: Exchange in first marriages and remarriages. *Demography*, *55*(3), 849–875.

Quintana, S. M., & Scull, N. C. (2009). Latino ethnic identity. In F. A. Villarruel, G. Carlo, J. M. Contreras Grau, M. Azmitia, N. Cabrera, & T. J. Chahin (Eds.), *Handbook of U.S. Latino psychology: Developmental and community-based perspectives* (pp. 81–98). SAGE.

Quintero, D., Cerezo, A., Morales, A., & Rothman, S. (2015). Supporting transgender immigrant Latinas: The case of Erika. In O. M. Espín & A. L. Dottolo (Eds.), *Gendered journeys: Women, migration and feminist psychology* (pp. 190–205). Palgrave Macmillan. https://doi.org/10.1057/9781137521477_9

Ramirez, M., III. (1967). Identification with Mexican family values and authoritarianism in Mexican-Americans. *The Journal of Social Psychology*, *73*(1), 3–11.

Ramirez, M., III. (1969). Identification with Mexican-American values and psychological adjustment in Mexican-American adolescents. *International Journal of Social Psychiatry*, *15*(2), 151–156.

Ramirez, M., III. (1998). *Multicultural/multiracial psychology: Mestizo perspectives in personality and mental health*. Jason Aronson.

Ramirez, O., & Arce, C. (1981). The contemporary Chicano family: An empirically based review. In A. Baron, Jr. (Ed.), *Explorations in Chicano psychology* (pp. 3–28). Praeger.

Rasheed, J. M., Rasheed, M. N., & Marley, J. A. (Eds.). (2011). *Readings in family therapy: From theory to practice.* SAGE.

Ratzinger, J., & Bovone, A. (1986). *Letter to the bishops of the Catholic church on the pastoral care of homosexual persons*, Vol. 1. Congregation for the Doctrine of the Faith Rome.

Ray, E. L. (2005). Mexican repatriation and the possibility for a federal cause of action: A comparative analysis on repatriations. *The University of Miami Inter-American Law Review, 37*(1), 175.

Restrepo, D., & Garcia, A. (2014). *The surge of unaccompanied children from Central America: Root causes and policy solutions.* Center for American Progress. https://www.americanprogress.org/issues/immigration/reports/2014/07/24/94396/the-surge-of-unaccompanied-children-from-central-america-root-causes-and-policy-solutions/

Rivera-Heredia, M. E., Obregón-Velasco, N., Cervantes-Pacheco, E. I., & Martínez-Ruiz, D. T. (2014). Familia y migración. Bienestar físico y mental. [Family and migration. Physical and mental wellness]. Editorial Trillas.

Rodriguez, C. (2018, June 05). *Seven things to know about mixed-status families.* Medium. https://medium.com/national-center-for-institutional-diversity/seven-things-to-know-about-mixed-status-families-92a18a714bb5

Rodriguez Vega, S. (2018). Praxis of resilience & resistance: "We can STOP Donald Trump" and other messages from immigrant children. *Association of Mexican American Educators Journal, 12*(3), 122–147.

Rogers, K., Shear, M. D., & Kanno-Youngs, Z. (2020, April 20). Trump plans to suspend immigration to U.S. *New York Times.* https://www.nytimes.com/2020/04/20/us/politics/trump-immigration.html

Root, M. P. (1996). *The multiracial experience: Racial borders as the new frontier.* SAGE.

Rosales, F. A. (1991). Review of the treaty of Guadalupe Hidalgo: A legacy of conflict. *Great Plains Quarterly, 11*(4), 279–280.

Rosenfeld, M. J. (2002). Measures of assimilation in the marriage market: Mexican Americans 1970–1990. *Journal of Marriage and Family, 64*(1), 152–162.

Rothbaum, B. O., Meadows, E. A., Resick, P., & Foy, D. W. (2000). Cognitive-behavioral therapy. In E. B. Foa, T. M., Kean, & M. J. Fiedman (Eds.), *Effective treatments for PTSD: Practice guidelines from the International Society for Traumatic Stress Studies* (pp. 320–325). Guildford.

Ruiz, D. M. (1997). *The four agreements: A practical guide to personal freedom.* Amber-Allen.

Rumbaut, R. G. (1994). The crucible within: Ethnic identity, self-esteem, and segmented assimilation among children of immigrants. *International Migration Review, 28*(4), 748–794.

Ryo, E. (2019, April 15). *How ICE enforcement has changed under the Trump Administration.* The Conversation. https://theconversation.com/how-ice-enforcement-has-changed-under-the-trump-administration-120322

Sandoval, C. (2013). *Methodology of the oppressed*, Vol. 18. University of Minnesota Press.

Savenije, W. (2007). Las pandillas trasnacionales o "maras": Violencia urbana en Centroamérica. [Transnational gangs or "maras". Urban violend in Central America. *Foro internacional*, 637–659.

Seltzer, J. A. (2004). Cohabitation in the United States and Britain: Demography, kinship, and the future. *Journal of Marriage and Family, 66*(4), 921–928.

Shapiro, F. (1987). *Eye movement desensitization and reprocessing (EMDR) therapy: Basic principles, protocols, and procedures.* Guilford.

Sidun, N., & Flores, Y. (2020). Human trafficking vulnerabilities, human rights violations, and psychological consequences. In N. Rubin & R.L. Flores (Eds.), *The Cambridge handbook of psychology and human rights* (pp. 273–287). Cambridge University Press.

Sigal, P. (Ed.). (2003). *Infamous desire: Male homosexuality in colonial Latin America.* University of Chicago Press.

Sinnar, S. (2003). Patriotic or unconstitutional? The mandatory detention of aliens under the USA Patriot Act. *Stanford Law Review, 55*, 1419–1456.

Skop, E. H. (2001). Race and place in the adaptation of Mariel exiles. *International Migration Review, 35*(2), 449–471.

Sluzki, C. E. (1979). Migration and family conflict. *Family Process, 18*(4), 379–390.

Smith, C. A., Ireland, T. O., Park, A., Elwyn, L., & Thornberry, T. P. (2011). Intergenerational continuities and discontinuities in intimate partner violence: a two-generational prospective study. *Journal of Interpersonal Violence, 26*(18), 3720–3752.

Smith, L., & Winslade, J. (1997). Consultations with young men migrating from alcohol's regime. *Dulwich Center Newsletter, 2*(3), 16–34.

Somos Familia. (n.d.). *Resources.* https://www.somosfamiliabay.org/resources/

Sorrentino, J. (2016, October 11). *"Las patronas" gives hope to Central American refugees.* Atavist. https://uscatholic.atavist.com/laspatronas

Southern Poverty Law Center. (2014). *Culture shock: The exploitation of J-1 cultural exchange workers.* https://www.splcenter.org/20140201/culture-shock-exploitation-j-1-cultural-exchange-workers

Souza, C. (2001). Esta risa no es de loca. In *Latina Feminist Group* (Ed.), *Telling to Live: Latina Feminist Testimonios.* Duke University Press, 114–22.

Stiglitz, J. E., Cortina, J., & Ochoa-Reza, E. (2013). Introduction. In J. Cortina & E. Ochoa-Reza (Eds.), *New perspectives on international migration and development* (xv–xx). Columbia University Press.

Stevens, G., & Tyler, M. K. (2002). Ethnic and racial intermarriage in the United States: Old and new regimes. *American diversity: A demographic challenge for the twenty-first century*, 221–242.

Straus, M. A., & Gelles. R. J. (1989). *Physical violence in American families: Risk factors and adaptations to violence in 1845 families.* Transaction Books.

Suarez-Orozco, C., Birman, D., Manuel Casa, J., Nakamura, N., Tummala-Narra, P., Zarate, M.,Vasquez, M. & Chatman, A. (2013). Crossroads: The psychology of immigration in the new century. *The 2011 APA Presidential Task Force on Immigration.* https://www.apa.org/topics/immigration/executive-summary.pdf

Suárez-Orozco, C., Gaytán, F. X., Bang, H. J., Pakes, J., O'Connor, E., & Rhodes, J. (2010). Academic trajectories of newcomer immigrant youth. *Developmental Psychology, 46*(3), 602–618.

Substance Abuse and Mental Health Services Administration. (2019). *National survey report.* https://www.samhsa.gov/data/data-we-collect/nsduh-national-survey-drug-use-and-health

Sue, D. W. (2010). *Microaggressions in everyday life: Race, gender and sexual orientation.* Wiley.

TANA. (n.d.). *Home page.* https://tana.ucdavis.edu/

Teachman, J., & Tedrow, L. (2008). The demography of stepfamilies in the United States. In J. Pryor (Ed.), *The international handbook of stepfamilies: Policy and practice in legal, research, and clinical environments* (p. 3–29). John Wiley & Sons, Inc.

Teachman, J. D., Tedrow, L. M., & Crowder, K. D. (2000). The changing demography of America's families. *Journal of Marriage and Family, 62*(4), 1234–1246.

Tello, A. M., Castellon, N. E., Aguilar, A., & Sawyer, C. B. (2017). Unaccompanied refugee minors from Central America: Understanding their journey and implications for counselors. *Professional Counselor, 7*(4), 360–374.

Tello, J. (1994). *Cara y corazón, face and heart: A family-strengthening, rebalancing and community mobilization process.* National Latino Children's Institute.

Tello, J. (2008). El hombre noble buscando balance: The noble man searching for balance. In Ricardo C. & Jerry T. (Eds.). *Family violence and men of color: Healing the wounded male spirit.* (pp. 37–60).

Tervalon, M., & Murray-García, J. (1998). Cultural humility versus cultural competence: A critical distinction in defining physician training outcomes in multicultural education. *Journal of Health Care for the Poor and Underserved, 9*(2), 117–125.

Torres, D. (2014). *Latinos and the facade of whiteness. La Respuesta: A magazine to (Re) Imagine the Boricua Diaspora.* https://repeatingislands.com/2014/09/09/la-respuesta-a-magazine-to-reimagine-the-boricua-diaspora/

Torres, L. (2016). In remembrance of the Orlando Pulse nightclub victims. *Latino Studies, 14*(3), 293–297. https://doi.org/10.1057/s41276-016-0012-4

Trujillo, C. (2003). *What night brings.* Curbstone Press.

Unger, J.B. & Molina, G. (1999). Educational Differences in Desired Family Size and Attitudes Toward Childbearing in Latina Women. *Population and Environment.* Volume 20, 343–351.

U.S Census Bureau, U. C. (2014, September 8) *Facts for features: Hispanic Heritage:* Sept. 15–Oct. 15. https://www.census.gov/newsroom/facts-for-features/2014/cb14-ff22.html

U.S Census Bureau, U. C. (2015, September 14) *Facts for features: Hispanic Heritage.* https://www.census.gov/newsroom/facts-for-features/2015/cb15-ff18.html

U.S. Census Bureau. (2019). *America's families and living arrangements.* https://www.census.gov/data/tables/2019/demo/families/cps-2019.html

U.S. Citizens and Immigration Services. (n.d.). *i-601, application for waiver of grounds for inadmissibility.* https://www.uscis.gov/i-601

U.S. Customs and Border Protection. (2020). *U.S. Border Patrol southwest border apprehensions by sector fiscal year 2020* https://www.cbp.gov/newsroom/stats/sw-border-migration/usbp-sw-border-apprehensions?_ga=2.139772211.128475407.1588556121-270283644.1588556121

U.S. Department of the Treasury (2012). Treasury Sanctions Latin American Criminal Organization. 10/11/2012 *Designation Targets Latin American Gang Mara Salvatrucha (MS-13).* Treasury.gov

Valencia-Garcia, D., Simoni, J. M., Alegría, M., & Takeuchi, D. T. (2012). Social capital, acculturation, mental health, and perceived access to services among Mexican American women. *Journal of Latina/o Psychology, 1*(S), 78–89. https://doi.org/10.1037/2168-1678.1.S.78

van der Kolk, B. A. (1994). The body keeps the score: Memory and the evolving psychobiology of posttraumatic stress. *Harvard Review of Psychiatry, 1*(5), 253–265.

van der Kolk, B. A. (1997). The psychobiology of post-traumatic stress disorder. *Journal of Clinical Psychiatry, 58*(9), 16–24.

van der Kolk, B. A. (2005). Developmental trauma disorder. *Psychiatric Annals, 35*(5), 401–409.

van der Kolk, B. A., & McFarlane, A. C. (Eds.). (1996). *Traumatic stress: The effects of overwhelming experience on mind, body, and society.* Guilford.

Vespa, J., Lewis, J. M., & Kreider, R. M. (2013). *America's families and living arrangements: 2012. Current Population Reports, 20*(2013), P 20-570. https://www.census.gov/prod/2013pubs/p20-570.pdf

Waldegrave, C. (2003). *Just therapy—A journey: A collection of papers from the just therapy team.* Dulwich Centre Publications.

Waldegrave, C. (2009). Cultural, gender, and socioeconomic contexts in therapeutic and social policy work. *Family Process, 48*(1), 85–101.

Walsh, F. (1996). The concept of family resilience: Crisis and challenge. *Family Process, 35*(3), 261–281.

Weisner, T. S., Beizer, L., & Stolze, L. (1991). Religion and families of children with developmental delays. *American Journal on Mental Retardation, 95*(6), 647–662.

White, M. & Epston, D. (1990). White, M., & Epston, D. (1990). *Narrative means to therapeutic ends.* W. W. Norton.

White House. (2012). *Remarks by the president on immigration.* Obamawhitehousearchives.org https://obamawhitehouse.archives.gov/the-press-office/2012/06/15/remarks-president-immigration

Williams, D. R., & Collins, C. (1995). U.S. socioeconomic and racial differences in health: Patterns and explanations. *Annual Review of Sociology, 21*(1), 349–386.

Williams, D. R., & Mohammed, S. A. (2009). Discrimination and racial disparities in health: Evidence and needed research. *Journal of Behavioral Medicine, 32*(1), 20–47.

Williams Institute. (2013, October 2). *LGBT Latino/a individuals and Latino/a same-sex couples.* https://williamsinstitute.law.ucla.edu/publications/lgbt-latinx-indv-and-ss-couples/

Williams, N. (1990). *The Mexican. American Family: Tradition and Change.* Rowman & Littlefield.

Wolf, S. (2012). Mara Salvatrucha: The most dangerous street gang in the Americas? *Latin American Politics and Society, 54*(1), 65–99.

Wong, C. F., Schrager, S. M., Holloway, I. W., Meyer, I. H., & Kipke, M. D. (2014). Minority stress experiences and psychological well-being: The impact of support from and connection to social networks within the Los Angeles house and ball communities. *Prevention Science, 15*(1), 44–55.

Yoshikawa, H. (2011). *Immigrants raising citizens: Undocumented parents and their children.* Russell Sage Foundation.

Yosso, T. J. (2005). Whose culture has capital? A critical race theory discussion of community cultural wealth. *Race Ethnicity and Education, 8*(1), 69–91. https://doi.org/10.1080/1361332052000341006

Zavella, P. (1989). The problematic relationship of feminism and Chicana studies. *Women's Studies: An Interdisciplinary Journal, 17*(1–2), 25–36.

Zavella. P. (2001a). Night Terrors. *Telling to live: Latina feminist testimonios.* In Alarcon, N. et al. (Eds). Duke University Press, 277–285.

Zavella, P. (2001b). Silence begins at home. *Latina feminist testimonies.* Alarcon, N. et. al. (Eds). Duke University Press, 43–54.

CPSIA information can be obtained
at www.ICGtesting.com
Printed in the USA
LVHW060557081222
734784LV00003B/16